GLOBAL ECONOMY

Ulrich Duchrow

GLOBAL ECONOMY

A CONFESSIONAL ISSUE FOR THE CHURCHES?

Translated by David Lewis

Original title:
Weltwirtschaft Heute: Eine Welt für bekennende Kirche?
Chr. Kaiser Verlag, Munich, 1986

Cover design: Rob Lucas

ISBN 2–8254–0876–X

Typeset by Input Typesetting Ltd, London SW19 8DR

Printed in Great Britain by Cox and Wyman Ltd

"He (your father) helped the weak and the poor to obtain justice. Was not that *really* to know Me? says the Lord. But you have eyes and thoughts only for profit, for the innocent blood you shed, for your deeds of oppression and extortion" (Jer. 22:16f.).

"All those who fail to offer counsel and aid to people in need, to those in physical danger even of death, God rightly calls 'murderers', therefore. On the Day of Judgment He will pass a most terrible sentence on them, as Christ himself declares: He will say, I was hungry and thirsty but you gave me no food or drink, I was a stranger but you did not welcome me, I was naked but you did not clothe me, I was sick and in prison but you did not visit me (Matt. 25:42f.). In other words, you were willing to let me and mine die of hunger, thirst and cold, be torn to pieces by wild beasts, rot in prison or perish of want. What is that if not to accuse such people of being murderers and bloodhounds? You may not have actually committed all these crimes but you have for your part left your neighbour to pine and die in distress. It is just as if I were to see someone drowning and at his last gasp, or trapped in a blaze, and I could save him simply by stretching out my hand, but did not do so. How else would the world regard me but as a murderer and a criminal?"

Martin Luther
on the commandment "Thou shalt not kill!",
in *The Large Catechism*

Acknowledgements

I would like to express my deep gratitude to my friend and translator, David Lewis.

I would also like to thank the Commission on the Churches' Participation in Development and its director, the Rev. Jacques Blanc, for helping to finance the translation of this book into English.

U.D.

Table of contents

Foreword

The choice of the first commandment with its abjuration of all forms of idolatry as the "golden text" for the year 1986 brings to a strangely impressive, forceful and even perhaps disconcerting focus the recent series of major commemorations, including above all the fiftieth jubilee of the Barmen Confessing Synod and Theological Declaration of 1934, and the spate of interpretative articles in parish magazines and scholarly journals it has brought in its train. But will the message get through? Shall we be able to recognize, identify and abjure the new worldwide idols of our own time, the golden calves we substitute today for Yahweh the one true God? Our major problem fifty years ago was not so much the wickedness and godlessness of the Nazis. Our problem then was the fanatical or deceitful falsification and corruption of the substance of the Christian faith and the devastation this wrought on the life and witness of the people of God. What corrupted the church and destroyed its credibility and acceptability in the sight of the hunted victims of the false gods fifty years ago was not the swastika but the "coordination" of the swastika and the cross.

Is something similar happening today? Different only because the substitutes for Christ's name today are incomparably more global in character? Yes, says the author of this book. Something of the kind *is* happening today and it pursues him relentlessly day and night whichever way he looks in theology or in his encounters in East and West and still more in North and South. He begins, therefore, with an analysis of trends in the Old Testament and New Testament scholarship, and pursues his expert probing by examining first Luther's position and then the emphases of neo-Lutheranism. He carefully notes what the ecumenical movement has been doing and the responses to this in Germany and Europe.

He presents us Roman Catholic positions *pro* and *contra* in both Europe and the two Americas. He arrests our attention with his analysis of the ways in which saving faith is dissolved into ethics and with his unmasking of seemingly pure ethicizing as undiluted fanaticism and idolatry; and all this not fifty years ago but right in our midst here and now; the claiming of Christ's name on behalf of false gods accompanied by utter blindness for his defenceless brothers and sisters.

With even greater boldness he tackles the tangled and as yet hardly penetrable jungle of ecosystems, military and economic orders, lent respectability by being labelled "Christian" or excused as bulwarks of "the Christian West". Who bothers to study these things? The author permits neither himself nor his readers any scepticism as to the availability of viable alternatives here. He refuses to abandon hope. While realizing that the dangers indicated by the prophets of doom really exist, he is more mindful still of the gospel promises. He asks questions and then some more; he himself conducts experiments to discover tracks along which even our hidebound churches may be led to make the first vital decisions.

We are not expected simply to accept the positions and analyses presented in this book. But we are required to share its probings and as individuals and churches to commit ourselves to a process leading to decisions. If it is the case that our German church — the putative heir of Barmen — is confronted today with the challenge to confess its faith in the one God and to abjure all other gods — including the idol of the modern market economy — we may well be grateful that someone has at length ventured the first steps down this path and refused to let its difficulty deter him.

In my view, this is a key book. Its theme is of vital concern and interest to the whole church today.

EBERHARD BETHGE

Introduction

At its Sixth Assembly in Vancouver in 1983, the World Council of Churches invited its member churches to join in 'a conciliar process of mutual commitment (covenant) to justice, peace and the integrity of creation'.[1] This process has been launched and the purpose of this book is to make a modest contribution to it.

Anyone who tackles seriously any of the main questions facing humanity today — whether that of injustice, the arms race, or the destruction of the created world — immediately comes up against the economic problem. But not all churches or theological traditions throughout the world have yet addressed themselves to, let alone solved, this problem. Indeed, there is a curious lopsidedness in the way churches and theologians in different parts of the world view this problem.

On the one hand, many churches and theologians in the "two-thirds world", especially in Latin America, have tried to deal with the economic problem in their theologies of liberation. They have felt the impact of the present global economic system too closely and too severely not to address themselves to this problem. Their church members and the people they live among are growing daily poorer. The question *why* this should be so (i.e. the economic question) can no longer be relegated to the margin of specialized ethical studies but has to be brought within the all-embracing horizon of biblical and theological reflection. The God of the Bible is encountered once again as the God who leads the poor and oppressed people to freedom. The ecumenical movement has made this new emphasis and approach its own.

On the other hand, there are the churches and theologians in the rich industrial countries or those identified with the middle and upper classes in the two-thirds world. These either wrap themselves in "the innocence which makes people guilty" (Allan Boesak) by claiming that the church has nothing to do with politics, or else see the "market economy" as part of the Christian credo to be defended at all costs. Either way, the critical analysis and reflection is conspicuous by its absence.

The situation in the Anglo-Saxon world, particularly in the USA, is somewhat different.[2] In France and Holland, too, we find a number of critical approaches.[3] But in the German-speaking area, the issue has hardly yet been joined. One indication of this is the fact that only in 1984 did a German-speaking author produce an "economic ethics" in the Protestant tradition, the last previous attempt to do so dating back to as long ago as 1927.[4]

How is this lopsidedness to be dealt with in the "conciliar process"? What is the significance of the fact that oppressed members of the body of Christ are crying out for justice and freedom while rich members of the same body shut their ears to this cry for help or react to it defensively? How are the latter to be sensitized to their real situation, converted to the cause of liberation and committed to action in this direction? The traditional German and even European way would be to analyze the problem in abstract universal terms and supply a theological interpretation. I prefer not to take that way but rather to tackle the problem deliberately in "contextual" terms.

What precisely is it which hinders the acceptance of the challenge of the global economic crisis by and within the German tradition, and, more specifically, in the West German situation? What are the fetters which hold us captive in *our* "Egypt"? And, on the other hand, what traditional theological resources are there to help strengthen our determination to seek deliverance from these fetters? In this issue of the global economy, what is God's concrete command and inescapable credal question to us as ministers and members of the churches in the rich industrial countries, for example, in the Federal Republic of Germany? Are there concrete steps which could be taken *here*, in the global context?

But how would this be relevant for other readers in other parts of European and world Christendom? One answer would be that reading this book could be like looking in a mirror, with the West German challenge as a sort of parable. Is this not what is required of us in the conciliar process for justice, peace and the integrity of creation? Do we not need to speak *out of* our own particular context so as to speak also, indirectly, to other contexts? It could also be helpful to us to understand why one part of Christendom fails to join others in the common ecumenical way and to learn of the fruitful possibilities available to us in some other unfamiliar tradition. The German tradition, for example, includes not only warnings but also certain valuable experiences such as those of the Confessing Church in the Nazi period. In this book, an effort is made to build on such positive elements.

In short, in this book we seek to accept the universal challenge of the global economic system by viewing the West German situation and tradition contextually in the hope that this may contribute to the ecumenical conciliar process. I realize only too painfully the leeway to be made up here. If only it were possible to refer to consensus proposals based on the assured findings of many years of preliminary study and experiment! Alas, we are not in that fortunate position. Only the urgency of the present situation in the industralized countries permits me to present my own tentative essays in this area to a wider audience. They are a revised and partly rewritten version of my book *Weltwirtschaft heute — Ein Feld für Bekennende Kirche?*[5] They are "essays" in the more literal sense, circling around the problems from various angles and inviting others to contribute their own insights for the benefit of the whole people of God. I am a theologian, not an economist. As a theologian, however, I have been engaged in intensive dialogue with economists. It is precisely the theological work which has been conspicuous by its absence in this field — in the German-speaking area at all events. A start had to be made and the first rough clearances hacked out!

NOTES

1. *Gathered for Life*, official report of the Vancouver Assembly 1983, ed. David Gill, Geneva, WCC, 1983, p. 255.
2. Especially important here has been the contribution of the Niebuhr brothers, Reinhold and H. Richard. Cf. also J. Ph. Wogaman, *The Great Economic Debate: an Ethical Analysis*, Philadelphia, Westminster Press, 1977, and Larry L. Rasmussen, *Economic Anxiety and Christian Faith*, Minneapolis, Augsburg, 1981.
3. Cf. "The Church and the Powers", a study document of the French Protestant Federation, *Study Encounter*, Vol. III, No. 3, 1972. Cf. also Harry M. de Lange, "Ecumenical Social Ethics for the Future", *The Ecumenical Review*, Vol. 37, No. 1, January 1985, pp. 106ff.; *idem.* "Towards an Economy of Enough", *The Indian Journal of Economics*, July 1981; *idem.* "Transnational Corporations in the

Light of the Vision of a Just, Participatory and Sustainable Society", *Churches and the Transnational Corporations*, Geneva, WCC, 1983; "Die Kirchen und die Einheit Europas", *Zeitschrift für Evangelische Ethik*, January 1983.
4. A. Rich, *Wirtschaftsethik. Grundlagen in theologischer Perspektive*, Gütersloh, 1984; G. Wünsch, *Evangelische Wirtschaftsethik*, Tübingen, 1927. But see also the works of Helmut Gollwitzer.
5. Munich, Chr. Kaiser Verlag, 1986.

PART ONE

The fetters of oppression
in the affluent economy of Egypt

A few years ago I asked Paulo Freire when he was going to write a sequel to his *Pedagogy of the Oppressed* with the title "Pedagogy of the Oppressors". After some moments of reflection, he replied: "No one could write it!"

Remembering the plagues which the God of the Hebrew slaves sent to warn the Egyptians but which proved quite ineffective, one is inclined at first to think that Freire was right. Our own personal experiences and those of our compatriots only serve to reinforce this impression. To make us who are rich and powerful abandon our resistance to God's liberating work would obviously require such disasters as the overwhelming of the Egyptians in the Red Sea. But the story of the people of Israel down to the Babylonian captivity also demonstrates that not even freed slaves are able to keep their freedom despite a massive dose of the divine "pedagogy". They, too, succumb to the idol Baal — and this name "Baal" means "lord and master". The desire for sovereignty and possession erodes freedom until there is none left.

On the other hand, God does not abandon God's creation or creatures. Even in the exile of the Jewish people, there are four horizons of hope to which we too can cling:

1. The prophet Ezekiel proclaims that God no longer reckons guilt collectively but that every individual human being, warned by God's message through the prophets, is confronted with the choice between justice and injustice, between life and death: "When a wicked man gives up his wickedness and does what is just and right, he shall live" (Ezek. 33:19). Woe betide the prophet who fails to warn the wicked man, therefore! "If you do not warn him to give up his wicked ways and so save his life, the guilt is his; because of his wickedness he shall die; but I will hold you answerable for his death" (Ezek. 3:18).

2. First Jeremiah (Jer. 31:33f.) and then Ezekiel (Ezek. 36:22f.) promise the people of God that it will no longer require instruction in order to know and do God's will but that God will give it a new heart and a new spirit. From the New Testament we know that under this new covenant God gives the Holy Spirit to recreate human beings. Although it is, humanly speaking, impossible for a rich person to enter the kingdom of God, nevertheless this is possible with God (Mark 10:24f.). The evangelist Luke, in particular, includes in his Gospel several narratives illustrating God's power to convert even rich people to God and God's justice (e.g. Zacchaeus, Luke 19:1ff.).

3. Moreover, the priestly document, likewise the fruit of the

Babylonian captivity, formulates the hope that, despite the continued desperate wickedness of the human heart, God will not destroy but rather uphold and maintain it: "Never again will I curse the ground because of man, however evil his inclinations may be from his youth upwards. I will never again destroy every living thing as I have just done" (Gen. 8:21).

4. Finally, it is also in the later prophecy and apocalyptic tradition of Israel that the hope emerges of the kingdom of God and a new creation, the work of God's Messiah. Inviting people to believe in Jesus as the Messiah necessarily means inviting them to cooperate in God's kingdom and new creation wherein justice dwells.

The corollary of all four biblical insights is that as rich persons and members of rich churches we need to be summoned to repentance and conversion, to deliverance from the fetters which chain us to false gods and consequently to injustice. Part of this metanoia is the recognition of our bondage. In respect of our West German situation and analogous situations elsewhere, we single out specifically the ideological and institutional assimilation of the church to the idolatrous Baalism of wealth and power. Every theological and ecclesiastical tradition is in danger of misuse as an ideological agent of accommodation to political and economic forces. This is what has happened in the case of the theological concept of the "two kingdoms" in the Lutheran tradition. Not only in the German context but also on a world scale this concept has acquired enormous ideological importance. From this example, therefore, we can learn just how churches distort the biblical and ecclesiastical traditions to evade conflict with political and economic forms of power. The simplest form of a mistaken "two kingdoms doctrine" is the "axiom" that the church has nothing to do with politics. In Chapter 1 we shall be dealing with this specific distortion.

When we decide to face up to the critical question of what hinders our own church in its specific context from hearing God's call to liberation in the form of a concrete challenge, our starting point for self-criticism will be not only our ideological complexes but also the question of the church's institutional form. In what institutional form has my own church lived and does it continue to live? In this institutional form, in what ways has it become assimilated to the social, economic and political institutions and interests of its social context? In recent German history, no one posed this question with greater acuity than Dietrich Bonhoeffer. In Chapter 2 we shall examine this question with his assistance.

1

An ideology for the rich and powerful: the distorted "two kingdoms doctrine" in the light of Luther's own teaching

To talk of a "Lutheran two kingdoms doctrine" suggests that Luther himself propounded some such doctrine and that this has been faithfully handed down to us through the centuries. But if anything is clear from exhaustive research and discussions over at least the last twenty years, it is, firstly, that Luther himself never formulated systematically something he referred to as a "two kingdoms doctrine" and, secondly, that much of what Luther himself said and wrote on this theme was subsequently forgotten and, to the extent that it was later rediscovered at the end of the nineteenth century, was then altered almost past recognition.[1]

1. Luther and the neo-Lutheran tradition

Certain developments in theology, church life and in the political realm in his own life-time were branded by Luther as dangerous and even heretical from a biblical standpoint. His arguments were essentially four:[2]

a) Critique of the church and clericalism

By analogy with the imperial hierarchy, the medieval church had come to understand itself as the "spiritual power" (potestas spiritualis). In sharp antithesis to this, Luther showed that "spiritual power" belongs exclusively to the Holy Spirit who by grace creates faith, love and hope. With its charisms and institutions, the church is called to serve; it is called to serve, following the example of its

---

● This is a revised version of my essay "The Doctrine of the Two Kingdoms as Resource for Our Time: Help or Hindrance", presented first at a conference in Chicago in 1980 and published in English in *Luther et la Réforme allemande dans une perspective oecuménique*, Geneva, 1983, pp. 249–262.

crucified Lord. Its form of "power" is that of the powerless and persecuted word and life of truth and justice. In the context of the concept of God's "regiments", in other words, justification *sola fide* is inseparable from the vulnerable and necessitous mode of existence of the church which proclaims this message of justification. This amounted to a clear repudiation of the praxis of the medieval church: a rejection of the accumulation and defence of privilege and wealth in the political realm by the expansion of clerical power.

b) Critique of totalitarianism

Luther's purpose in writing his basic treatise "On Secular Authority" was not to promote an uncritical subservience and obedience to the secular powers but, on the contrary, to define the limits of the obedience owed by Christians to the princes of that day. One of the occasions which prompted him to write it, indeed, was the act of the princes prohibiting the sale or purchase of the German version of the New Testament. This moved Luther to warn the princes not to encroach on freedom of conscience since God alone is sovereign over people's consciences and rules them by God's spiritual regiment. Another of Luther's purposes in writing this work was to show Christians how they could cooperate with God's "secular regiment", which was concerned not with people's faith but with their actions (works). Luther frequently expounded this positive aspect in the context of another traditional doctrine, that of the three "estates": *oeconomia* (economy and family), *politia* (politics) and *ecclesia* (church). It is God's will that the life of human beings should be sanctified in each of these three "estates".[3]

c) Critique of monasticism

In the medieval church, work in the economic and political realms and institutions was considered to be less holy than participation in specifically ecclesiastical and Christian activities. In Luther's view, on the contrary, the necessary corollary of the justification of a human being by grace and faith was the recognition of secular callings and institutions as, above all, opportunities for demonstrating faith and Christian love of the neighbour and as areas to which the church's critical and constructive witness and service are to be addressed. Luther himself counselled people in their "secular" callings, helped in the establishment of a new order of peace based on law, promoted the development of an educational system and protested against the embryonic stages in the development of "multi-national" financial and trading monopolies (e.g. the Fuggers) as well as against the princes' abuse of power, etc.

d) Critique of "utopian enthusiasm"

Though Luther strongly urged and himself practised active participation in economic and political matters by Christians and the church in its public witness, for the defence of the neighbour and to the glory of God, he equally strongly opposed any idea that this world as a whole could become the church before the coming of the perfect kingdom of God. Luther made use here of the Augustinian tradition with its division of humanity into two parts: the *civitas Dei* under the rule of God and the *civitas diaboli* under the rule of Satan. This distinction enabled Luther to view history as the scene of the divine struggle against evil in the form of sin and destruction. The goal of the historical process is the kingdom of God in its fullness; but this kingdom already begins among human beings by the power of the Holy Spirit who recreates them and church communities in conformity with the Sermon on the Mount. On the other hand, however, because Satan is still at work, the weak need the protection of a provisional political order (Rom. 13:1-7). This institutional defence is graciously furnished by God via God's "secular regiment". In these public political institutions, Christians and the church do not contend indeed for their own rights but, when these rights are violated, bear witness for justice and truth. But Christians and the church — especially in the persons of those working in the political institutions, which are indeed specifically created for the common good — do struggle with their own weapons "for others" and for justice and peace. It was precisely at this point that Luther opposed the "utopian enthusiasts" who urged either complete withdrawal from political life or else its transformation by force into the "kingdom of God".

Since Luther's position in this respect has so often been misconstrued as supporting uncritical subservience, one passage at least must be quoted to illustrate his real intention. In an exposition of the passion narrative, Luther has a passage on "Jesus brought before Pilate" in which he declares:

> Christ here shows and teaches us that we must not be silent about the truth in the presence of the "big shots" and the nobility but on the contrary warn and criticize them when they commit injustice . . . For there is a world of difference between suffering injustice and violence and keeping quiet about them. We should suffer injustice and violence

but we should not keep silent about them. For a Christian must bear witness to the truth and be willing to die for it if need be. But if we are to die for truth and justice, we must freely and openly bear witness to them . . .

For the princes and "big shots" find it quite tolerable that the whole world should be criticized if only they themselves are exempted from this criticism. But they must certainly be criticized too and anyone entrusted with the office of preaching owes it to them to point out where they act unjustly and do wrong, even if they protest that such criticism of rulers will lead to rebellion.'[4]

Luther's various statements could perhaps be systematized as follows: *Firstly*: Like Augustine, Luther distinguished between two groups of people: the one group acknowledges and submits to God's rule, the other group is subject to the power of evil; there is the kingdom of God and there is the kingdom of Satan. These two kingdoms are locked in an eschatological struggle throughout history until the final, complete and visible triumph of the kingdom of God.[5]

Secondly: Into this history of the struggle between two opposing kingdoms, Luther introduces the idea of distinct, complementary forms of divine government (regiments) whereby God opposes the power of evil; he picks up here the medieval doctrine of two authorities, one spiritual, the other secular, but only after a critical revision of this doctrine.[6] God's spiritual regiment is not the church hierarchy but God acting through the word (law *and* gospel). Church authority thus becomes purely ministerial, analogous to the "servant form" of the crucified Jesus. God's spiritual governance produces faith (relationship to God), freedom *from* the obsession of self-expression (relationship to oneself), and freedom *for* the service of one's fellow creatures (relationship to the world). God's secular governance permits even those who have not yet responded to the Spirit by faith to create institutions which defend not only the economic and political life of society against the power of evil, but also the church itself.[7]

Thirdly: Following medieval tradition, Luther labels these institutions, designed to give God's governances concrete form, hierarchies or estates: church (*ecclesia*), political community (*politia*), family and economy (*oeconomia*). In all these "estates", according to Luther, all human beings are called simultaneously to obey the will of God — voluntarily if they have been renewed by the Spirit of Christ, but involuntarily if they continue in sin. The political institutions have to reckon with such resistance by the use also of lawfully established coercive measures ("force": due process of law, defensive war, resistance in carefully defined conditions). As far as possible, however, political government must operate rationally and equitably, i.e. be based on reason and justice. In other words, since few live by the voluntary love which is the fruit of the gospel, the main concern in the political realm is external conformity to the divine law (*usus politicus legis* — the political use of the law). But according to Luther, the criterion for this law to which human beings are subject, by which they must be guided and which they must obey, and which they know as the 'law of nature', is the revealed Decalogue (the Ten Commandments) and its fulfilment in the law of Christ (i.e. love). This law, therefore, is not autonomous, not independent of God's revealed will. While, therefore, there is an obvious tension between, on the one hand, the obedience of Christians to the Sermon on the Mount in their own personal lives and as members of the church and, on the other hand, their action for others as responsible members of the community in every aspect of its life (as defined, e.g. in Romans 13), the bond uniting these two 'realms' is love. Just as the "estates" fulfill their divine mission and assist one another in promoting human prosperity and wellbeing, so too the church, the church especially, not only serves God's spiritual governance but God's secular governance as well, by critically and constructively testing which institutions and modes of conduct correspond most nearly to the divine will (and conversely, of course!) even if this means, finally, public and vocal resistance. Here, again, there cannot be any dichotomy or autonomy!

The factor which gives coherence to the doctrine of the "kingdoms", "governances" (regiments), "hierarchies" or "estates" is Luther's vision of the divine cooperation with human beings: in all things, God is the one exclusive operator, the all-encompassing One, the source of all possibilities. But God's chosen mode of operation also embraces the divine purpose that we human beings should cooperate with God in all the "regiments" and "estates" to combat the forces of evil.[8] There is no rivalry, therefore, between a theocentric and an anthropocentric interpretation of the two kingdoms doctrine in Luther.

Even from this brief résumé, it is clear that no simple "doctrine of two kingdoms" is to be found in Luther. On the contrary, he employs a whole set of interconnected distinctions to bring out at various key points the real tension between the divine kingdom and the forces of evil in human history and to encourage us to become "fellow workers" with the God whose will it is that the whole of creation should have life and have it abundantly.

2. Neo-Lutheranism

The other result of recent studies and discussions is the recognition that the nuances and subtleties of Luther's position were almost completely lost sight of until the close of the nineteenth century and that a few of them were then picked up again in a vastly different context, of course, and mostly in a distorted and even heretical form. The oblivion which overtook Luther can be explained by certain historical currents, particularly in Germany. From the end of the Reformation period onwards a system developed in Germany which can be defined as a post-Constantinian version of caesaropapism. In the German territorial churches, the prince was at the same time the chief bishop. Within this symbiosis of church and state, only the doctrine of the three "estates" remained operational, though here too in a debased form. The different offices in empirical society were distinguished in such a way that people were divided into three categories: those active in the public service, those active in the service of the church and those active in industry and commerce. There were some exceptions, of course, to this general trend; for example, the resistance tradition within Lutheranism as developed in North America in particular.[9]

Towards the end of the last century, liberal theologians began to take a renewed interest in certain elements and terms in Luther's account of the two kingdoms and the two governances (without, however, differentiating between them). The way liberal theology did this had roots far back in modern Western history. Philosophically and socially, this development was strongly marked by various dichotomies and dualisms. It was Descartes who first developed the philosophical dichotomy between a self (the "I", the subject, the mind) independent of the "world" and a machine world (object, matter) without mind. This approach was developed by Newton into the classic mechanistic physics which unleashed the enormous torrent of modern technology. Bourgeois society made a clear-cut division between the private personal sphere and the public sphere of politics. The political institutions which had been regarded as responsible for the common good of society in medieval and reformation doctrine were now deprived of the possibility of controlling the private proprietors of the means of production. These were left free, therefore, to expand their possessions by the industrial technological exploitation of natural resources and human labour.

The intention of the late nineteenth century liberal theologians, of course, was to defend the Christian faith as much as they could. All they managed to save was the inner faith, the inner attitude, the Sunday service, personal relationships. Science, technology, economics, industry, the imperialistic policies of national governments, and even public and legal political institutions were regarded as autonomous realms with no concrete relationship whatever to God's loving purpose in Jesus Christ. In the German language area we have in mind here such theologians and scholars as Wilhelm Herrmann, Rudolf Sohm, Friedrich Naumann and Max Weber. It was this group, moreover, which insisted that these dichotomies went back to Luther himself. According to them, Luther made a clear-cut distinction between power politics and other areas of secular life, on the one hand, and on the other hand a Jesus Christ interested only in saving souls until the coming of the transcendent kingdom of God one day in some unspecified future. They believe this view to be supported by Johannes Weiss's exegetical discovery that the eschatology of Jesus was wholly apocalyptic and transcendent.

The position of this group, which constituted the "Protestant Social Congress" can be epitomized by a passage from Freidrich Naumann:[10]

> The more purely Jesus is preached, the less politically instructive he is, and whenever Christianity has coveted a constructive rôle, i.e. wanted to be politically instructive and culturally dominant, it has then been the farthest removed from the gospel of Jesus.
>
> This means in practice that, in building our political structures, we do not use the cedars of Lebanon but materials fetched from the Roman Capitol. But within this house Jesus is still to preach his gospel today as he did long ago in the house that Rome built. It is not to Jesus that we turn, then, with our questions of political and economic policy and planning. That may sound harsh and abrupt to anyone brought up as a Christian yet it seems to me authentically Lutheran. In the major struggles of his time, Luther did not always display a consistent clarity and firmness in this difficult question. We find him at one time trying to convert biblical ideas into political rules but at another time, when confronted with the fundamental problem and particularly in the struggles with Karlstadt and Münzer, relentlessly and splendidly forthright and clear, vigorously distinguishing between spiritual and secular matters with the full authority of his mind and temper. According to Luther, political matters are not to be settled by an appeal to the gospel;

they can be decided by Jews and Gentiles just as well as by Christians, since reason alone, and not revelation, is required for their solution.

This Lutheran division of the realms, which seemed to me for a time a restriction of the range of Christianity's influence and a subtraction from its due authority, has on closer inspection of the matter proved correct. In regarding political matters as outside the scope of the proclamation of salvation, we are returning to the grand old teacher of our German faith. I vote for and champion the German fleet not because I am a Christian but because I am a citizen and because I have learned to abandon the idea that fundamental political issues are to be settled by the Sermon on the Mount.

That this attitude lacks an inner coherence, I have already admitted . . .

But the view of the relation of politics to the gospel which I have presented as a politician, indeed had to present in order to answer your question, is at the same time my answer to many similar questions. The lawyer must take the same attitude to the law, the merchant to his enterprise. And is there a single one of all those who earn their living today not also a merchant? Our living conditions are realities which confront us willy nilly and we have little room left to fashion things closer to our heart's desire. Yet it is precisely in this little area of freedom that our most personal selfhood moves; here is the place where the tidal wave from Jesus floods most directly into our activity. In many matters, every one of us is a slave obedient to inflexible compulsions, some external force or a logic inherent in the very nature of things; but there in that small place of our freedom, where this coercion and this logic cease, where we realize that our itinerary is not fixed and absolute, there is that part of our life where we want most of all to be the servants of Jesus.

This passage establishes beyond doubt that the basic philosophical pattern into which Luther's ideas are being pressed here is the Cartesian divorce between the free self (*ego*) and "things" (matter), with an automatic autonomous logic on both sides of the great divide. The concept of autonomy stems from Max Weber:[11]

Just as rational economic and political action obeys its own inherent laws, so too every other form of rational action within the world remains inescapably tied to the conditions of the world which are inimical to fraternity but which must necessarily be its means or ends, and thus finds itself in a relationship of tension with the ethics of fraternity.

Crisis overtook this development in the twenties and thirties of our century when confessional Lutheranism appealed to these dichotomies to justify its support of nationalism and national socialism.

It exploited Luther's distinction between law and gospel to this end. The gospel was restricted to the forgiveness of individual sins while the law became a system of autonomous "orders" of creation and history. A classic example of this is a passage from the *Ansbach Recommendation* published by Erlangen theologians in 1934 in opposition to the *Barmen Theological Declaration* of the Confessing Church:[12]

> 2. The word of God addresses us as law and gospel. In its proclamation, the church must follow suit. The gospel is the message of Jesus Christ who died for our sins and was raised for our justification.
>
> 3. The law, "namely, the unchangeable will of God" (Formula of Concord, Epitome VI, §6) meets us in the total reality of our life as illuminated by the divine revelation. It binds each one of us to the estate into which we have been called by God and obligates us to the natural orders to which we are subject, such as family, nation, race (i.e. blood ties). For we are certainly assigned to a definite family, a definite nation, a definite race. Since, moreover, God's will is always concerned with our here and now, it also binds us to the definite historical moment of our family, nation, race, i.e. to a specific moment in their history.
>
> 4. But what the natural orders reveal to us is not only God's will as demand. Constituting as they do the basis of our entire natural existence, these orders in their totality are also at the same time the means whereby God creates and sustains our earthly life. Anyone assured of the grace of the Father through faith in Jesus Christ also experiences in these natural orders "pure, fatherly divine goodness and mercy". As Christians, therefore, we thank God for every order, i.e. every civil government, respecting it as an instrument of the unfolding divine purpose even when it is a distorted instrument. As Christians, however, we also distinguish between good and eccentric rulers, between healthy and debased orders.
>
> 5. Recognizing this, as faithful Christians we thank the Lord God for bestowing on our nation in its time of need the leader, Adolf Hitler, to be its "pious and faithful governor" and for his desire to grant us a régime of "discipline and honour" in the form of the National Socialist State. We therefore acknowledge our responsibility in God's sight to support the Leader's work in our respective callings and professions.

This text speaks for itself.

An important agent in the transition from dichotomic thought of the liberal variety to dichotomic thought of the confessionalist variety was Paul Althaus, himself one of the authors of the *Ansbach Recommendation*. He had himself made the transition from a liberal to a confessionalist and nationalist theology. It was in controversy with Althaus that Karl Barth minted the polemical term: "the *Lutheran* doctrine of the two kingdoms".[13] Even in the thirties, of course, there was still a certain flexibility in the terminology defining this dichotomy (two spheres, two realms, etc,) but only until 1938, when Harald Diem wrote his book on *Luther's Doctrine of the Two Kingdoms*.[14] Diem's aim was to defend Luther against the heretical distortion of his teaching by the majority of German Lutherans who divorced secular matters completely from God's purpose of justice and salvation for all God's children. It was only from this relatively recent time onwards that the technical term "two kingdoms doctrine" became generally current. In other words, it originated in an attempt to reformulate Luther's teaching, though a very questionable reformulation since in fact it still hinders the acceptance of the kingdom of God in Lutheran circles as the dominant concern of the church and Christians and their recognition of the divine purpose of justice and love as the criterion for every area of human life — economic, social, cultural, political and scientific.

Even after the disaster which overtook Lutheranism in the Hitler era, this false trail has to a large extent still been pursued. White Lutherans in South Africa have used not only the term "two kingdoms doctrine" but also its underlying dualism to defend or conceal the inherent injustice of apartheid.[15] Chilean Lutherans who support Pinochet and helped send Bishop Frenz into exile argue along the same lines. These neo-Lutheran dualisms and dichotomies helped to quieten the consciences of Lutherans in the Federal Republic when they attacked the WCC Programme to Combat Racism, while at the same time approving or tolerating military violence. Consciously or unconsciously, the neo-Lutheran doctrine of the "two kingdoms" is still being used by many Lutherans in different parts of the world as their basis for a double standard of morality — a Sunday morality and a weekday morality.

This is not to deny that many Lutherans have also acquired from their tradition a real concern for faithfulness in their Christian discipleship. But the point here is whether they have been sufficiently critical in their theology and practice here to see the real side-effects and structural implications of their respective economic, social and political systems. I have been speaking of Lutherans and the ways in which they in particular are tempted to evade the imperatives of the gospel, but Christians of other traditions will need to examine themselves in like manner and with equal severity.

International research shows that only in isolated cases in recent history have Luther's own views been respected in keeping with his own basic intentions and in fidelity to the biblical tradition. One such case was the Norwegian church's resistance to the Nazi occupation in the Second World War.[16] Study of the theological basis of this resistance has shown that Bishop Berggrav appealed directly to Luther's works in support of the resistance struggle. He used Luther's teaching on God's two governances or regiments (*not* "kingdoms"!) to show that governments, too, are subject to God and therefore have their divinely appointed limits and that there are situations in which the church and Christians are called upon to engage in resistance as a matter of Christian conscience and not only as a political decision. This example deserves special mention since it concerned a predominantly Lutheran nation and the persecution of a Lutheran national church. It furnishes a key for understanding why neo-Lutheran views normally tend to abandon various areas of life to their own supposedly autonomous laws. Either they lead to identification with the dominant forces in society and an accommodation with them or a sense of being so small a minority within society tends to inhibit any kind of resistance.

Another exceptional case is provided by the church in the German Democratic Republic. Examples of the misuse of the two kingdoms doctrine could be cited here too, of course. But some East German theologians have employed this doctrine in a quite legitimate way.[17] While stressing, on the one hand, the independence of the church, they have also been able, on the other hand, to adopt a positive approach to constructive elements in a socialist society. This approach they call "critical solidarity".

A survey of historical examples of the use and abuse of Luther's views on the "kingdoms" or "regiments" enables us to distinguish as follows:[18] The *misuse* of Luther's views is connected at its core with an illegitimate accommodation to existing power relationships, whether cultural, economic or political. Especially grave is the fact that the neo-Lutheran "two kingdoms doctrine" was developed specifically as a legitimization of that modern abuse of power which today is pushing us steadily towards the brink of disaster.

The *legitimate use* of Luther's views may assume one of the following three forms, depending on the specific context:
a) critical but constructive cooperation in emancipation from false dependencies and in the creative deployment of power;

b) critical and active resistance to blatantly incorrigible power;
c) critical and passive resistance to blatantly incorrigible power.

3. A help or a hindrance for the church today?

What light does this brief historical survey shed on our present responsibilities? The reintroduction of the traditional concept of the "two kingdoms" both by neo-Lutherans and their critics as a shorthand term for a dualistic social ethics saddled this term from the very outset with a negative and even heretical connotation. The preference of the Norwegians for the term "two regiments or governances" instead of the term "two kingdoms" is significant here. But even the efforts of Lutheran scholars and churchmen to recover the authentic ideas and terminology of Luther himself were undertaken defensively, i.e. to defend Luther from neo-Lutheran distortions, so that the critical and constructive approach which they discovered was a secondary rather than a primary use of the term as theological shorthand.

This source of the concept in the context of neo-Lutheran errors and possibly even heresies of practice in respect of economics, politics, militarism and imperialism is the chief and most complete hindrance to its positive use today. By "positive" here, I mean a use whereby reformation and biblical insights and themes can be given free and creative rein among Lutheran Christians today. Even within the ecumenical community of different churches and traditions, the neo-Lutheran "two kingdoms doctrine" has been and remains, for those who seek to be obedient to Christ in all areas of human life, shorthand for an illegitimate accommodation to the *status quo*.

The same cannot be said of other reformation and biblical ideas which have been rediscovered in our time or even of the new theological concepts which have been hammered out in the present century to define the fundamental relationships of the church and Christians to the world. Let me give just a few examples. At the very moment when most German Lutherans were falling in behind Hitler and using their dualistic formulations to justify this capitulation, Karl Barth and the Confessing Church developed the concept of *Christ's royal sovereignty* in such a way as to relate it to all areas of human life (*Barmen Theological Declaration*, Article 2). In articulating their opposition to the neo-Lutheran doctrine of the two kingdoms they defended at the same time Luther's original intention. The rediscovery of the term *status confessionis* in the early stages of the church struggle in the thirties in Germany was related, from the very beginning, to the defence of the Bible and the church's credo. The same applies to the reintroduction of this term at the Dar-es-Salaam Assembly of the Lutheran World Federation in 1977 in reference to the apartheid heresy in South Africa.

Another shorthand term of this positive sort is *discipleship*, one of Dietrich Bonhoeffer's key concepts. But all theologies which make the *kingdom of God*, i.e. the central term in the message of Jesus of Nazareth, their starting point have a built-in criterion warning them against illegitimate accommodations to the *status quo*. The same applies to such terms as *liberation theology* and *black theology* since these terms impel us to deeper explorations of the fundamental biblical truth that God adopts the cause of oppressed human beings as God's own cause. Even such recent ecumenical terms such as *the responsible society* or a *just, participatory and sustainable society*, for which there is no direct precedent in the ancient church tradition, lead us directly into reflection on the Bible and to responsible Christian action in the world.

All of these terms can be misused and misconstrued, of course. From historical and contemporary experience as well as from theological reflection, we know the dangers and errors their misuse entails. We have only to think of the misuse of Reformed theology in South Africa. But the point I am making is that the positive terms mentioned here were rediscovered or tailored to undergird a required Christian witness at a given time and in a given place. But the "two kingdoms doctrine" was created and subsequently often used as a neo-Lutheran "flag of convenience" precisely for the avoidance of the required Christian witness and even as a stick with which to beat those who wanted to bear this required witness and to follow Jesus even at the price of suffering.

What conclusions are we to draw from this hermeneutic reflection? In the view of some Lutheran theologians, the doctrine of the two kingdoms or two regiments is quite useless as a guide in the twentieth century and should therefore be abandoned. While this position is understandable, there are two reasons which make it unacceptable in my view. The first is that we cannot simply shrug off our own history. If we have fallen into error or heresy, repentance and change are called for; not just a change in terminology, of course, but also a conversion of our lives. But lives are governed by creeds. The life of the Lutheran and United churches in Germany has been dominated by something of a "two kingdoms mentality". If we are to be faithful members of our church (Lutheran or United) we must somehow come to terms with this "two kingdoms" syndrome if only because of the hindrance it has proved in our recent history. Such a clarification is also required in relation to the ecumenical community.

The second and far more important reason is that Luther's real thinking on these matters is so rich, and deals so sensitively and illuminatingly with certain fundamental issues, that I am loth to dispense with his insights and signposts. Not that I insist on the use of the terms "two kingdoms" or "two regiments". It is probably true that these terms are now permanently archaic and unhelpful. But we are still far from having exhausted the utility of Luther's insights for our contemporary problems, as I hope to show in a later chapter.

NOTES

1. U. Duchrow, *Christenheit und Weltverantwortung. Traditionsgeschichte und systematische Struktur der Zweireichelehre*, Stuttgart, 1970 (2nd ed. 1983); U. Duchrow and H. Hoffmann (eds), *Die Vorstellung von Zwei Reichen und Regimenten bis Luther* (Vol. 17 of Texts on the History of the Church and Theology), 2nd ed., ed. C. Windhorst, Gütersloh, 1978; U. Duchrow (ed.), *Lutheran Churches – Salt or Mirror of Society? Case Studies on the Theory and Practice of the Two Kingdoms Doctrine*, LWF Department of Studies, Geneva, 1977; U. Duchrow and W. Huber (eds), Die Ambivalenz der Zweireichelehre in lutherischen Kirchen des 20. Jahrhunderts (Vol. 22 of Texts etc.) Gütersloh, 1976; N. Hasselmann (ed.), *Gottes Wirken in seiner Welt. Zur Diskussion um die Zweireichelehre*, Vol. 1; *Dokumente einer Konsultation*, Vol. 2; *Reaktionen (Zur Sache* 19 and 20), Hamburg, 1980; J. Rogge and H. Zeddies (edd.), *Kirchengemeinschaft und politische Ethik. Ergebnis eines theologischen Gespräches zum Verhältnis von Zweireichelehre und Lehre von der Königsherrschaft Christi*, Berlin, 1980; G. Scharffenorth, *Den Glauben ins Leben ziehen, . . .* Munich, 1982; Thomas William Strieter, *Contemporary Two Kingdoms and Governances Thinking for Today's World: a Critical Assessment of Types of Interpretation of the Two Kingdoms and Governances Model, Especially within American Lutheranism*, Diss, Chicago, May 1986.
2. Cf. Duchrow, *Christenheit und Weltverantwortung*, chapter IV.
3. Cf. W. Maurer, "Luther's Doctrine of the Three Hierarchies and their Medieval Background" (in German in *Proceedings of the Bavarian Academy of Sciences*, History of Philosophy Class, No. 79, 1970), Munich, 1970.
4. WA 28; 360, 25–28. 361, 33–39. (The English translation of each reference to WA in this book is by David Lewis.)
5. Cf. Duchrow, *Christenheit und Weltverantwortlung*, pp.181ff. and 441ff.
6. *Ibid*, pp. 321ff. and 479ff.
7. Cf. Luther, *Von weltlicher Obrigkeit*, 1523.
8. Cf. Duchrow, *Christenheit und Weltverantwortlung*, pp. 512ff. and H. E. Tödt, "Die Bedeutung von Luthers Reiche- und Regimentenlehre für heutige Theo-

logie und Ethik", in N. Hasselmann (ed.), *op. cit.*, pp. 52–126 (in my opinion the best summary of the present stage of research).

9. Cf. O. K. Olson, "The Revolution and the Reformation", in W. Lazareth (ed.), *The Left Hand of God*, Fortress Press, Philadelphia, 1976, pp. 1–30.

10. On the group as a whole, cf. Karl H. Hertz, *Two Kingdoms and One World*, Augsburg Publishing House, Minneapolis, Minnesota, 1976, pp. 86ff. On Naumann, cf. pp. 163f.

11. M. Weber, *Gesammelte Aufsätze zur Religionssoziologie*, I, Tübingen, 1963, p. 552. Cf. W. Huber, "The Barmen Theological Declaration and the Two Kingdom Doctrine. Historico-Systematic Reflections", in Duchrow (ed.), *Lutheran Churches — Salt or Mirror in Society?*, pp. 28ff. Cf. D. Conrad, Max Weber's conception of Hindu Dharma as a paradigm, in D. Kantowsky (ed.), *Recent Research on Max Weber's Studies of Hinduism*, Cologne, Werk Forum Verlag, 1986, pp. 169–192. Conrad argues that Weber first used the concept of autonomy in his second essay on Hinduism and specifically in his description of the scales of values in the different castes in the Hindu social system, though in the process reading his own idea of the conflict of pluralistic value systems into this system. From the ideological standpoint, his interest both historically and systematically is focused on the legitimation of power (i.e. war) politics and the capitalist market.

12. Cf. Karl H. Hertz, *op. cit.*, pp. 184ff.

13. *Ibid.*

14. Cf. Huber in Duchrow, *Lutheran Churches etc.*, p. 35.

15. Cf. W. Kistner, "The Context of the Umpumulo Memorandum of 1967", in Duchrow, *Lutheran Churches etc.*, p. 165.

16. T. Austad, "The Doctrine of God's Twofold Governance in the Norwegian Church Struggle from 1940 to 1945. Fifteen Theses", in Duchrow (ed.), *Lutheran Churches etc.*, pp. 84ff.

17. Cf. H. Falcke, "The Place of the Two Kingdom Doctrine in the Life of the Evangelical Churches in the German Democratic Republic", in Duchrow (ed.), *Lutheran Churches etc.*, pp. 61ff.

18. Cf. Duchrow, in Duchrow (ed.), *Lutheran Churches etc.*, pp. 300ff.

2

The assimilated institutional church of the rich in the light of Bonhoeffer's practical ecclesiology

We turn now to focus more closely on the character of a church institution which seeks a privileged place in society, in the light of Bonhoeffer's critical ecclesiology.

I. Bonhoeffer's ecclesiology of concrete community

Christian community is the starting place, the leitmotif, the boundary and the social intention of Dietrich Bonhoeffer's theological ethics. "Jesus Christ existing as community" is the Jesus in whom Bonhoeffer believed and the community in which he believed. His recognition of the concrete communal locus of Christian faith — obedience, life, and the reflection on these which is theology — is the richest and most radical of Bonhoeffer's insights.

These are the opening words of Thomas I. Day's book *Conviviality and Common Sense*, far and away the finest study of Bonhoeffer's ecclesiology to date.[1] It would be impossible to present this ecclesiology in all its richness within the compass of the present essay, nor is it necessary to do so. The main outlines of this ecclesiology are clearly presented in Day's basic theses which introduce us immediately to the questions we shall be concerned with.

According to Day, the first point to note is that for Bonhoeffer, throughout his entire life, the church remains the sign outside the bracket of every theological statement. "Theology presupposes the empirical church. But the church also remains a theme of theology.

● An earlier and fuller version of this essay was presented at a Bonhoeffer Consultation in the Research Centre of the Evangelical Studies Association (FEST) on 9 and 10 February 1978.

As such it is to be dealt with first in theology."[2] It is no mere chance that both Bonhoeffer's earliest work *(Sanctorum Communio*, 1927) and his last, unfinished work on which he was working shortly before his death, were devoted to ecclesiology.[3]

Day's second thesis is that Bonhoeffer's ecclesiology in particular, like his theology in general, was developed not as an exercise in the logical deployment of abstract concepts but as a response to the concrete community circumstances in which he found himself.

In the very first chapter of *Sanctorum Communio*, Bonhoeffer insists that dogmatic theology can only be a committed theology *(cum ira et studio)* and that both the concept of church and the theological concept of "person" have a social dimension.[4] In *Akt und Sein* he underpins this epistemologically. As Bonhoeffer puts it succinctly in his 1932 address on "The Nature of the Church": "There is no theological reflection in isolation from community. The isolation of the individual is the basic error of Protestant theology."[5] "Theology is an auxiliary, a means, not an end in itself."[6] The statement in *Discipleship* to the effect that "an insight cannot be isolated from the life in which it is achieved" is described by Bethge as the "master key" to Bonhoeffer's entire theological thinking, method and articulation.[7] A false neutrality ends up by transforming theology into an ideology and leads to mystification rather than to the truth.[8] Bonhoeffer liked to quote Luther's words: "It is by living, even by dying and being damned, that one becomes a theologian, not by understanding, reading and speculating" *(vivendo, immo moriendo et damnando fit theologus, non intelligendo, legendo aut speculando).*[9] Only by an obedient and radical respect for the Creed, the Sermon on the Mount and Christian worship can theology be true to itself and be renewed in the service of the Confessing Church.[10] It is wholly consistent with this view of theology and the dangers of individualizing it, idealizing it, and pursuing instead a camouflaged ideology, that Bonhoeffer should himself have foregone "the privileges of an academic rostrum"[11] in order the better to serve the church as a theologian.[12]

Given this understanding of theology, how does Bonhoeffer develop his ecclesiology? He does so in terms of the following community situations in which he found himself: (1) that of his family as a patriarchal community but one in which mutual concern and assistance as well as a strong sense of political and academic responsibility were a lived reality (period down to 1930); (2) that of involvement in the national and international struggle of the Confessing Church from Berlin, London and Finkenwalde (following his realization of the church's responsibility for justice and peace as a result of his period in the United States from 1930 to 1931); (3) that of direct participation in the political resistance movement (again in the context of the family); (4) that of exploratory reflections on the concrete church of the future after the collapse of the Third Reich: thoughts in prison on the poor church for others.

The whole of Bonhoeffer's life work is pervaded by the question of the *church without privileges*. Endorsing Bethge's conclusion, Jan Smolik can affirm that "Bonhoeffer's whole life can be defined as the quest for the church without privileges".[13] Smolik reviews Bonhoeffer's various utterances on this theme as well as the secondary literature.[14] Despite very important insights in detail, however, the *systematic* place of this question in Bonhoeffer's *historical* experiences and reflections is still not brought out sufficiently clearly here, it seems to me, and this is especially important when examining why Bonhoeffer's type of ecclesiology is received (or not received) in the present situation in Federal Germany and in other Western countries.

In his 1932 lecture on "The Nature of the Church", Bonhoeffer himself tells us where he locates this question systematically. He does not locate it, as we might have expected, in the supposedly secondary question of church structures or in the question of church and state. It is, on the contrary, in the very *first* section of this address, prior to *all other* questions of the church's "what" or "how", that Bonhoeffer raises the question of its "where", the question of the church's *place*.[15] It is important for us to have clearly in mind here these sections of Bonhoeffer's manuscript: (A) on the place of the church in the world, and (B) in Christendom:

(A) In the world
 . . . The new situation of our church today is defined, on the one hand by its *displacedness*. It wants to be everywhere and is consequently nowhere. Being impalpable it has become unassailable. Never and nowhere is it wholly itself. It exists only in disguises. It has become the world without the world's becoming the church. Displaced existence is the existence of Cain, of the fugitive. Fleeing from itself, the church today has become an object of profound contempt. Sects are taken more seriously than the church for they at least occupy a definite place. A thing can only be described if it has a definite place. Its nature and claim thereby acquire profile. The definite place being occupied, no one else can lay claim to it. But it is not only the church which is

without claim and place, everywhere and nowhere, but also the concept of God. The church no longer supported the sense of loneliness in its specific place.

On the other hand, having lost its specific place, the church is now only to be found at privileged places in the world. It now feels more comfortable in this place rather than that. Its option for certain places rather than others reflects different degrees in its capacity for adaptation. It has lost the yardstick for its *proper* place. The church is now hated because of its preferred places . . .

What is the church's proper place? It is impossible to specify it concretely in advance. It is the place of the present, the contemporary, Christ in the world. It is the will of God which chooses this or that place for this purpose. It cannot therefore be indicated or taken up by us human beings in advance. God designates it by his gracious presence. It has to be adopted by him. The church has been given no authority to declare a historical place to be the place of God . . .

. . . No one knows in advance where this place, this centre, will be. Historically speaking, it may be right on the fringe, as was Galilee in the Roman Empire or Wittenberg in the 16th century. But God will make this place visible and everyone then has to include it in his itinerary. All that the church can do is to attest the centre of the world which God alone decides. It must try to make space for God's work.

(B) In Christendom

Church and Christendom are not identical. How are we to explain the hatred of the church which is obviously not directed against Christians as such? Is it provoked by the fact that the church stands for the most part only at the periphery of life? The high points or transitional stages of the individual life (birth, confirmation, marriage, death) are also high points of church activity. It is there that the church is mainly encountered. Nature and celebration go together, it is said. The church serves as a link between them. What we are offered, therefore, are church nature festivals. The church becomes what is exceptional in daily life, i.e. celebration; people seek and desire the church in order to interrupt the daily monotony. Everyday thoughts are given a veneer of solemnity. The rôle of the church is to divert, deepen, ennoble . . .

What is the proper place of the church in Christendom? Answer: the daily life of the world in all its aspects and not just one single isolated aspect, be it ethical or religious. It is just such isolation which leads to this "celebration" view of the church. But we have to learn to view the daily life of the world as it really is, under the judgment of God. Religion, even the Christian religion, comes to terms with this exceptional character — but God does not come to terms with it! With the thought of God, we do not "celebrate". God pervades and lays claim to reality in *all* its dimensions . . .[16]

The vital point, then, is that the church at the privileged places of the world is at the same time the displaced church which is unwilling to be the obedient church of the present Christ at the places decided by God. The choice is not between this or that way of organizing the church's life but between being the church or not being the church or even, at worst, being an anti-Christian church. Even more surprising, the place of the contemporary Christ is not the devout religious community which busies itself with "essential church matters" (and adapts itself to society and its culture in an "indulgent peace"[17]) but "reality in all its dimensions". Behind these terse affirmations about the place of the church, therefore, is a comprehensive verdict on the historical rôle of the Western European churches and on religious practice in the modern period down to our own day.

A few months after this address, God chose the place for the church in Germany: namely, the Jewish question. Bonhoeffer kept the appointment. The Confessing Church and even Barth, on the contrary, hesitated to follow the *Christus praesens* here (into suffering). The Confessing Church, not to speak of the "German Christians" and the national provincial churches of Germany, renewed their attempts to draw a neat dividing line between the ecclesiastical and the political realms. Bethge tells of the repeated attempts to play off the national church's fears for its existence against the developing radical stance within the Confessing Church. "Concern for the survival of the National Church has already virtually replaced concern for the undisguised Word of Truth."[18] Not surprisingly, therefore, Bonhoeffer was obliged to trust his own conscience alone in deciding to participate in the conspiracy against Hitler (in the company of only very few others) and could no longer look for the support of his church in this decision.[19]

Bonhoeffer's basic theological conception has far-reaching practical consequences for his dealings with the empirical church. He does not develop any broad plan of church reform nor urge the creation of a "pure" sect.[20] On the contrary, the starting point for action of any kind is precisely recognition of the secularization of the church and concrete repentance based on obedience to God's word in the given situation. "The Confessing Church would surrender the promise it has been given if, alongside obedience to the truth revealed by the Holy Spirit, any other entities of any kind were introduced in order to revive the life of the church."[21]

The solution of becoming a sect is also ruled out, however,

because the contemporary Christ is to be sought, found and attested in *all* dimensions of reality. Because the corrupt national church fails to do this, it is just as much a sect as any religious community which is concerned only with "essential church matters".

In this context, a critical question also has to be addressed to Bonhoeffer himself. So strongly did he stress the universality of the church that he failed to make a distinction at one important point which we are having to wrestle with today. "The church's place", he says, "is not only with the poor but also with the rich . . ."[22] That, of course, is true — but in what sense? One of the basic hermeneutic rules for understanding scripture, which Bonhoeffer himself repeatedly stressed, is the rule of concreteness. The central question here is who speaks to whom.[23] God declares God's grace and command in different ways to the poor and to the rich, i.e. to the poor as poor, and to the rich as rich.

This is a troubling question, particularly when we think not only of rich and poor individuals but also of the structural processes whereby the impoverishment of the poor is the consequence of the enrichment of the rich. Bonhoeffer touches on this question but fails to follow it through.[24] God had pointed him in his day to other questions as primarily the place of the present Christ.

But in the light of this question, it is already clear that those who follow the contemporary Christ obediently in all dimensions of life, not magisterially but ministerially, by doing so deliberately, put at risk their own privileges and those of the church. The sequence is: discipleship leads to the loss of privileges and to suffering. This is not to say that in order to do this there is no need to develop practical alternative forms of church life. The preachers' seminaries of the Confessing Church (e.g. Finkenwalde) were concrete steps to make it possible to teach church theology, practise confessional fidelity, train pastors and engage in a common spiritual life, independently of the state universities. Pastors faithful to the confession had to be supported exclusively by voluntary gifts from the congregations, to forego their pension rights, etc.

In Bonhoeffer's view, after the collapse of the Hitler régime, the German church would have to make a fundamentally new start. He would spend his remaining days down to his death drafting in outline the future of this church distilling all the experiences of the church struggle. The question arises: did the German church avail itself of this future?

II. Can the national church in the FRG become a confessing church?

The question with which the last section ended is sometimes considered as purely rhetorical, but the matter is not as simple as that. After the Second World War there is not just a Federal German Republic but also a German Democratic Republic,[25] where, in an avowedly atheistic state, the churches are far more aware of what it means to live as disciples of Christ and to practise the presence of the contemporary Christ in a "religionless world" than are the churches in the West. How far the churches in the East have succeeded in doing so in accordance with the criteria proposed by Bonhoeffer it is not my purpose to examine in detail here. The oft-used slogan of the "shrinking national church"[26] seems on the whole to imply a negative verdict. Yet there are many signs here that the way from this shrinking national church to a confessing minority church is being sought and affirmed fairly generally despite all the temptations on the right hand and on the left, the temptation to migrate (inwardly or even literally) on the one hand, and the temptation to take the easy way of conformity, on the other.

In the Federal Republic of Germany, too, some of the lessons of the era of the church struggle appear to have been taken to heart. The evangelical academies, the church conference *(Kirchentag)*, and the committees of the Evangelical Church in Germany (the Commission for Public Responsibility, for example) do seem to be asserting the claim of Jesus Christ to all areas of life. But are they doing so within the context of the binding confession of faith, the militant "action of the just" and the prayer which waits and listens for God's decision as to where the church should be? But if we look beyond these hopeful signs and consider the remaining aspects of reality of the national church, we are bound to ask whether the picture today is really any different from that painted by Bonhoeffer in his 1932 address, which can be summed up as a state of displacement in the interests of the privileged places.[27] Church sociologists and theologians, moreover, are becoming increasingly concerned to justify the existing national church system without even asking the questions raised by Bonhoeffer and others. The most notorious recent examples of this trend are furnished by the standard use of the EKD programme "How stable is the Church?"[28] and the study published by the Theological Commission of the United Evangelical Lutheran Church of Germany entitled "National Church — Church of the Future?"[29]

Does this mean that it is impossible for a church like that in the Federal Republic of Germany to accept Bonhoeffer's theoretical and practical ecclesiology in the given conditions of the present national church? Are its stakes in social privilege too high for it to be willing to pay the price of becoming an obedient confessing church? Humanly speaking, the answer is probably yes. What then is to be done? Join a free church? Are voluntary churches as such more truly the church of Jesus Christ? According to Bonhoeffer, who was himself sometimes tempted to join a free church, we must choose another way.[30] As long as the word of God is preached within it, the present empirical church is where the struggle for the true church of Jesus Christ is to be waged. But, if struggle there must be, at what precise point is it to be joined?

For Bonhoeffer, there is only one possible starting point: we must wait attentively and prayerfully to see where God chooses; the place of the *Christus praesens*, the place where confessing the faith and the doing of justice are mandatory.[31] It is my firm conviction that one of the foremost places where we are to look for the *Christus praesens* today is the global economic system since this place is central for injustice, wars and the destruction of the creation.

But even if this is accepted, what concrete form would the community of the church have to take today to allow it to approach these problems in the way proposed by Bonhoeffer? Some Christians and Christian groups are engaged in serious efforts to help solve this problem. What is not yet generally recognized, however, is the confessional significance of these questions, what it would mean concretely to be a church of disciples of Jesus Christ truly obedient to God's commandments, and how the forgiveness of sins would bring joy into the doing of justice and prayer.

Since June 1977 there has been a glimmer of hope. Meeting together then for the Sixth Assembly of the Lutheran World Federation, deputies from the Lutheran churches of the world declared the system of apartheid in South Africa to constitute a *casus confessionis*, an imperative challenge to Christians to confess their faith. Will our churches in Germany, and elsewhere in the rich Western countries, likewise recognize themselves as material accomplices in the maintenance of a global system of apartheid just as are the white South Africans, a world system of injustice in which human beings are ceaselessly being despised and killed?[32]

The ecumenical movement has become clearer on this point than it was in Bonhoeffer's time. On the other hand, the refusal of the

West German churches to accept the WCC's Programme to Combat Racism also made clear their reluctance to accept a commitment of this kind. Nor has the World Council of Churches itself wholly succeeded in establishing its social and political options as wholly consonant theologically with its fidelity to the confession of Jesus Christ as God and Saviour, and in understanding and accepting these options therefore in complete unanimity. Nor has the authoritative ecumenical council desiderated by Bonhoeffer in the thirties yet become a reality.

Yet only one way is open to us today: we must confront the empirical churches with the concrete question of the confession of faith, in ecumenical solidarity and in all possible ways. For, if it is salvation in Jesus Christ which is at stake here and not simply supposedly "optional" political questions, it is publicly in the setting of the whole church that these issues must be resolved. Important auxiliary examples are proved here by alternative ways of believing, living and acting on the part of both individuals and groups. For a visible demonstration is needed that, for those who follow Christ faithfully, his yoke is easier and his burden lighter than the murderous laws of our exploitative system and society.

Can Bonhoeffer's ecclesiology (theoretical and practical) be received in a situation of the kind that exists in the Federal Republic of Germany? Humanly speaking, the answer is no (Mark 10:27). But if it is the case that "one holy Christian church will be and remain for ever" and if this church is "the assembly of all believers among whom the gospel" (including God's gracious command!) "is preached in its purity and the holy sacraments administered according to the gospel" (CA 7), then even in situations of this kind there will be the church which listens for God's living word and is willing to betake itself to where God shares in the sufferings of the world. Not yet have we tried seriously at all levels of the life of the church to face up to the question of the confession of our faith and of the form this confession requires of the church today.

NOTES

1. Dissertation, New York, 1975 (Xerox University Microfilms, Ann Arbor).
2. D. Bonhoeffer, *Das Wesen der Kirche* (Kaiser Traktate 3), ed. O. Dudzus, Munich, 1971, p. 31. Cf. Bonhoeffer, *Sanctorum Communio. Eine dogmatische Untersuchung zur Soziologie der Kirche*, Munich (1930)³1960, p. 90.

3. Dietrich Bonhoeffer, *Letters and Papers from Prison*, the enlarged edition, ed. Eberhard Bethge, SCM Press Ltd., London, 1971, pp. 380ff.

4. Cf.Day, *op. cit.*, p. 18 and p. 57.

5. *Op. cit.*, p. 30.

6. *Gesammelte Schriften* (abbrev.*GS*). Vol. III, p. 432. Cf. Day, *op. cit.*, p. 2.

7. Bonhoeffer, *The Cost of Discipleship* (Germ.*Nachfolge*, Munich, 1937, p. 8). cf. E. Bethge, "Freedom and Obedience in Bonhoeffer" (in German), in C. Frey and W. Huber (eds), *Schöpferische Nachfolge*, p. 345.

8. *GS* I, p. 248; cf. Day, *op. cit.*, p. 20.

9. E. Bethge, *Dietrich Bonhoeffer: a Biography*, Collins, 1970, p. 792.

10 "I am hopelessly torn between staying here, going to India, and returning to Germany to take charge of a preachers' seminary shortly to be opened there. I no longer believe in the University, and never really have believed in it — a fact which used to rile you. Young theologians ought now to be trained throughout in conventual seminaries where the pure doctrine, the Sermon on the Mount and worship are taken seriously as they never are (and in present circumstances couldn't be) at university. It is high time we threw off a restraint that is grounded in theology — and which is, after all, only fear — towards the conduct of the state. 'Open your mouth for the dumb' — who in the church today realizes that this is the least of the Bible's demands? And then there's the matter of military service and war, etc. etc. . . . " (Bethge, *op. cit.*, p. 334).

11. Bethge, *op. cit.*, p. 165 and p. 192.

12. A detailed reflection on the relationship between theology and the congregation can be found in *GS* III, pp. 421–425.

13. *Genf '76*, p. 132. Cf. Bethge, *op. cit.*, pp. 779–780.

14. Especially E. Feil, *Die Theologie Dietrich Bonhoeffers. Hermeneutik — Christologie — Weltverständnis*, Munich — Mainz 2, 1971; A. Dumas, *op. cit.*, H. Müller, *op. cit.* See Day, *op. cit.*, pp. 92, 175f., 220, 259, 452ff.

15. *Op. cit.*, pp. 19ff. (see note 2 above).

16. *Op. cit.*, pp. 21–25.

17. Cf. E. Bethge, "Christian Faith without Religion. Was Dietrich Bonhoeffer Mistaken?" (in German), *Evangelische Kommentare*, July 1975, p. 397.

18. Bethge, *Dietrich Bonhoeffer*, p. 414. Cf. also p. 329 and pp. 418f. (especially against the Lutheran provincial churches which misused the confession of faith in order to rescue the national church), pp. 516f.

19. Cf. Bethge, *Dietrich Bonhoeffer*, pp. 699f. Contrary to misinterpretations current today, it is clear that Bonhoeffer did not rule out in principle acceptance of responsibility by the church for active resistance on the part of its members in special situations. But he knew that his church was *not yet* in a position to do so in his case and therefore he assumed sole responsibility for it in his own conscience.

20. Cf. *Das Wesen der Kirche*, pp. 70ff.

21. *GS* II, pp. 215f. On the Holy Spirit as subject of the actualization of the *Christus praesens*, cf. already *Sanctorum Communio*, pp. 94f.

22. *Das Wesen der Kirche*, p. 71.

23. Cf. K. Stendahl, *Paul among Jews and Gentiles*, Fortress Press, Philadelphia, 1976, p. 106.

24. See e.g. the section in *Sanctorum Communio* on "Church and Proletariat" to which R. Seeberg objected and which was not included in the first edition (*Sanctorum Communio* pp. 247ff.). On the problem as a whole, cf. Day, *op. cit.*, pp. 104f., 137, 163, 193f., 197f., and in our third chapter below.

25. Cf. Day, *op. cit.*, p. 459.
26. G. Krusche, "Neubestimmung des Verhältnisses von Staat und Kirche (in den sozialistischen Ländern)", in V. Vajta (ed.), *Die lutherischen Kirchen. Vergangenheit und Gegenwart* (Die Kirchen der Welt, Vol. XV), Stuttgart, 1977, pp. 301–319.
27. Cf. Day, *op. cit.*, p. 458.
28. Ed. H. Hild, Gelnhausen-Berlin, 1974.
29. Eds. W. Lohff and L. Mohaupt, in *Zur Sache*, No. 12/13, Hamburg 1977.
30. Cf. Bethge, *Dietrich Bonhoeffer*, p. 239 and pp. 266f.
31. "Our church, which has been fighting in these years only for its self-preservation, as though that were an end in itself, is incapable of taking the word of reconciliation and redemption to mankind and the world. Our earlier words are therefore bound to lose their force and cease, and our being Christians today will be limited to two things: prayer and righteous action among men. All Christian thinking, speaking and organizing must be born anew out of this prayer and action" *(Letters and Papers from Prison*, p. 300). Cf. also Day, *op. cit.*, pp. 456f.
32. Cf. M. Buthelezi and U. Duchrow, "Does the Bible also Speak to White Men?" (in German in WPKG, No. 64 1975, pp. 434ff); and U. Duchrow, "From the Theology of Liberation via the Ethics of Liberation to the Church of Liberation" (in German) in *Orientierung*, reports and analyses from the work of the North Elbian Evangelical Academy No.5, December 1977, pp. 49ff.

PART TWO

Remembering the God of Abraham, Isaac and Jacob: the call to freedom and discipleship

"Then Moses said to God: Suppose I go to the Israelites and tell them the God of their forefathers has sent me; they're sure to ask me his name. What am I to tell them? God answered: I AM, THAT IS WHO I AM. *Tell.* them I AM has sent you!" (Ex. 3:13f.)

This dialogue from the story of the burning bush from the midst of which God called Moses to be the instrument of God's divine liberation is meant to help us, as it helped Moses, to address a people which is hard of hearing. However accustomed our congregations and churches may have become to the fleshpots of Egypt and however much we may have tied ourselves down by ideological and institutional conformism, experiences of the promises of God lie hidden within our past and our present.

Just as the tribes of Israel were reminded of the promises given by God to their ancestors, so we too can be reminded of these past and present experiences of God. This reminder is obviously an essential part of our conversion and our ventures into freedom. Indeed, the more radical the need for conversion and the courage to venture forth, the greater the need too for a rocklike assurance and continuity of faith. Access to this assurance and continuity is not via generalizations nor the experiences of quite different historical traditions. It is no help to be told that God generally acts in this or that way. It is little help for a German to be confronted with the wealth and strength of Eastern Orthodox experiences of the Blessed Trinity. Each tradition has to help those who stand within it.

For Germans, the important thing is to know the experiences and promises hidden within their own tradition. Here the names of Luther and Bonhoeffer have a special and exemplary rôle. These "fathers" have considerable authority and this can therefore give us confidence in taking the necessary steps towards conversion and a new departure. Both wrestled with the question of what churches and Christians are to do when economic and political institutions degenerate and decay and we are required to resist and to seek new ways. In Chapter 3 we shall be concerned with this remembering and listening to the "God of our spiritual ancestors" which will indicate to us the initial approaches to knowledge and action in the context of the global economic system today.

But Yahweh, the God who made himself known to Moses, the God of the slaves and of those who are banished to the margins of history (who in those days were called "Hebrews"), points not only to the past but reveals himself as the God who is today and will be tomorrow. Yahweh's name can also be rendered as "I WILL

BE WHO I WILL BE". This God is present when we hear the cry of the oppressed. This God is present as the One who confronts and opposes those who abuse and corrupt their power.

Today, too, therefore, this God is present among us in all parts of the world. Moreover, the ecumenical community has begun to perceive God as such. The churches in the Federal Republic of Germany are called to perceive God as such just as are the churches and Christians in other rich countries and in the rich sectors of the poor countries. The call to freedom has been sounded. The price of ignoring this call can only be the continued death of countless fellow human beings from hunger and from other such "plagues" threatening humanity today. In Chapter 4, therefore, we shall try to summarize the experiences and insights of the ecumenical community from the standpoint of the victims of the present global system.

3

What to do if the driver is drunk: the answer of Luther and Bonhoeffer

When economic or political institutions are notoriously perverted, both Luther and Bonhoeffer have a clear answer to the question of what is to be done: "If the coachdriver is drunk, we have to put a spoke in the wheel."[1] In other words, the church is summoned to resist in order to prevent disaster. We now have to see what that signifies in respect of the present global economic system.

Both Luther and Bonhoeffer adopt a twofold approach to the ethical problem with different sets of questions uppermost in each approach. *Firstly*, they ask how Christ becomes a reality in our midst. This is the question of the body of Christ, the operation of the Holy Spirit within this body, and the consequences this has for the life of Christians themselves and for their conduct within the human community as a whole. *Secondly*, however, they approach the question from the standpoint of the human community and its actual institutions. The question now is what are the requirements for a successful common life? What concrete form should its institutions have and what is the proper use of these institutions? These are questions for both Christians and others. As theological questions, of course, they are also interested in how God chooses to work through these institutions and how human beings are to deal with them in obedience to God. Luther deals with this second set of questions under the rubric of the "three estates": i.e. *ecclesia* (church), *oeconomia* (embracing family

---

● Revised version of a paper read by the author to the Bonhoeffer Committee of the Federation of Protestant Churches in the GDR on 2 October 1981 in Ferch, near Potsdam, and to the Theological Faculty of the University of Vienna on 13 January 1982. Printed in Chr. Gremmels (ed.), *Bonhoeffer und Luther* (International Bonhoeffer Forum 6), Munich, 1983, pp. 16–58.

and the economy), and *politia* (the political commonwealth or state). Bonhoeffer sees them as questions concerning the four "mandates": church, marriage and family, work, government.

The two approaches to the problem of ethics, one from the standpoint of the body of Christ, the other from the standpoint of social institutions, are combined by Luther and Bonhoeffer in different ways, depending on the level of experience or the particular aspect of faith in the Triune God that is uppermost.

They are bridged in the *first* place by the fact that in Luther and Bonhoeffer the body of Christ, viewed from the angle of human institutions, also has its place in the doctrine of the "estates" or "mandates" as the question of the *ecclesia* (the church). We must be careful here to avoid the mistake of neo-classic Protestant dogmatics and not equate the three "estates" with three separate groups of people. For Luther and for Bonhoeffer, the "estates" or "mandates" are different dimensions of life in which every Christian or human being operates and is answerable to God and called to cooperate in the achievement of God's good purpose.[2] In other words, we are answerable to God not only as individual persons but also in a whole set of diverse inter-related dimensions.

The *second* bridge between the two approaches is God's command. In the first approach I ask how God's will is accomplished by the Holy Spirit in and through the body of Christ. In the second approach I enquire into the concrete reality of the world within which God's commandments challenge the conscience and direct it to good conduct (*usus theologicus* and *usus politicus legis*).

A *third* possible bridge would be the doctrine of God's "regiments" (or "governances"). In the first approach, it would then be a question of God's ecclesiastical regiment which challenges the conscience but also liberates the human being by the act of justification in Christ. Enjoying this gift of freedom, we are constrained by the Spirit of Christ to daily renewal and struggle to do God's will voluntarily within the concrete reality of the "estate" or "mandate". In the second approach, it is a question of summoning both Christians and others to submit to God's "ecclesiastical regiment" but also, even should this summons be rejected, of summoning them to ensure and make possible a common life under God's "secular regiment" in the family, economics and politics. For even if sin has rendered us more or less blind and thus limited our capacities for action (cf. Rom. 7:14ff.), God has nevertheless given us minds to use to this end.

Finally, a *fourth* bridge between the two approaches is provided by Christology. Luther establishes this bridge more indirectly but Bonhoeffer quite explicitly. In the first approach, it is a question of the saving, liberating, justifying and redeeming Christ who assembles a people under the rule of God and endowed with all the gifts of the Holy Spirit. In the second approach, it is a question of Christ the mediator in creation, the Cosmocrator, already established secretly as the present Lord of the whole cosmos, who will bring all things under the sovereignty of God's love. This Christological connection between the church and the reality of the world, between faith and reason, is the strongest and most basic criterion for our responsibility as Christians for the world, enabling us to test every claim to autonomy against the declared will and purpose of God.

In all these four bridges a tension remains between the two approaches: the tension of God's eschatological struggle to establish divine sovereignty over the destructive and self-destructive forces of evil. This struggle embraces both the body of Christ and all human institutions. Just because the body of Christ is not yet "all in all" prior to the kingdom of God in its fullness, it is still necessary to differentiate between the two approaches to the problem of ethics.

These four bridges, sketched here in outline only, must be kept clearly in mind as we develop the twofold approach to Christian ethics by Luther and Bonhoeffer in the next two sections (so as to avoid a false dualism). In a third section we shall look at the concrete question of the church and the economic realm today.

I. The body of Christ as basis for Christian ethics in Luther and Bonhoeffer

1. MARTIN LUTHER

To show the continuity and consistency of Luther's approach, the following presentation will examine two of his writings, one early and the other late: *A Sermon on the Blessed Sacrament . . . and on the Fraternities* (1519)[3] and *On Councils and Churches* (Part 3, 1539).[4]

1.1. *A sermon on the blessed sacrament . . .*

In a quite traditional fashion, the Augustinian monk Luther begins this early work with an array of Augustinian definitions. The keys to his interpretation of the Lord's Supper are the three terms "sign", "significance", and "faith". The core of the exposition is found in the second section, on the *significatio* or significance. He explains this exclusively in terms of *communio*, the communion in the body of Christ:

> And *communicare* in the Latin means "to receive this communion" or "to go to the sacrament" as we say in German. For Christ with all his saints constitutes a spiritual body, just as the inhabitants of a city constitute a community and a body, each individual citizen being a limb of every other and of the whole city. All saints, therefore, are members of Christ and of the church, which is a spiritual and eternal city of God. It can be said of anyone accepted into the city of God that he is accepted into the communion of the saints, incorporated into Christ's spiritual body and thereby made a member thereof.
>
> *Excommunicare*, on the contrary, means "to expel from the community, to amputate a member of this body" and in German we use a term meaning "to banish or excommunicate", though with qualifications, as I shall explain in the next sermon on the *anathema*. To receive this sacrament in bread and wine, therefore, is simply to receive a sure token of this communion and bodily bond with Christ and all his saints, just as a citizen is given a token, a certificate or document of some sort certifying that he is a citizen of this city, a member of this community. As St Paul says in 1 Corinthians 10:17: "We are all one bread and one body, for we all share one bread and one cup."

This approach makes one assumption and has two implications which while self-evident for Luther are not so for us. The *assumption* is that Christ and his saints constitute an indivisible unity. Luther's procedure is not first of all to examine what happens at the Lord's Supper between Christ and the individual or even just his or her soul and only then go on, in a second stage, to bind the individual so united with Christ to other Christians and human beings generally. For Luther, the Lord's Supper is at one and the same time incorporation in Christ as Head of the body and in the saints as its members. Further on in the sermon, therefore, Luther can even employ such unexpected words as these:

> In this sacrament, therefore, we have been so granted the boundless mercy and grace of God that we may cast off all wailing and all temptations and trials from us and lay them on the church and especially on Christ.

In the Lord's Supper, therefore, I enter in a real sense above all into the one visible community in which Christ is present, of course, as Head. Not a breath of spiritualism here. Visible bodil iness. Flesh and blood human beings in a community with a historical structure. This is to be maintained and asserted in spite of the atomized and abstract society in which we live today and which separates us from the relatively simpler conditions of Luther's time.

The *first consequence* of this approach is described by Luther as follows:

> This communion is constituted by the fact that all the spiritual blessings of Christ and his saints are imparted to and become the possession of the one who receives this sacrament. Conversely, all sufferings and sins also become common to all, so that love is quickened and united with love. Keeping to the rough physical image: just as all the citizens of a city bear the city's name, share its fame, freedom, trade, customs, morals, services, support, protection and the like, so too, conversely, they share every danger, fire, water, enemies, death, injury, taxes, and the like. For if we wish to share the joys we must also share the costs and return love for love. If anyone injures one citizen, clearly he injures the whole city and all its citizens; anyone who does good to a citizen deserves the gratitude and respect of all the other citizens. So is it also in our physical bodies, as St Paul points out in 1 Corinthians 12:25f., where he explains this sacrament in a spiritual sense. The members care for one another; if one suffers, all the others suffer with it. If one member is joyful, all the others rejoice with it. We can verify this for ourselves: if my foot hurts or even only my little toe, my eyes at once investigate, my fingers reach out to it, my face registers anguish and my whole body bends down to help — and all this for the sake of my little toe, the tiniest of my members! And conversely, of course: if I take good care of my body, all its members are the beneficiaries.

Once we have been incorporated into the body of Christ by baptism, once we have become citizens of this city, we are bound up in the bundle of life with this community and have rights and duties in a living process of giving and receiving. When sin, evil thoughts, a bad conscience, suffering or fear assail us, "let us, if we wish to be rid of these things, simply go rejoicing to the sacrament of the altar, lay our burden before the community and seek the aid of the whole membership of the spiritual body!"

Conversely, and this aspect is dealt with by Luther in some detail, love also constrains the member of the community to lend his or her aid whenever misfortune befalls "the truth and word of God" in the community, and to do so, indeed, "everywhere in the world", i.e. in the universal body of Christ, in Christ's poor and persecuted brothers and sisters:

Your heart, therefore, must devote itself to love, learn that this sacrament is a sacrament of love, recognize the love and support that are bestowed on you and that you in return should love and support Christ in his suffering members. All dishonouring of Christ in his holy word, all distress in Christendom, all the undeserved suffering of the innocent, will make you suffer. You will find all this suffering and distress in every part of the world. Here you will defend, work, pray, urge, and when there is nothing more you can do, show heartfelt compassion. You must know that this too is what it means to bear the misfortunes and trials of Christ and his saints. For then is Paul's saying fulfilled: "Bear one another's burdens and so fulfill the law of Christ!" (Gal. 6:2). For if you bear the burden with them all, they in turn will all bear the burden with you and so all things are shared, good and evil. All things then become easy: the evil spirit cannot then overcome the church. When Christ instituted his sacrament, he said: "This is my body, given for you. This is my blood, shed for you. As oft as you do this, you remember me" (Luke 22:19f.). As if he wished to say: I am the head. I will be the first to sacrifice myself for you, to make your suffering and misfortune my own and to bear them for you, so that in return you may do the same for me and for one another, so that you may share all things together in me and with me. And I leave you this sacrament as a sure sign for all this so that you may never forget me but in this way may daily be exercised and reminded of what I have done for you, so that you may be able to strengthen and support one another.

The horizon of the Lord's Supper, then, is the distress and oppression in the whole of Christendom which dishonours Christ himself. Anyone who has been made a member of this body has no other choice but to counter this distress and oppression with resistance, work, exhortation, and where outward circumstances exclude these, with solidarity in suffering. Then the evil spirit is denied a foothold in the church. Then the body is obedient to the Head who instituted the sacrament with the words: "Given for you!"

In this solidarity in suffering — and this is the *second consequence* — we see why the Lord's Supper, unlike baptism, is celebrated frequently, and what the proper use of the sacrament is. Baptism is "a beginning, an entrance into a new life". But this new life meets with overwhelming resistance and temptations because of sin and suffering, our own and others', because of the devil, the world, desires and fatalism. This is why we need *daily* support and reinforcement. The Lord's Supper exists for the hungry and fearful (Magnificat, Luke 1).

Indeed, it is only when we receive the Lord's Supper conscious of our own and others' need and distress within a real fellowship of mutual sharing that we receive it worthily and are strengthened by it (1 Cor. 11!):

> For if we are willing, as we should be, to make the misfortune of Christ and of all Christians our own, if we want to help to bear the pain of the distress of the innocent and of all Christians, we shall find misfortune and distress in plenty; not to mention what our own evil character, the world, the devil and sin daily make us produce ourselves. It is also God's will and plan that he should hunt and chase us with so many hounds and prepare so many bitter herbs for us, just so that we may long all the more for this strengthening, and take delight in the holy sacrament, become worthy of it, i.e. desirous of it.

So it was that the early Christians, in a very down-to-earth way, collected articles and food (*collecta*) and money to give to the poor. This also helps us to understand why so many were prepared to become martyrs. This was also why Luther later on in his new "church orders" treated the question of the poor as a vital matter.[5]

Luther's criticism is not only of the church of his own time, for its failure to practise real fellowship, but also of those whose *only* desire is to profit from the communion with Christ and his saints, *only* to hear but not to do likewise. These he warns against such use of the sacrament:

> But they are unwilling to practise fellowship themselves, unwilling to help the poor, to be patient with sinners, to care for the needy, to suffer with the suffering, to pray for others, unwilling also to defend the truth, to seek the betterment of the church and all Christians at their own cost; and this unwillingness springs from fear of the world, fear of having to endure unpopularity, injury, shame or even death, even though it is God's will that love of the truth and of the neighbour will drive them to desire this sacrament with all its resources of grace and comfort. These are selfish people for whom this sacrament profits nothing . . . For where love does not daily increase and so transform the human being that he or she *has fellowship with every other individual*, this sacrament is fruitless and meaningless.

A little later, Luther adds, in criticism of the medieval view of the Lord's Supper: " . . . the nobler the sacrament is, the greater the damage its misuse does to the whole church . . . "

To sum up: Genuine and fruitful partaking of the sacrament of the Lord's Supper is identical with real participation in fellowship with Christ and his saints. This participation in the one body of Christ brings abundant comfort, strength and support to the participant, but only if the latter in turn joins in a life of resistance, action, intercession and compassionate solidarity for the sake of Christ and his saints.

1.2. On councils and churches

Whereas the target of Luther's early sermon was the piety of the medieval church and the idea that the sacrament of the Lord's Supper was automatic in its effects, in his later work *On Councils and Churches* he was obliged to attack this same position in his own ranks, i.e. in opposition to the so-called "antinomians", and therefore in a different form. The "antinomians" considered the Law to be obsolete for the Christian community and applicable only to unbelievers.

In this later work, Luther developed his ecclesiology not in terms of the body of Christ but with reference to the clause in the Apostles' Creed: "I believe one holy Christian church, the communion of saints", i.e. in terms of the *sancta Catholica Christiana*. This, he says, is

> a Christian, a holy people which believes in Christ. Hence it is called a *Christian* people and has the Holy Spirit who sanctifies it daily not only by the forgiveness of sins obtained for them by Christ (as the antinomians foolishly assert) but also by removing, sweeping away sin and putting it to death. Hence it is called a *holy* people.

The exposition of the real communion of Christ and his saints in the 1519 sermon is replaced in the 1539 tract by an exposition of the real effects of the work of the Holy Spirit in the communion of saints or, as Bonhoeffer expresses it, the realization of the reality of Christ. The Holy Spirit "accomplishes this life-giving and sanctifying work by daily sweeping away sin and bestowing new life".

This advances our enquiry in that here, in contrast to the 1519 sermon, the fulfilment of the Ten Commandments (the two tables of the Mosaic Law) is regarded as the purpose, goal and effect of the work of the Holy Spirit. For it is in the context of the concrete fulfilment of the Mosaic Law that Luther deals theologically with the question of economics and other institutional forms of human life. As I have already pointed out, we have here a bridge between the two approaches to the ethical problem (the one starting from the body of Christ, the other from the doctrine of the "estates"). In terms of the first table of the law (love to God), the Holy Spirit bestows true knowledge of God, strength and comfort for the conscience, victory over the devil, praise and thanksgiving to God: in other words, faith, hope and love. But the fulfilment of the second table of the law (love to the neighbour) is also the gift of the Holy Spirit, and includes the renunciation of profiteering, covetousness and fraud; in place of which forms of disobedience we have "delight in lending, giving and assisting".

This is the work of the Holy Spirit who also sanctifies the body and quickens it to this newness of life until it is consummated in the life of the other world. This is what is meant by Christian sanctity. And there will always be people of this kind on earth even if only in twos and threes or only children. Grown-ups are fewer here, alas. But no one who fails to live this kind of life is to regard him or herself as a Christian; nor should we comfort them by pretending they *are* Christians, by talking idly of the "forgiveness of sins" and of the "grace of Christ" as the antinomians do.

For just as these people reject and misconstrue the Ten Commandments, so too they talk loudly of the grace of Christ. But they strengthen and comfort those who persist in their sins by telling them not to worry since these sins have all been washed away by Christ. They see people commit notorious and public sins but let them go on doing so with no change or improvement in their lives. It is quite clear from this that they do not really understand the Christian faith and Christ, abolishing them even as they preach them. For how can anyone rightly talk of the works of the Holy Spirit in the first table, i.e. of comfort, grace, pardon of sins, if he neither heeds nor practises the works of the same Holy Spirit in the second table, which he can grasp and experience whereas the former he has neither proved nor experienced? Obviously, therefore, they neither have nor understand either Christ or the Holy Spirit. Their idle chatter is mere empty mouthing. And, as I have said, they are really Nestorians and Eutychians who confess and teach Christ in the substance but deny him in the consequence. They teach Christ and in teaching him eliminate him.

According to Luther, then, anyone who preaches Christ without at the same time preaching the real fulfilment of the second table of the Mosaic Law (love of the neighbour), "abolishes" Christ, "eliminates" Christ. He develops this further in terms of the outward marks of the church (*notae ecclesiae*). These he sub-divides: seven marks for the first table and seven for the second.[6] For our theme, the fulfilment of the commandment "You shall not steal!" as one of the marks of the true church is of particular importance, including its relevance for the economic structures of our life. To suppress this necessary mark of the church is to abolish and eliminate Christ. Luther was perfectly clear whom he was addressing:

those who propagated the Roman and neo-Reformation "anti-nomian" heresy of "cheap grace" (cf. Bonhoeffer in *The Cost of Discipleship*), a religion and a church which imagine they can bear Christ's name without solidarity and communion with the poor and persecuted, without love for truth and justice.

2. DIETRICH BONHOEFFER

From a formal standpoint, Bonhoeffer's starting point for Christian ethics is the same as Luther's as just outlined on the basis of the 1519 sermon and the 1539 tract: namely, the body of Christ. Bonhoeffer defines the problem of Christian ethics as "the relation of reality and realization, past and present, history and event (faith), or, to replace the equivocal concept by the unambiguous name, the relation of Jesus Christ and the Holy Spirit".[7] In Bonhoeffer's view, the New Testament image best qualified to express the realization of the reality of Christ is "the picture of the body of Christ himself who became man, was crucified and rose again".[8]

Given the historical differences between Luther and Bonhoeffer, on the other hand, it should not surprise us to find that, for all the similarities between his approach and Luther's, Bonhoeffer has ventured further clarifications both in substance and in the arguments deployed. Two such clarifications call for special mention:

2.1. *The context of resistance*

It is permissible to connect the first clarification with the situation in which Bonhoeffer writes, namely, that of his coalition with a secular conspiracy. Luther's 1519 sermon and his 1539 tract were both written from a situation within the church; in opposition to heresies, to be sure, yet the context of Luther's writings is still the body of Christ in the stricter sense of the assembled community engaged in the struggle for sanctification. It was in this context that Bonhoeffer too wrote his dissertation *Sanctorum Communio* and his book on discipleship. But the context of Bonhoeffer's *Ethics* is clearly that of the quest for standing ground as a member of the church of Jesus Christ without the backing even of the Confessing Church itself.[9] We find a reflection of this context not least in bold statements — going almost to the limits of the permissible — concerning the cosmic universality of the reality of Christ, i.e. of the body of Christ.

> In the body of Jesus Christ, God is united with humanity, the whole of humanity is accepted by God and the world is reconciled with God.

In the body of Jesus Christ, God took upon himself the sin of the whole world and bore it. There is no part of the world, be it never so forlorn and never so godless, which is not accepted by God and reconciled with God in Jesus Christ . . . The church is divided from the world solely by the fact that she affirms in faith the reality of God's acceptance of man, a reality which is the property of the whole world. By allowing this reality to take effect within herself, she testifies that it is effectual for the whole world.

The body of Jesus Christ, especially as it appears to us on the cross, shows to the eyes of faith the world in its sin, and how it is loved by God, no less than it shows the church as the congregation of those who acknowledge their sin and submit to the love of God.[10]

What emboldens Bonhoeffer to venture statements of this kind is the tradition of the "cosmic Christ" in the New Testament: in the letter to the Colossians (especially the hymn to Christ in 1:15ff.) and in St John's Gospel (the prologue, c. 1). The Barthian tradition in the Confessing Church, with its clear recognition of Christendom's responsibility for the world on the basis of the royal sovereignty of Christ, served him well here. But no one else ventured so far forth into the sufferings of Christ "outside the camp" as to dare to take up the struggle against the persecution of the Jews or to join in the conspiracy against Hitler — as Bonhoeffer did — as the very cause of Christ himself.

2.2. Opposition to the compartmentalization of the world into "two spheres"

The second clarification contributed by Bonhoeffer in his development of the basic approach to the ethical problem which he shared with Luther was his opposition to the "compartmentalized thinking" which in various forms pervaded the history of the Western church and its theology and which therefore stood "like a Colossus" barring the way to the single reality of the one God who revealed himself in Jesus Christ. Bonhoeffer can put his finger on the precise place where he agrees with Luther and where he differs from him:

Just as the secular realm was used polemically by Luther against the sacralizing of the Roman Church, so too the secular realm itself must be resisted polemically on the basis of the Christian or "sacral" realm when the former is in danger of assuming absolute autonomy, as it did soon after the Reformation in a movement which culminated in the culture-Protestantism of the nineteenth century. In both of these polemical protests the process is the same: the reminder, namely, of Jesus Christ as the reality of God and the reality of the world. But just as it was *in the interests of a better Christian realm* that Luther used the secular realm in protest against a Christianity which by seeking to be autonomous was cutting itself off from the reality in Christ, so the polemic of the Christian realm against the secular realm today must be *in the interests of a better secular realm* and prevented from leading us back again to a static sacrality as an end in itself. Only in this sense, i.e. as a polemical unity, are we entitled to accept Luther's doctrine of the two kingdoms, and it was doubtless in this sense that it was originally intended.[11]

Bonhoeffer's actual opponents here are the pseudo-Lutherans with their false doctrine of the "autonomy of the orders", as well as "culture Protestantism" which Bonhoeffer considers to be based on the same heresy and which, in addition, "can exercise this right of autonomy in its dealings with the spiritual sphere".[12] Bonhoeffer rightly discerns behind these theological false tracks the positivist empirical approach to reality[13] and the modern secularization process with its demonic perversion of the freedom given in Christ.[14] But, if we disregard the conflict with the medieval church, which is not really Bonhoeffer's problem, the purpose of both Luther and Bonhoeffer is the same. This is illustrated in the fragmentary section on "Personal and Real Ethos"[15] which must date from the same period as the "Fourth Approach", i.e. 1940/1941. Here Bonhoeffer traces the doctrine of autonomous spheres back to the heresy of fundamental *adiaphora* with its roots in antinomianism:

> To sever the world of things from the commandments of God is to proclaim its autonomy; this constitutes the abandonment of the dominion of Christ over one sphere of life, and that means antinomianism.[16]

There is only one point which, though not absent in Bonhoeffer, is not brought out as clearly in his approach as it is in Luther's, probably because Bonhoeffer was concentrating on the political situation and the resistance it demanded, namely: the constitutive connection between membership of the body of Christ and "resistance, action, intercession and compassionate solidarity" on behalf of the poor and needy.[17] This criticism applies both to the approach in terms of the body of Christ and to the extension of the lines in the direction of the poor. Nevertheless, the common ground between Bonhoeffer's approach and Luther's remains. For Bonhoeffer's death was the end of a consistent way of "resistance, action, intercession and compassionate solidarity" on behalf of the victims of persecution and injustice, and, in Luther's view, this was the supreme form of participation in the body of Christ and his saints.

My sole concern here is to establish the economic question within the approach to ethics in terms of the body of Christ. And here I am inclined to see a relative difference between Luther and Bonhoeffer, one which is connected with their different historical contexts and also, perhaps, with other factors, such as the fact that Luther tackles the question of the poor and the question of economics directly. When we come to the other approach to ethics, i.e. in terms of the "estates" or "mandates", and examine the way the economic question is tackled there, we shall have to check whether these observations on the "body of Christ" approach are confirmed or not.

Firstly, however, we have to ask how far the approach found in both Luther and Bonhoeffer is viable in our own historical situation, i.e. in particular, our own situation in the western sector of the northern industrial societies.

3. THE BODY OF CHRIST TODAY — DIVIDED AMONG THIEVES, PROFITEERS AND THE ROBBED

For the Lutheran churches in South Africa and within the Lutheran World Federation, the South African question only became really explosive when it dawned on them that apartheid was reflected within the church even to the point of dividing Christians at the Lord's Table and in the organized church life of one and the same confession. Formally, therefore, the starting point for keener sensitivity to apartheid within the churches was similar to that which had led to the emergence of the Confessing Church under the Nazi régime in Germany. It was not the economic, social and political injustice of apartheid as such which prodded the churches into action (in the way that the Jewish question had clarified the vision of only a very few individuals like Bonhoeffer in the thirties) but its inroads into the church itself.

Once this approach to the discussion of apartheid in South Africa had been discovered, it was not long before the walls erected by the neo-Lutheran pseudo-doctrine of the "two kingdoms" between the churches and their social and political responsibility in this situation began to tumble. It was Manas Buthelezi, in particular, who kept on asking what was the good of blacks and whites being able to sit down together occasionally at the Lord's Table if they were then prevented by law from having a cup of tea together in the nearby café.

The upshot of this learning process — at the level of theological and church pronouncements, at any rate — was the decision of the Dar-es-Salaam Assembly of the Lutheran World Federation in 1977, "on the basis of faith and in order to manifest the unity of the Church", to declare apartheid an issue which constitutes a *status confessionis*:

> Confessional subscription is more than a formal acknowledgement of doctrine. Churches which have signed the confessions of the church thereby commit themselves to show through their daily witness and service that the gospel has empowered them to live as the people of God. They also commit themselves to accept in their worship and at the table of the Lord the brothers and sisters who belong to other churches that accept the same confessions. Confessional subscription should lead to concrete manifestations in unity in worship and in working together at the common tasks of the church.
>
> Under normal circumstances Christians may have different opinions in political questions. However, political and social systems may become so perverted and oppressive that it is consistent with the confession to reject them and to work for changes. We especially appeal to our white member churches in southern Africa to recognize that the situation in southern Africa constitutes a *status confessionis*. This means that, on the basis of faith and in order to manifest the unity of the church, churches would publicly and unequivocally reject the existing apartheid system.[18]

In other words, the Lutheran churches have come to recognize, via the concept of the *status confessionis*, in a circuitous way and for the present mostly only in a verbal way without practical consequences, that participation in the body of Christ excludes systematic oppression and exploitation of certain groups of people within the church or in society generally.

Some theologians, therefore, including myself, are seeking, in the light of the New Testament doctrine of the body of Christ, to understand, analyze and influence the international economic processes and mechanisms which experience shows are already catastrophic in their effects and are becoming increasingly so with each passing day, costing every year the lives of roughly thirty million human beings. The northern industrial countries (including the two Germanies, if in differing degrees) are growing steadily richer at the expense of the majority of the people in the countries supplying the raw materials, who are becoming steadily poorer. This is due in part to the conditions prevailing in respect of tariffs, trade and transport. In ecclesiological terms, this means that

Christians and churches in the "North" enjoy their growing (or at least protected) prosperity in part at least at the expense of the Christians and churches in the countries supplying the raw materials. In other words, if we are in any real sense still the one universal body of Christ, this body of Christ is divided among active thieves, passive profiteers, and deprived victims. It is an illusion — another example of "compartmentalized thinking" — to picture the one single reality as divisible into a "wicked world", on the one hand, and a "not so bad church", on the other, indeed a church which does so much for development aid, to give just one example! Even someone unable or unwilling to accept the cosmic approach or the prologue to the Fourth Gospel and the letter to the Colossians, or the Christian ethics of Dietrich Bonhoeffer based on the universal body of the cosmic Christ, can hardly deny that the body of Christ in the narrower sense of the empirical church is divided today among thieves, profiteers, on the one hand, and the deprived and the robbed, on the other!

One of the first to recognize this was Ernst Lange who, in his commentary on the Louvain Faith and Order Conference of 1971 wrote as follows:

> In some at least of the problems dealt with in the sections (sc. of the Louvain conference), it is open to dispute whether it was simply a matter of the *bene esse* and therefore a question of renewal, or a matter of the *esse* and therefore a question of institutional repentance and a necessary surgical operation on the substance of traditional doctrine and order. If it is true that "the Christ of the eucharist and the Christ of the poor are one and the same Christ", then what is really at stake in this indissoluble connection between sacramental understanding and practice, on the one hand, and the principle of social justice, as the indisputable standard for the domestic ordering of the church and for its action in the world, on the other, is not simply the degree of the church's credibility but the reality of the church as church. So far as racism within the church is concerned, the problem of Judaism in the New Testament is undoubtedly an anticipation of this issue and we all know that Paul's judgement was that what was at stake here was gospel or no gospel and therefore salvation or no salvation.[19]

These brief remarks on the present entanglement of the body of Christ with the anti-body of a thieving and murderous machinery of oppression and exploitation will be expanded later on in this book. But we can already ask the question: What would the consequences be for the Christian ethic and, indeed, for the church as church, if they should be true? Would we be confronted simply with a question about the normal Christian way of dealing with social, political and economic institutions, or, on the contrary, with a situation in which, for the sake of Christ, Christians and churches have to recognize that, from the standpoint of the church and the gospel, a *casus confessionis* clearly exists, and that, from an economic and political standpoint, they have to join the resistance, i.e. must try "to put a spoke in this wheel"?[20] And, if so, how?

The question is one which concerns the very being of the church as church. Are we in our own church simply engaged in the normal "struggle for sanctification" or are we involved in a struggle against an "erring" or even a "false" church?[21]

But if we are to deal with the question of Christian participation in economic resistance, the inadequacy of our previous ecclesiological approach has to be recognized and the necessary correctives applied. Indispensable as it undoubtedly is to approach Christianity wholly and deliberately on the basis of the revealed reality of Christ, i.e. on the basis of the "body of Christ and his saints", it is just as essential not to short-circuit the argument by deducing the reality of the world directly from the reality of the church or ignoring the former completely. The very fact that it is theologically forbidden us to interpret or deal with the reality of the world on its own in isolation from God's revelation in Christ, makes it all the more important theologically to understand it in its own structural reality and potential. Luther takes this inviolable difference from, yet dialectical relationship to, the one God revealed in Christ into account by his doctrine of "regiments" (governances) and "estates". Bonhoeffer does so with his doctrine of the "mandates" within the context of God's eschatological struggle against the forces of evil. Before we can tackle at long last the question of "where" and "how" we are to practise economic resistance, we must take another look at the institutions, social, economic and political, and enquire into their real significance and rôle.

II. Western capitalist economy in the light of the doctrine of the "estates" and the "mandates"

As I have already pointed out, in both Bonhoeffer and Luther, the body of Christ and his saints is connected to the reality of the world and responsibility for this reality in at least three main ways: via the fulfilment of the Ten Commandments, in content identical with the "law of Christ" (love to God *and* love to the neighbour); via the difference and relationship between the various "regiments" (i.e. "governances", "ways of ruling") of God and between various "estates" and "mandates" in which, answerable to God, human beings can perceive the commandments concretely in a world reality which has a diversity of institutions; and via the nexus of Christ's rôles as mediator in creation, as redeemer, and as cosmocrator.

Luther expounds the Ten Commandments with considerable historical concreteness in the Small and Large Catechisms. He presents the "regiments" and "estates" in a number of individual works which have also been much discussed in scholarly circles.[22] Bonhoeffer deals in detail with the commandments in his *Ethics*, particularly in the passage on "The Confession of Guilt" (written in 1940).[23] He deals with the doctrine of the "mandates" and Christology in the already mentioned "Fourth Approach"[24] and later again in the uncompleted "Fifth Approach".[25]

The only formal difference between Luther and Bonhoeffer here is that the latter divides Luther's classic *oeconomia* into "family" and "work". I am persuaded, moreover, that Bonhoeffer grasped Luther's purpose perfectly in emphasizing, in opposition to all "compartmentalized thinking" the unity of the mandates despite their differences. In other words, economics and politics cannot in principle claim any autonomy which would exempt them from responsibility to God's command. Any such claim would be self-destructive, i.e. would entail their destruction by the forces of evil whenever human beings and institutions surrender to these forces. In the "estates" and "mandates", therefore, the order of the day is not the acceptance of the *status quo* but the struggle for life. From the Christological standpoint, the unity of the "estates" and "mandates" is the reflection of the truth that Christ is the mediator, redeemer and consummator of the creation. From the standpoint of the body of Christ, it is the church and not simply the individual Christian that carries full responsibility for the integral salvation of the world in Christ, including the social, economic and political aspects of human life.

Instead of pursuing further the theoretical aspects of the doctrine of the "estates" and "mandates" here, I prefer to focus attention rather on the concrete problems of the economic institutions in Luther's own day, in Bonhoeffer's lifetime, and in our own day and situation.

1. BONHOEFFER ON ECONOMICS

I begin this time with Bonhoeffer because it seems to me that, in respect of our contemporary questions, he represents no essential advance on Luther and in some respects even falls behind Luther. Whereas Luther wrote whole volumes on this set of questions, it would seem that no "word from the Lord" was granted to the prophet Bonhoeffer at this point, no authoritative declaration within the corpus of his writings, despite the importance of these questions for both the church and politics. Nevertheless, these writings of Bonhoeffer, though general in character, do indicate the proper questions.[26] For Bonhoeffer has also been criticized in the strongest possible way even by those most in accord with him.[27] Let us briefly review a few relevant passages to show that in what follows, far from contradicting Bonhoeffer's basic approach, we are simply drawing out more critically and in greater detail certain inchoate questions raised by Bonhoeffer himself and of vital importance for us today.

I shall not linger on the detail of Bonhoeffer's aphorisms on the theme of "the church and the proletariat" in *Sanctorum Communio*[28] but simply note that his conclusion here, at all events, is that the church of the future can be neither bourgeois nor socialist in any artificial sense, even though he finds a clear affinity between "socialism" and the Christian idea of community. But the argument here is hardly advanced by constant references to the paternalism of this well-connected young doctoral candidate's animadversions!

Much more important is whether, in respect of the economic question, Bonhoeffer grew out of the dreadful comments he allowed himself as an assistant pastor in Barcelona, as he certainly did in respect of the question of war. His comments then were in the nationalist liberalist tradition (Naumann!), including the assertion, wholly in the style of the laissez-faire theoreticians of that time with their social Darwinism: "We are living today in an economic and social order in which the weaker are bound to be ruined by the stronger; if we wish to participate in the life of society we have no choice but to cooperate with it in this direction."[29] All Bonhoeffer at that time could offset against this is charitable assistance and "reverent and humble amazement at the wonderful ways of God".

From 1930 to 1931, during his stay in America, Bonhoeffer came into contact with the poor and even with workers in a quite new way. He saw how capitalists had a vested interest in a fundamentalist type of Christian piety and recognized the necessity of making an empirical analysis of society and politics. Nevertheless, Day's conclusion hits the nail on the head: "Bonhoeffer did not explore the implications of such facts, but he had begun to see them".[30]

> In 1932, at any rate, Bonhoeffer was able to make the sort of statement found in his comments on P. Schütz's book on *Secular Religion*. Schütz differentiates between two types of secular religion: (a) the imperialist type and (b) "the mammonistic religion". "Capitalism and assurance of salvation are foster brothers. The grasping for goods is a grasping for God. Election finds expression in economic success of a worldly kind. This throws fresh light on the Russian revolution. It is a protest against a capitalist Christ, not against Christ as such. But the West has known him and still knows him only as the capitalist Christ. Protest against this Christ is more than justified. We find a similar situation in the protest of the young American negroes against the white Christ. They want a black Christ. Their boycott is directed against the Christ whom the whites claim as theirs and use as a cover for their lust for domination."[31]

These comments stem from Bonhoeffer's period as a lecturer in Berlin. But though he engaged at that time in practical work with the unemployed he made no clear ideological decision against capitalism, repelled as he was by the collectivism of the only socialism he knew.[32] The question of peace seemed to him more urgent than the economic and social question.[33] At that time it was to the Indian example (Gandhi) that he looked for a way out of and beyond Western civilization based on violence and the domination of human beings and nature, not to a critical and constructive study of economic questions.[34]

In 1935, he was still hoping for an ecumenical council which would speak an authoritative word about war, racial hatred and social exploitation,[35] in other words, on the problems of our century to which today we need only add the ecological question. In 1940 in his *Ethics* he adds: "The New Testament, too, refers to *political and economic forms which in themselves conflict with the commandment of God* (Rev. 13)."[36]

But even in the part of his doctrine of the "mandates" intended to deal with the "mandate of work", Bonhoeffer did not push forward to a concrete analysis.[37] Surprisingly enough, the fundamental connection between the technology which tyrannizes rather than serves, on the one hand, and the industrial mode of production, on the other, seems to escape Bonhoeffer even in his in other respects illuminating statements on technology in the section "Inheritance and Decay" in his *Ethics*.[38]

The furthest Bonhoeffer goes, it seems to me, is in his 1940 passage on "The Confession of Guilt" in which he includes this as yet undecoded and unsolved set of problems. In this never subsequently equalled confession, he summarizes our situation vis-à-vis the commandment "You shall not steal" in the following lapidary words: "The church confesses that she has witnessed in silence the spoliation and exploitation of the poor and the enrichment and corruption of the strong."[39]

It could be summed up by saying that Bonhoeffer's pilgrimage in this question begins with a tragic sense of impotence and ends with an impotent confession of guilt.

2. LUTHER

In Luther's case, the picture is quite different. Not that he or his contemporaries had solved the problem. Far from it. But Luther at least speaks clearly and takes up the struggle boldly.

The first point to be noted is the theological context in which Luther tackles economic matters (*oeconomia*) as an "estate" in which God calls the human being to faithful obedience. The context is the interpretation of the commandment "You shall not steal!" and the Sermon on the Mount, which are here too regarded by Luther as a unity, as a statement of God's will of love. They are not interpreted, therefore, in an individualistic and privatizing sense; as Luther sees the matter, they are relevant "wherever business is transacted and money exchanged for goods or labour" (*Large Catechism*).[40] This accords with Luther's basic view of the preaching office whose functions he also divided between the two tables of the Mosaic Law as an office related directly both to God and to the organized life of society. In his sermon on "Keeping Children in School" (1530), he says of the preacher that " . . . he instructs and counsels all estates how to behave to one another in their offices and estates in order to do justice in the sight of God . . . "[41]

Against this background it is easy to see why Luther frequently intervened vigorously in the debate on the economic problems of his time. An excellent concise summary of Luther's statements and theological method here is given by Gerta Scharffenorth in her essay on "The Sermon on the Mount in Luther's contributions to the ethics of economic life".[42] All I need to do at this point, therefore, is to select one or two problems of importance for our present purpose.

Firstly, one or two comments on the interpretation of the commandment "You shall not steal!" in the *Large Catechism*. When we recall that Luther's purpose here was to provide "instruction for children and uneducated people" and to assist heads of households who had to examine the members of their household once a week at least on their knowledge of the catechism, it comes as something of a surprise to find that Luther's exposition of this commandment focuses not so much on the private sin of petty theft but attacks, rather, the "great and powerful arch-thieves". In Luther's view, the whole world in all its estates is "nothing but a vast wide stable full of great thieves". He is referring here not just to the small weekly market but to those "who turn the free public market into a carrion pit and robbers' den" where "daily the poor are defrauded", "new burdens and high prices are imposed" and "everyone misuses the market in his own wilful, conceited, arrogant way . . . " The arch-thieves are those "who daily plunder not only a city or two but all Germany", and "the head and protector of all thieves" is "the Holy See at Rome".[43]

What lies behind this term "arch-thieves"? For the answer we turn to Luther's "Large Sermon on Usury" (1520), reprinted as the second part of the tract "On Trade and Usury" (1524).[44] The people Luther has in mind here are the "joint stock companies" which emerged in early capitalism and which in turn enjoyed huge trade monopolies: for example, the Fuggers and the Welsers. According to Gerta Scharffenorth, Luther addresses himself mainly to the following six problems:

> (1) The charging of interest, which was tolerated despite the canonical ban on usury; (2) the growth of mendicancy as an economic problem (preponderance of the non-working over the working population; (3) the practice of price-fixing in the merchant guilds; (4) the increase in sureties which, while stimulating the freer flow of money, also created a network of dependencies; (5) trade monopolies making it possible for trading companies to control the "free public market"; (6) the speculative purchase of commodities so as to make the charging of higher prices possible in times of scarcity and the consequent exploitation of the needs of the purchasers.[45]

But the decisive point of Luther's analyses and interpretations, and one quite unfamiliar to neo-Lutherans, is the affirmation, after thorough examination, that the economic institution of *the transnational banks and trading companies as such is in conflict with the will of God* as expressed in both the natural and revealed will of God. In conscience, therefore, not only the use of these institutions is to be rejected but these institutions themselves as institutions:

> I ought, of course, to speak in detail of the companies, but the whole business is so abysmally and unfathomably full of sheer miserliness and

injustice as to leave nought to be said with a good conscience. Or is anyone naive enough to fail to see that these companies are simply plain wicked monopolies? Even the secular heathen laws prohibit such things, not to mention divine justice and the Christian law. For they all control and do as they please with goods and quite shamelessly commit all the crimes just mentioned, raising or lowering prices to suit their own book and squeezing and bankrupting all the small enterprises, just as the pike treats all the little fish in the water, as if they alone were the lord of all God's creation, exempt from all the laws of faith and love . . .

Let no one ask, therefore, how he can belong to such companies with a good conscience. The only possible advice, the only thing to do, is to have nothing whatever to do with them. Nothing good can come of them. If the trading companies are to survive, right and honesty must perish. If right and honesty are to survive, the trading companies must perish![46]

Luther is not content just to unmask the mechanisms which produce increasing poverty on the one hand and increasing wealth on the other. Nor does he content himself simply with attacking those who manipulate these levers, though considering the pusillanimity of the Western churches today when it comes to speaking out on economic matters and in particular to challenging the multinational firms and banks, this too was a considerable achievement. (In the final analysis, of course, even the church's money depends in fact on this economy.) In addition to this direct confrontation, however, Luther also urges all the other "estates", i.e. the political institutions and the church, to cooperate in putting an end to this scandalous state of affairs. Responsible as they are for the whole of human society and not just for the rich and powerful, governments should take legal measures against these private interests in order to establish justice for the ordinary people.[47] Luther calls on the church to dissociate itself from the banks and their practices not just verbally but also in its own (institutional!) financial affairs and thereby to "set a good example" for the secular "estates". A church which accepts the normal interest should stop calling itself the church.[48] When addressing his argument to the church and Christians, Luther deploys the full message of the Sermon on the Mount; when dealing with those whose appeal is to reason alone, he deploys the "Golden Rule" (Matt. 7:12).[49]

Luther is well aware, of course, that the political and church institutions have been bought and coopted by the economic powers. They have a stake in them. It is common knowledge that the election of Charles V as Emperor, for example, was made possible only by the financial backing of the Augsburg banks and that this made him susceptible to blackmail on their part. *Luther's aim, therefore, is to find ways whereby congregations and "ginger groups" could set an example of active resistance to poverty and new and constructive ways of combatting it.* This left an indelible mark on the Protestant church orders.[50]

3. THE WORLD SITUATION TODAY

The theory which in my view best describes the present world situation is the "dependence theory". There are, of course, rival attempts to analyse the situation and to find suitable development strategies, as for example, the "liberal" theories. These affirm that the only way to reverse the steady impoverishment of the "developing" countries is to integrate them completely into the world market. The facts give the lie to this view, however, and indeed demonstrate quite the opposite, i.e. that wherever a country is integrated into the capitalist world market, the result is the impoverishment of the majority of its population, bled white by the economic, political and military power centres, while only the small sections of society which cooperate with these centres benefit.[51] The result is the well-known or rather "infamous" scissor movement — within countries and internationally — whereby the rich grow richer and the poor grow poorer and more than forty millions die of starvation every year.

It is this situation that the "dependence theory" seeks to analyze and interpret. Its assumptions and conclusions are as follows: If we examine the global political and economic system, we find it divisible into power centres (metropoles) and power peripheries (satellites). By making and keeping the peripheries economically, politically, culturally and militarily dependent, the centres develop at their expense. This was the case not only in the overt colonial period; it continues to be the case in the present period of indirect colonialism, for the former colonial powers have in many cases succeeded in establishing centres in the former colonies, i.e. in the peripheries. These sub-centres ("elites") in the poorer countries cooperate with the main power centres in the industrial countries, to their own benefit but also to the detriment of the peripheries in their own countries.

This helps to explain, for example, why the USA, one of the main centres in the world, prefers to cooperate with corrupt and oppressive regimes and "élites" in Asia, Africa and Latin America; at the present time, in South Korea, El Salvador or South Africa, for example. This is not simply a "traffic accident" of USA foreign policy but is inherent in the system itself. When an administration such as that of President Jimmy Carter seeks to take modest measures to correct this normal course, therefore, the economy nevertheless continues to widen the gap between centres and peripheries, between rich and poor. The repudiation of Carter in favour of Reagan speaks for itself here. The industrialized Soviet Union follows basically the same patterns in respect of the global economic system, as the UNCTAD conferences clearly show, and the same applies to all the other industrialized countries in varying degrees. For it is the extension of power by modern science and technology which has created the single process whereby a minority of the world's population "develops" and the majority remains underdeveloped, and the gap between the "haves" and the "have-nots" widens daily.

It is not that we have become more wicked and sinful than previous generations. Relationships of dependency have always existed: between feudal lords and serfs, between men and women, and so on. Because of the expansion of the effects of sin by a technology and industry based on modern science, the global development which exploits the scientific and technological approach is patently becoming a deadly threat both for the human family and for its home, the earth. The dilemma is that not only the modern industrial economy but also science and technology increase the power of those who use them without regard for their side-effects. This was noted already by Descartes at the beginning of this development. Humanity is seen as "master and owner of nature" (*maître et possesseur de la nature*). It is also generally recognized that this modern approach was justified by an appeal to Gen. 1:26–28: nature was intended to be subjected to humanity as the image of God. But the question is in the image of *which* God in modern times? Answer: in the image of a God who is a projection of the human being who makes full use of one's power without regard for the consequences of this for others. In other words, in the image of a "god" who is the exact opposite of "the God and Father of our Lord Jesus Christ".

If, then, the modern Western approach to nature and to the fellow human being has been and still is the effort to become "lord and owner", this means that humanity is thought of as an omnipotent "operator" who acts accordingly both individually and collectively. The problem this poses is no minor ethical problem but a major theological one. What it adds up to is the absolute self-justification of humanity, or, in Bonhoeffer's definition: "the demonic corruption of the liberty bestowed in Christ". Only gradually do the quite destructive effects of this corruption emerge. It is on this precise point that the doctrine of justification should focus attention today. Since the modern approach is essentially idolatrous and arrogantly dismisses God's inclusive and prevenient grace (Luther: " . . . as if they alone were the lords of all God's creation, exempt from all the laws of faith and love . . . "), it is quite aberrant to seek and find atheism in communism alone. Atheism is inherent in the modern approach and much older than Marxism. In its humanistic aspects, indeed, Marxism even contains surplus elements which seek to eliminate tyrannical exploitation from human society, though of course combined with a theoretical underestimation of the rôle of sin in human life and therefore of the potential and actual institutional abuse of power in "really existing" socialism. "The alternative to the one true God is not atheism but idolatry" (Phil Anderson).

In addition to this, however, capitalist atheism manipulates the Christian religion in order to legitimize the extension of human power. What is suppressed here is the fact that this increase in human power has in the main helped the strong at the expense of the weak and of nature. It was precisely because of this masked rôle of bourgeois religion that Marx and his adherents were avowed atheists. In professing themselves atheists, they were expressing in theory what the capitalist tradition was doing in practice, i.e. in science, technology and in the economic field. But on this same basis, they sought to remedy the situation; for they assumed that the working class was the all-competent and omnipotent "operator" in the creation of a better future for humanity in its natural environment.

The theological question would therefore seem to be the following: How are we to move away from the one approach to another? From that of the universally effective operator to that of the "*co*-operator"? I use this term "cooperator" for two reasons: (1) It is central to Luther's analysis of the way in which human beings share in God's work of ordering and governing his creation in the different "governances" and ways.[52] (2) In using this term, we touch on the basic problem of modern civilization: its basis in the idolatrous apotheosis of "operating" to which it gives a "religious" certificate.

Can this premise of humanity's absolute power be transformed in such a way that full justice is done to God's care for the whole creation, or do we have to struggle for a clear alternative? This critical question does not contradict Bonhoeffer's recognition of the world as world, since it is precisely this world as world that he wishes to claim for Christ, precisely this world which he wants to assume its responsibilities, and because it is on this basis that he also reaches his critical questioning of the modern trend.

We cannot here go further into the critical theoretical questions arising in this connection (see Chapter 7) or deal with the differences between market capitalism and state capitalism as systems which are both based on the "operative" approach. In the neo-colonial phase of the Western system, at all events, the main question seems to me to be the following: Given that the economic (and indirectly also the political) institutions based on the divine "mandates" so manifestly fail to meet the fundamental needs of human beings, what implications does this have for the various "social forms" of the church? If the service of Christ in the persons of his needy, poor and oppressed brothers and sisters is part of the very essence of the sacramental body of Christ, has the time come when the church, faced with this manifest failure of the economic institutions, must in obedience to its faith "put a spoke in the wheel"? If the foregoing argument has made clear both the call to resistance and the focal point of this resistance, the question of ways and means remains.

III. Economic resistance by the church in its different forms today — why and how?

Taking the body of Christ as our starting point, the question arose as to whether, in respect of the present world economic system and of the church's direct or indirect complicity in this system, we are confronted with a clear *casus confessionis* calling imperatively for a clear decision. If so, the church is faced with a vital question, failure to respond to which will have long-term effects comparable to those which followed its failure to face up to the workers' question in the nineteenth century. It is a matter of urgency, then, to look at it in greater detail both theologically and contextually. Meanwhile, in its own financial and economic affairs the church must dissociate itself as radically as possible from this "Babylonian captivity" or else "stop calling itself the church" (Luther).[53]

Taking the economic institutional structures and the ideological decisions on which they rest as our starting point, we recognized a systematic and blatant corruption of the economy whose purpose, theologically speaking, is to serve the welfare of human beings. This demonic perversion of the economy is signalled by the increasing wealth of the rich at the expense of the steady impoverishment of the poor ("where wealth accumulates and men decay", O. Goldsmith) and by fresh millions dying of starvation year after year. Unless radical changes overtake this system soon, and there are no signs yet that this is happening,[54] the only course that remains for Christians and churches, according to Luther, is — resistance. At this point, however, we need to examine more closely what we mean here by the church.

H. E. Tödt mentions three agents of action: the individual, the group, and the church.[55] In respect of political or economic resistance, these three agencies can be differentiated still further.

A certain awareness of life-style has emerged among *individuals* in the economic field in industrial societies. This movement is attracting a growing number of individuals, though not yet in sufficient numbers. In any case, no real breakthrough is to be looked for from this approach alone. For one thing, in an individualistic bourgeois society, the life-style movement tends to get mixed up with other considerations (the slimming courses of an affluent society) and dwindles into the merely banal. It can also become a substitute for action, much as charitable relief work does when it makes the assistance it offers an excuse for evading the basic structural questions. The life-style movement only makes sense — but then it really *does* make sense! — if it forms the individual basis for economic and political action to change the structures of society, both nationally and globally.

For action of this kind, however, we have to look to the groups and to the church. Within these categories, of course, further distinctions have to be made. Tödt takes the church as a single entity and over against it sets the political resistance groups. In my own view, the resistance-setting makes it more necessary than ever to discriminate between the various possibilities open to different forms of the church.

With Dombois and Huber,[56] I posit four *social forms* of the church: (1) *local congregation*, (2) *universal church*, (3) *discipleship groups*, and (4) *regional church*. From the angle of the primitive church, two of these social forms of the church spring immediately to mind: the *community* which assembles in one place, "the *locally* delimited church"[57] ("all in Rome beloved of God, saints by God's calling" Rom. 1:7; "the church of God which is at Corinth", 1 Cor. 1:2; 2 Cor. 2:1, etc.). The totality of Christians in all places is the *church in its universal form (ecclesia universalis*: cf. 1 Cor. 1:2 — "To the church of God which is at Corinth, to those sanctified in Christ Jesus, called to be saints together with all those who in every place call on the name of our Lord Jesus Christ"). Today we describe the form of the universal church as "conciliar fellowship" (though conciliarity is also characteristic of all the other social forms of the church in different ways).[58] The earliest case of this kind of fellowship was the Council of Jerusalem (Acts 15). Throughout the centuries, both the local congregation and the universal church have developed a variety of concrete organized forms.

Already in the early church, however, alongside the local churches (of Ephesus or Corinth, for example) and the sum total of these local churches, there emerged regional associations of the church; for example, that of "the churches in Asia" (Rev. 1:4) or "the churches in Galatia" (Gal. 1:2). These *regional churches* subsequently came to be known as "particular" churches.[59] In the course of different historical epochs, this regional form of the church also assumed various organizational forms. This diversity was due mainly to the different cultural and political organization of the societies in which these regional churches lived. The specific rôle of this regional form of the church was to bear witness to the main political units under which the churches lived. Because the regional churches have largely had to adapt themselves to the cultural and political conditions of their respective societies and to maintain expensive institutions which make them financially dependent, they have frequently succumbed to an excessive conformity and assimilation to the culture and economy of their environment.

It is precisely at this point that Christian groups have again and again surfaced to stress the difference between church and society and to call for a renewal of the church's life. But already in various New Testament writings, such groups are clearly visible as an independent and distinct social form of the church. Jesus himself insisted that many who wanted to become his disciples should remain in their social contexts, such as family and local community. But even these disciples were not expected to carry on as before but rather to show the fruits of the kingdom of God in their lives. According to the Acts of the Apostles, the Jerusalem church even practised community of possessions. There is nothing in the New Testament, therefore, to devalue the local form of the life of the church. In addition to this, however, Jesus called a group of people like the twelve disciples out from all their social bonds, such as family and heritage, so that they might be somewhat more free to proclaim and live the new reality of the kingdom of God than the disciples who remained within their local community. Gerd Theissen's name for them in the Jewish Palestinian context of primitive Christianity is "radical charismatic travelling preachers".[60] With later church history in mind, Dombois speaks of "orders" and "special service communities",[61] while Huber prefers to speak of "initiative groups".[62] My own preference is for the term *discipleship groups*, and this for two reasons. On the one hand, the other terms proposed are too restrictive; on the other hand, "initiative groups" is too imprecise and fails to reflect the fact that we are here speaking of a form of the church or that the group's economic basis must, in embryo at least, be independent of the prevailing economic system.

This brings me to the question of the *criteria for discipleship groups*. These criteria are most clearly reflected in the case of the charismatic travelling preachers and in the case of the classic monastic rules: renunciation of property and family and complete self-determination so as to be unencumbered for witness to the kingdom of God and the call of the Spirit. Property and family accurately specify the economic dimensions of our human life (*oikonomia* derives from *oikos* meaning house or home). Within the total church of Christ there is obviously room and need for an independent look-out post. From Luther's time onwards, of course, it was necessary to insist that this social form of the church has no superior spiritual quality raising it above the local form of the church with its basis in the family. It is equally plain, however, that Protestantism, by its almost complete exclusion of discipleship groups as a social form of the church, firstly in feudal society and later on in bourgeois society, has been and remains in grave danger of becoming assimilated to the existing power structures and of losing the essence of the church as church. In this respect, too, the church struggle under National Socialism denoted a fresh beginning.

It is for this reason that I consider it most important to approach the existence of the groups ecclesiologically and not merely sociologically. In other words, I would differentiate between broad "initiative groups" (up to and including those concerned with political or economic resistance) and "discipleship groups" which regard themselves as a form of the one church and bear constantly in mind in their own church life as well as in their mission of discipleship the church in its totality. The broad "initiative groups" in the field of global economics include a wide diversity of "third world groups", groups with a special interest in a specific country, larger movements such as the Berne Declaration in Switzerland or the groups which campaign against some specific economic scandal such as that connected with the publicity for Nestlé's baby food. The same phenomenon can also be seen today in the ecology movement and the peace movement.

What are our reasons, then, in present circumstances particularly, for distinguishing in this way between these (quite legitimately) secular groups and other groups which see themselves as in some special and emphatic sense part of the one church even though the causes they espouse in practice may be similar to those of the secular groups? Are we simply following here in the footsteps of the "Christian" political parties or trade unions as distinct from similar associations of a secular kind?

Apart from the twofold approach to Christian ethics propounded earlier in this book (*sc.* in terms of the body of Christ and in terms of the institutional realities of our world) the need to make this distinction can best be grasped, within the German tradition at any rate, by reference to the experience of the Confessing Church in the "Third Reich".

Alongside the purely political or economic fields of action, it is essential that groups which keep radically in view the essence of the church as church should be formed and fulfill their mission within the church. Their importance is enhanced the greater the danger becomes that the church as a regional or even local institution may be assimilated or be tempted to assimilate to movements or conditions which obscure its essence as church or even threaten to destroy this essence altogether. The task of these groups as a discipleship movement is to hold the church to discipleship of Christ its Lord by setting it an example of penitence and renewal. Something of the sort was attempted by the "fraternities", and in the USA and in Germany communities and cells are being formed to pursue a similar course. Their main distinguishing feature, therefore, is their refusal to countenance the failure of the church in face of such credal issues as the Jewish question, world exploitation, racism or the threatened destruction of the earth by weapons of mass destruction, and their struggle to keep the church in faithful discipleship of its Lord. Following the tradition of the Confessing Church and in view of the re-emergence of the question of the *status confessionis*, these groups could also be called "confessing" discipleship groups. But the decisive thing is the radical discipleship they first practise themselves before inviting others to do the same. Nor need it only be radical monastic communities which practise this independence. The contours of a discipleship group begin to emerge whenever family, possessions and self-determination are set at risk for the sake of the kingdom of God and God's justice and the way of discipleship accepted. Even a family can become a discipleship group or form part of such a group, as is illustrated increasingly in the base communities. Discipleship groups, therefore, are not secular groups with a "Christian" veneer — in Reformation theology there is no such thing — but a genuine form of the church aware of the supreme importance of the kingdom of God and discipleship *for the world*.

A *second* feature of these groups, as of many of the classic "orders", is the *unity of struggle and contemplation, orare et laborare*, of politics and the Lord's Supper.[63] In face of the apocalyptic growth of the powers, to continue to live in hope and in praise of God is impossible unless the intensive Christian fellowship in the body of the crucified Lord is a daily experienced reality. (The ecumenical base communities in Latin America take the same view.) For the most part, our national church congregations do not offer this Christian fellowship — or do not yet do so — but it could well be that, after a period of pastoral education, the critical situation calling for decision would once again arise as it did during the church struggle and whole congregations would once again identify themselves with the confessing discipleship groups and thus become themselves the confessing church. But this situation would only arise should the institutionalized church become not simply the "erring" church but the pseudo-church, i.e. a "church" which persecutes the true church or allows the true church to be persecuted by political forces. We are not permitted to *desire* the establishment of the discipleship groups as the *true* church. We know from experience that that could only end in sectarianism and the mere transfer of all the problems of the institution to the groups themselves. The tension between the four social forms of the one church must be left to operate as long as possible; in the language of the sociologists this is the tension between mobile elements and the institution.

A *third* feature of the confessing discipleship groups is their *readiness* in principle *to cooperate with secular groups* working either in resistance or at alternatives in those issues which are identified as credal questions in the light of the gospel. In this respect, they do pioneering work on behalf of the whole church. Here is the theological anchorage of Bonhoeffer's decision to join the resistance movement. Here is where Luther, opposing the economic practices of his day, called for "civil initiatives" to tackle the problems of poverty.

Finally, the relationship of these groups to the universal church differs from that of most regional church bodies. For a growing and increasingly informal network of such groups is emerging and developing across the rigid political boundaries, especially in the global issues of exploitation and peace. The voice of the oppressed is heard here even when church authorities, pursuing the vested interests of the institution, make common cause with the powers that be or else keep silent. This could be illustrated particularly by the religious orders in Latin America and increasingly also in North America with experiences of and contacts with Latin America. The confessing discipleship groups have an important rôle to play therefore in the universal form of the church.

But the local and the regional church organizations also have their part to play in the resistance to existing mechanisms of exploitation. We are confronted here, of course, with the inherent limitations of the local and regional forms of the church as well as with those peculiar to rich churches with traditional national and state connections. As I have already said, the fundamental limitations here lie in the economic basis of these institutions which leaves no room for the radicalism and independence of voluntary poverty and tends to reinforce the assimilation of the church to society.[64] The peculiar limitations of a rich church are even more deep-seated. Humanly speaking it is "impossible" for a rich man to enter the kingdom of God and submit to its rules (Mark 10:24–27 and parallels). It is from this situation that we ourselves begin. "But with God all things are possible." In other words, only as we are radically converted by the Holy Spirit can our churches be pervaded by something of the spirit of independence and resistance of discipleship. The local form of the church takes precedence over the regional form, therefore. For the local church is the scene of mission and of training in Christian faith and practice. The plea commonly put forward by church authorities to the effect that "the congregations are not yet ready for this" must be turned round; it is the congregations which are really the starting point for the training of the church institutions in discipleship. For here we have the promise of the Holy Spirit, in word and sacrament, in prayer, fellowship and service. Our congregations, of course, have largely lost the habit of assuming responsibility. But too little is expected of them ecumenically, too. Much more can happen here than is the case at present, for questions of structure can be dealt with here in personal terms.

With respect to our particular question, three lines of advance seem to me especially important:

1. Local congregations or church districts can begin to see their own financial and economic practices as a theological problem and to draw practical conclusions which will make their Christian witness more credible.[65]
2. "Prophetic resistance" in this context can mean tackling the ideologies which the present system has been drumming into people's minds from childhood onwards and recognizing the idolatrous nature of these ideologies.[66]
3. The mechanisms of the global economic order which make the rich richer and the poor poorer are increasingly identifiable in the industrial countries themselves (the vulnerability of small businesses, the disappearance of jobs, urban and rural disparities, etc.). Its effects are visible locally and regionally. The global ramifications of the specific local economy can be studied and confronted with the ecclesial reality of the local church.

These lines of advance can be followed locally and regionally at the same time, as the example of solidarity with the oppressed in South Africa shows.[67] But local congregations, regional synods and church authorities are fundamentally dependent here on the pioneer work of the discipleship groups. These groups are not entitled, therefore, to be self-sufficient but have a duty to keep in touch with other social forms of the church.[68] This is all the more indispensable in view of the fact that, when a *casus confessionis* does present itself and resistance is called for, all the social forms of the church must be drawn into the conciliar process and eventually into the conciliar action. It is in this conciliar process that the decision as to whether this case of confession and resistance exists is made officially and authoritatively, with all the consequences this will entail, up to and including the church struggle.[69]

Besides this training in discipleship in all the social forms of the church, the question also arises of alternative economic institutions. For it is impossible for the church resistance groups alone to build a new economic and political system. Here, in fact, we have to combine the two approaches to Christian ethics: the one in terms of the body of Christ and the other in terms of the institutions themselves. There is only one possible rôle for church resistance groups and the "converted" congregations and regional churches here: namely, to persuade society as a whole, by their own resistance and example, to create and develop just and participatory structures in order to solve humanity's vital questions.

But how exactly is this to happen? It is clear from the history of the workers' movement that the propertied and ruling classes do not willingly share their privileges. Unjust power yields only to countervailing power in some form or other (the details are unimportant at this stage), though this certainly does not necessarily signify countervailing violence. On the contrary, the more effectively a countervailing power is organized (e.g. trade unions) the more likely it is that conflicts will be settled without countervailing violence.

Just as the "workers' question" was the issue for the nineteenth century, so, for our own century, the dominant issue is the discovery and critical and constructive support (with church resources) of possible countervailing power in the present global economic system.

As can be seen from South Africa, Latin America and many other places, advances in this direction can be costly and taken even at the risk of death. We Christians in the centres of power have hardly yet taken even the first step in this direction. Whether this witness will achieve an institutional alternative or, on the other hand, the juggernaut of our present global economic system will hurtle onwards to disaster is not in our hands. But it *is* our business, trusting in God's gracious activity in the midst of our world, to participate in his work and to try to halt the juggernaut by "putting a spoke in its wheel".

NOTES

1. Cf. D. Bonhoeffer, *GS* II, pp. 48f.
2. Cf. W. Huber, *Kirche und Öffentlichkeit*, Stuttgart, 1973, pp. 57ff.
3. WA 19, 482–523. Cf Bonhoeffer, *Sanctorum Communio* pp. 127ff. On the sermon, see also J. Dantine, "Some Reflections on Martin Luther's Doctrine of the Lord's Supper" (in German), in *Martin Luther*, journal of the Austrian Friends of the Luther Society, Vol. 18, Vienna, 1981, pp. 13ff.
4. WA 50, 624–644.
5. Gerta Scharffenorth, *Kirchordnungen der Reformation*, 1976, pp. 20–23. ET in U. Duchrow (ed.), *The Identity of the Church and its Service to the Whole Human Being*, LWF Dept. of Studies, 1977, pp. 732–765; cf. also Scharffenorth, "Baptism and Church Membership in Luther's Theology and in the Church

Orders of the Reformation" (in German), *Den Glauben ins Leben ziehen. Studien zu Luthers Theologie*, Munich, 1982, pp. 71–121, 114ff.

6. Cf. WA 50, 643. It is a mistake to say, therefore, as I have myself been guilty of doing, that in *On councils and churches* Luther recognizes only seven *notae ecclesiae*, since this typically ignores the fulfilment of the commandments of the second table, dealing with human life in community, as also marks of the true church.

7. Dietrich Bonhoeffer, *Ethics*, ed. E. Bethge, tr. N. Horton Smith, Collins, 1964, p. 190.

8. *Ibid.*, p. 205.

9. E. Bethge, *Dietrich Bonhoeffer*, ET Collins, 1970, pp. 619ff.

10. Bonhoeffer, *Ethics*, pp. 205f.

11. *Ibid.*, p. 199.

12. *Ibid.*, pp. 196f.

13. *Ibid.*, pp. 193f.

14. *Ibid.*, pp. 96f.

15. *Ibid.* pp. 320f.

16. *Ibid.*, p. 327.

17. This statement is exaggerated and is to be qualified above all in view of Bonhoeffer's *Life Together (Gemeinsames Leben*, Munich, 1939, repr. 1979).

18. *Dar-es-Salaam Report 1977*, pp. 179f. On the historical antecedents to this, see C. J. Hellberg, *A Voice of the Voiceless*, Lund, 1979; on the theological interpretation, see U. Duchrow, *Conflict over the Ecumenical Movement*, WCC, Geneva, 1981, pp. 74f. and pp. 252f.

19. Ernst Lange, *And Yet It Moves . . . Dream and Reality of the Ecumenical Movement*, CJL and WCC, Geneva, 1979, p. 98. Cf. Duchrow, *op. cit.*, in n. 17, pp. 341f. and Ch. 3 n. 20.; also Duchrow, "The Confessing Church and the Ecumenical Movement", *The Ecumenical Review*, Vol. 33, 1981, pp. 212ff.

20. Bonhoeffer uses this phrase in his essay on "The Church and the Jewish Question" (*GS* II, 48) to describe the possibilities of church action in face of a government which is a threat to the preaching of the Christian gospel: "The third possibility consists in not merely binding the wounds of those crushed beneath the wheel but in putting a spoke in the wheel itself. Such action would be direct political action on the part of the church and is only possible and mandatory when the church sees the state failing in its function of creating justice and order . . . " (the printed German text reads "indirect", an obvious error). Whether we have here a genuine citation from Luther, as Bishop Berggrav of Norway asserted (without giving chapter and verse) in 1946 in his famous essay "*When the Driver is Drunk: Luther on the Duty of Disobedience*", I have been unable to establish despite exhaustive enquiries. In the same context, Bonhoeffer uses the term *status confessionis* for the first time: "Here the church of Christ would find itself in *statu confessionis* and here the State would be caught in the act of negating itself" (*op. cit.*, p. 49).

21. See my *Conflict over the Ecumenical Movement*, pp. 16–23. The consequences of these ecclesiological reflections for our own church situation in face of developments in the present global economic system will have to be examined separately in subsequent chapters of the present book. This question is not as sharply posed by A. Rich in his important and nuanced essay on "Material Pressures and Structural Evil in the Economy" (in German) in ZEE 26, 1982, pp. 62–82. He simply asserts that "the struggle against structural evil forms an essential part of the Christian life" (*ibid.*, p. 78).

22. For the literature, see Chapter 1 above, notes 1 and 8.
23. Bonhoeffer, *Ethics*, pp. 110f.
24. *Ibid.*, pp. 188ff.
25. *Ibid.*, pp. 263ff.
26. See Bethge's biography in the few passages relative to this question.
27. Cf. e.g. T. Day, *Conviviality and Common Sense*, Diss., New York, 1975, p. 105 and frequently.
28. *Sanctorum Communio*, pp. 274ff. On this cf. Day, *op. cit.*, pp. 104ff.
29. *GS* V, pp. 174ff. Cf. Day, *op. cit.*, p. 137; T. R. Peters, *Die Präsenz des Politischen in der Theologie Dietrich Bonhoeffers*, Munich/Mainz, 1976, p. 156 (too positive); H. E. Tödt, "Theologisches Denken und politischer Lernprozess. Dietrich Bonhoeffers Entscheidungen in der Endzeit der Weimarer Republik", in G. Grohs and others, *Kulturelle Identität im Wandel*, Stuttgart, 1981, pp. 52ff.
30. Day, *op. cit.*, p. 163. Cf. Bethge, *Dietrich Bonhoeffer*, Chapter 5 on the period in America. On the "social gospel" movement and Bonhoeffer's encounter with it, cf. *GS* I, pp. 104–112.
31. *GS* V, p. 317; cf. Day, *op. cit.*, p. 193.
32. Cf. Day, *op. cit.*, p. 194 and E. Bethge, *op. cit.*, pp. 121ff.
33. *GS* I, pp. 175ff.
34. *GS* III, pp. 261–267; cf. Day, *op. cit.*, pp. 197f.
35. *GS* I, p. 261.
36. *Ethics*, p. 325. Cf. *ibid.*, p. 208 where Bonhoeffer assumes in principle in respect of all the mandates that their divine mandate lapses when the assigned task is persistently and arbitrarily violated.
37. *Ethics*, pp. 207–213.
38. *Ibid.*, pp. 98f.; pp. 101f.
39. *Ibid.*, p. 115.
40. *Large Catechism*, p. 395 in Tappert's *The Book of Concord*, 1959.
41. WA 30, 537.
42. In C. Frey and W. Huber (eds), *Creative Discipleship. Festschrift for H. E. Tödt* (in German, *Texte u. Mat. D. FEST* A 5), Heidelberg, 1978, pp. 177–204; in a revised and expanded form in *idem, Den Glauben ins Leben ziehen*, pp. 314–338. Cf. also more recently F. W. Marquardt, "God or Mammon: Theology and Economics in Martin Luther", in German in *Einwürfe 1*, Munich, 1983, pp. 176–216. See Chapter 7 below.
43. *Large Catechism*, The Seventh Commandment, pp. 395–399.
44. WA 6, 36ff. and WA 15, 293ff.
45. Scharffenorth, *op. cit.*, p. 193.
46. WA 15, 312.
47. *Op. cit.*, p. 196.
48. WA 6, 50ff., esp. 6, 59.
49. *Op. cit.*, p. 188.
50. *Op. cit.*, pp. 196ff.
51. On what follows, see Duchrow, *Conflict over the Ecumenical Movement*, pp. 60ff. The best recent account of theories of underdevelopment is provided by W. Ochel, *The Development Countries in the Global Economy* (in German), Cologne, 1982, pp. 65ff.
52. Cf. Duchrow, *Christenheit und Weltverantwortung*, pp. 512ff. Cf. D. J. Hall, *Imaging God: Dominion as Stewardship*, New York, 1986.
53. WA 6, 50ff., esp. 6, 59.
54. Cf. the irresponsible attitudes of the industrial states to recent attempts by

UNO to ensure that the riches of the oceans are accessible most equitably to all the nations in the world community, by the adoption of a new international law.

55. H. E. Tödt, "Conscientious Resistance: Ethical Responsibility of the Individual, the Group and the Church", in J. Godsey and G. Kelly (eds), *Ethical Responsibility: Bonhoeffer's Legacy to the Churches*, New York, 1981, pp. 17–41.

56. On what follows, cf. Duchrow, *Conflict over the Ecumenical Movement*, pp. 42ff. and pp. 350ff.

57. Cf. H. Dombois, *Das Recht der Gnade. Ökumenisches Kirchenrecht* II, 1974, pp. 35ff. p. 184.

58. Cf. Duchrow, *Conflict* . . . , pp. 329ff. and pp. 350ff.

59. Cf. W. Huber, *Kirche*, Stuttgart/Berlin, 1979, p. 45; Dombois, *op. cit.* p. 37.

60. G. Theissen, *Sociology of the Jesus Movement* (in German), *ThExh* 194, Munich, 1985, 4th ed.

61. H. Dombois, *op. cit.*, pp. 39f. Cf. also the excellent essay by G. Kretschmar, "The Ecumenical Significance of the Orders" (in German), in *Erbe und Auftrag* 56, 1980, pp. 256–273 and 371–376.

62. W. Huber, *op. cit.*, pp. 46f.

63. Cf. also N. Greinacher, *In the Presence of Mine Enemies — Supper of Peace. On the Political Dimension of the Lord's Supper* (in German), GTB 1051, Gütersloh, 1982.

64. On what follows, cf. U. Duchrow, "The Church between Assimilation and Discipleship" (in German), in *Una Sancta*, 36, 1981, pp. 161–173.

65. Cf. the decision of congregations and church districts in the Rhineland Church to allocate church-tax income to the Special Fund of the WCC's Programme to Combat Racism and the controversy over this decision at the January 1982 regional church synod and subsequently.

66. Cf. Cees Hamelink, *The Corporate Village*, IDOC International, Rome, 1977. The author summarized the theses of this book in "A Key to the Exercise of Power" (in German), in *Überblick* 4, 1976, pp. 29ff.

67. Cf. in addition to the procedures just referred to in the Rhineland Church the decisions of the Baden Church Synod in the spring of 1981 ("Message to the Congregations"), in Appendix I below.

68. Networks with this as their objective include, in addition to the traditional fraternities, for example the "Westphalian Church of Solidarity" and the "Ecumenical Network in Baden", see Chapter 9 below.

69. Cf. D. Bonhoeffer: "The necessity of direct political action on the part of the church is to be decided as occasion arises by a 'Protestant Council' and can therefore never be planned casuistically in advance" (*GS* II, 49; cf. footnote 19 above).

4

Ecumenical criticism
of the present global economy:
The call to freedom and discipleship

The system by which our churches are financed is interwoven with our national economies and these in turn are an integral part of the global economic system. Whether we realize it or not, we Christians and churches in Europe are inextricably connected with Christians in all other countries not only by our communion in the one body of Christ but also by the global system of economic and financial processes. Whether at congregational or church leadership level, most of us in the churches are aware of this connection, at least as donors of funds to people in need. How we are individually and collectively connected with others by the economic *structures* remains outside our perception or is deliberately ignored. But this is not the case in the ecumenical fellowship of the churches as it has taken shape in the World Council of Churches. For here the voices of those who suffer from the global economic system in its various regional and national forms can be raised and heard. They must be listened to if we are to join God's liberating action for justice.

Various studies have been made of the history of this ecumenical conscientization process.[1] The main landmarks in this history can be identified: the 1928 Jerusalem meeting of the International Missionary Council and its critique of capitalist structures; the second world conference of the Life and Work movement in Oxford in 1937 which marked the beginning of a new attitude of the non-Roman churches to the workers' movement; the founding assembly of the World Council of Churches in Amsterdam in 1948 which introduced the concept of a "responsible society" as a "middle axiom" for ecumenical social ethics; the Third Assembly of the World Council of Churches in New Delhi in 1961, when Western domination of the ecumenical movement was modified by the entry into membership of the WCC of a large number of Orthodox churches and "younger churches" of Asia, Africa and Latin America; the 1966 Church and Society Conference in Geneva which suddenly alerted church constituencies to this new current by calling for radical "structural changes"; and, finally, the Fourth WCC Assembly in Uppsala in 1968 on whose recommendation the Commission on the Churches' Participation in Development (CCPD) was created as an instrument and a programme to concentrate ecumenical theological thinking on economic questions.

Founded in 1970, this Commission generated an astonishing energy and creative impetus. Unfortunately its work has still to make the impact it deserves on congregations, church leaders and theological educators in Germany and elsewhere in Western Europe although it has been taken up here in a number of action groups and specialist teams. One reason for this lukewarm reception has been the Commission's replacement of the traditional emphasis on charitable appeals by an insistence on the question of justice and the root causes of injustice. This it did, moreover, by a fresh concentration on the biblical message comparable with that of the Reformers of the sixteenth century. Since the Fifth WCC Assembly in Nairobi in 1975, the Commission's work has been governed by the following programme priorities:

— To assist churches and their constituencies to manifest in their theological outlook, styles of life and organizational structures, their solidarity with the struggle of the poor and the oppressed;
— to assist development agencies of the churches to evaluate and redirect their efforts in line with the criteria proposed by the Nairobi Assembly;
— to assist churches to provide support to organizations of the poor and oppressed;
— to assist churches to make their contribution towards the search for a just, participatory and sustainable society.[2]

In the Central Committee's report to the Sixth Assembly of the WCC in Vancouver in 1983, covering the work of the ecumenical body from 1975 to 1983, the passage just quoted is followed by the revealing comment: "This option in favour of the poor and the oppressed sometimes creates tensions because it questions not only the structure of society but also that of many churches themselves."[3]

In the view of many, the approach adopted here by the ecumenical movement, that of "the church in solidarity with the poor", represents a significant breakthrough in the history of the church. Theologically it marked on a broad front the end of the "Constantinian era" of the church's accommodations to political, cultural and economic power. Not surprisingly, therefore, it was not accomplished without tensions and conflicts with traditional power centres in the life of the church and its theology.

In a series of studies, the Commission has demonstrated the validity of this approach, biblically, historically, theologically, ecclesiologically and socially.[4] Yahweh, the God of the Bible and Jesus of Nazareth, are unmistakably on the side of the poor and the oppressed. The Christian community which wishes to follow Jesus is called to do likewise. Indeed, Jesus himself comes to us today in the persons of the poor and the oppressed (Matt. 25:31ff.). The poor and needy are thus special agents of evangelism, of God's mission in the world. This explains the emphasis placed on this approach in the world missionary conferences in Bangkok in 1973 and in Melbourne in 1980.[5] The significance of this for the life-style and organization of the churches has hardly yet been explored let alone implemented.

Leaving to one side the second and third programme priorities of the CCPD (the reorientation of church development agencies and support for organizations of the poor and the oppressed)[6], I turn to the fourth: the contribution of the churches to the search for a just, participatory and sustainable society (JPSS). These three keywords "just", "participatory", "sustainable", together with the principle of "the church in solidarity with the poor", furnish the overarching perspectives introduced into the ecumenical movement by the Commission. They replace the earlier concept of "the responsible society" which sought a way between capitalism and communism. These new criteria seek an alternative to both capitalism and communism which alike make growth and modernization the main criteria of development. In contrast to that:

> *Justice* has to do with an equitable system of production *and* distribution not only by and among people now but also between present and future generations. A just society presupposes the recognition that the people are the main subject of history. The pursuit of justice goes beyond distribution and involves *participation* of all people in decisions about what, how, for whom and by whom to produce. The structural changes required as preconditions for the creation of a more just, participatory and sustainable society will only be possible if political power is shared by the people. *Sustainability* is about humanity's dependence upon the earth and the way in which society organizes itself and its technology. It is also about humanity's demand for economic and

political systems in which justice, participation and peace are ensured for all in present and future generations.[7]

In its quest for a new political ethics, the Commission has studied these criteria closely.[8] But it has already tested them out as a composite norm for evaluating economic processes and developing alternatives. Its study of problems of economic theory in the light of basic theological and ethical insights has been mainly at three specific levels: (1) a staff working party on transnational corporations (TNCs) composed of representatives from the various WCC units and sub-units; (2) regional consultations and an international consultation (Bad Boll 1981) as well as discussions with companies and trade unions on the same theme; (3) an interdisciplinary "Advisory Group on Economic Matters" (AGEM).

The results of the work at these different levels have been published.[9] I shall concentrate on two documents: the final report of the working group on the TNCs and the final recommendation of the 1982 WCC Central Committee.

a) The question of *power* — the power whose impact on human beings is ambiguous.[10] TNCs, of course, are only one factor in this power complex but, in virtue of their size, a decisive factor. People are also directly affected by them. As defined by the ILO, the TNCs are public, mixed economy or private enterprises which possess or control productive, industrial, servicing or other forms of plant outside the country in which they have their headquarters.[11] According to a leading economist associated with the CCPD's research, their rationale and logic is marked by the following interests and aims:

1) "stability and survival (of the firm);
2) growth and expansion;
3) creation of surpluses (profits) and accumulation of capital (investments)."[12]

They therefore have two main characteristics in common:

> *individually*, they are centres of decision-making — and, therefore, of power — that control productive processes in more than one country, and that make plans regarding investment, production, marketing, finance and prices on a transnational scale; *collectively*, they have become the main agent of the transnationalization of production, finance, trade and information, as well as important channels for the expansion of an economic ideology which emphasizes "freedom of choice". As economic entities, they behave according to the logic of unlimited growth, hierarchical decision-making, global expansion and profit maximization . . .

One of the results of this process of transnationalization is an increasing thrust among decision-making centres to build the world order following the logic of modernization, which seeks efficiency and growth at any cost. Underlying this logic is the belief that growth is equivalent to progress and that the accumulation of material wealth is the key to human happiness and fulfilment. The result, however, is unevenness: coexistence of affluence and poverty, waste and hunger, over-production and underdevelopment.[13]

Above all, there is the powerful and sometimes determinative influence which the TNCs exercise on politics. This applies not only to the industrial countries but also to the power centres in the "two-thirds" world which are often only maintained in power with the aid of powerful police and military defence systems (which in turn provide a market for the TNCs' arms trade) while the poor in these countries become still poorer. In opposition to that, the WCC programme affirms:

Christian responsibility demands a struggle *against* partial (and, hence, incorrect) notions and practices of development, but *for* building solidarity with the poor (those who do not have "the freedom of choice") and development alternatives consistent with the search for more justice, participation and sustainability.[14]

Even more explicit is the final report of the international consultation on "Transnational Corporations, the Churches and the Ecumenical Movement", which *contrasts the transnational nature of the Christian ecumenical movement with that of the TNCs:*

The relationship between these two visions of transnationality is one of struggle and conflict. TNCs cannot be converted to ecumenism. Their economicist, exclusive and hierarchical logic makes this impossible. The ecumenical movement cannot compromise its commitment to a holistic, human-centred approach to development and its prime commitment to the poor . . . That requirement makes heavy demands on churches and Christians — both those who benefit from and are domesticated into TNCs and their logic, and those for whom bearing witness and struggling carries great risks to their livelihoods, positions, personal security and even lives. It is not the ecumenical movement as such but the Gospel of our Lord and his kingdom which enjoin Christians to accept such demands in the service of the struggle for justice in history, in solidarity with the poor.[15]

One of the main problems raised by the study is that of the power and accountability of the TNCs.

TNC power . . . turns on concentrated capacity to produce and sell, based on control over knowledge, technology and sources of finance, reinforced by alliances with governments and national ruling groups, and maintained by profit and investment flows. Its organizational structure is vertically oriented: hierarchical and exclusive. Very often, corporations holding this power are guilty of abusive and unjust practices . . . Power can be constrained only through accountability. TNCs by their own logic seek to avoid accountability except for senior managers and major sources of finance.[16]

The following are identified as the groups to which the TNCs are to be held accountable: the firms' own employees, the users of their products, suppliers, local administrations, the governments of their own and the host countries, peoples' organizations (e.g. environmentalist groups and other such civic movements), and the legal authorities. The principle of accountability cannot be limited to the individual morality of the industrialist; the decisive responsibility rests on the firm as an institutional unit.

General consensus emerged, as the programme was implemented, that TNCs should be rendered accountable to society and their power constrained. Among the types of TNC power constraints possible are market reform, information dissemination, government action, international restructuring, development of production and technology alternatives and building the power of people's organizations.[17]

b) This immediately touches on another emphasis of the TNC programme: *technology*, and the *organization* of those affected, particularly the *workers*. Since present productive capacity could meet the basic needs of all human beings, including the need for work (on condition, of course, that this capacity is really deployed to this end), hunger and unemployment are a scandal, not an inescapable fate. They demonstrate that the forces dominating the market are fundamentally incapable of ensuring an equitable distribution of the blessings of technological progress or else unwilling to do so.[18] Unemployment is the consequence of an industrial and government policy geared to an ideal model of global growth and global accumulation.[19] New technologies are used to economize on labour and to control the workers. The chief victims here are increasingly the women workers, up to and including the lucrative mass-prostitution organized by large-scale tourist agencies.

In recent years, both the CCPD and the Church and Society Sub-unit of the WCC have devoted special attention to detailed studies of alternative ways of developing science and technology based on the priority of the poor and the development of a just, participatory and sustainable society.[20] Of particular importance here are the experiments with "appropriate technologies" using the old cultural traditions and skills of the indigenous peoples as well as resistance strategies for workers' organizations and people's movements, including the defence of union rights, legislation proposals, and the creation of networks linking at the international level those directly affected by the operations of the TNCs.

c) What, however, are the *tasks of the churches* in all this?[21] Pride of place belongs here to the focus on Jesus Christ and on all the dimensions of his being and history as mediator in creation, redeemer, pattern, Lord of history and the powers, as the One who equips and enables his disciples to establish and to become living signs of the kingdom of God.

> To be faithful to Jesus demands a constant affirmation of our belief in the One Living God, and at the same time a permanent confrontation with those human realities which tend to become the objects of idolatry. In other words, the proclamation of Jesus as the Lord excludes the acceptance of idols such as mammon and false security, dominance of unlimited growth, irresponsible accumulation and profit backed by injustice and the violation of other people's rights.[22]

Justice is never to be divorced from Christian love; in other words, Christians must always be concerned with the structures of society. This is why the WCC Central Committee in 1982, after adopting the report of the TNC study, also urged the member churches as a matter of priority "to work, in close collaboration with those affected and involved in TNCs issues, on theological reflection on TNCs and related economic problems".[23]

Proof of the seriousness of our theological work here will be its *practical consequences*. It is no secret that the situation from which the churches begin here is marked by a wide range of views and even deep divisions.[24] Attitudes towards the present world economic system range from unqualified defence to total repudiation. Leaving aside for the moment the unqualified support of the world economic system, i.e. the defence of the *status quo*, the following emerge from the TNC study as possible approaches:

1. When TNCs are approved in principle as agents of growth and progress, the usual recommendation is the establishment of *codes of conduct*. "Most often, churches holding this position have funds invested in TNCs or have influential business executives as part of their constituencies."[25] Churches in the two-thirds world reject this approach in the absence of any governmental or other effective instrument for monitoring or enforcing respect for such codes.

2. Other churches use their weight or economic influence to challenge particular firms over manifestly unjust measures either by initiating *discussions* with them or by lobbying shareholders. This is an honest approach only if the church concerned is clearly determined to withdraw its funds from firms or banks which persist in a course recognized and warned against as unjust and actually does so when this case arises.

3. A growing number of churches are initiating or joining in *study and research projects to monitor* TNC activities. On the basis of the clarifications thereby obtained, support can be given to political, trade union or civil campaigns.

4. To an increasing extent, churches are identifying themselves publicly with labour organizations and popular movements campaigning for justice, participation and the protection of the natural environment. This amounts to support for the creation of a *countervailing power* to offset the largely uncontrolled power of the TNCs.

5. Another form of church action is the public denunciation of oppressive practices and exploitation on the part of industrial concerns.[26] When such practices are flagrantly persisted in, churches have also supported *consumer boycotts*.

6. The most radical approach is that adopted by churches — mostly in the "South" — which campaign for *radical structural changes* in the present system. The idea of a "new international economic order" which is usually canvassed in this connection is quite inadequate and can even be exploited as a disguise for a new deal with power élites in the "South". Nor can "really existing socialism" qualify directly as a possible alternative. Even leaving aside the question of participation and ecology in such socialist systems, the question of justice in respect of the world economy is also far from being clearly answered here:

> The achievements of socialist economies are generally relevant from the point of view of a development aiming at the satisfaction of the basic human needs of the majority of people and the attainment of sustained full employment. TNCs based in capitalist countries, while operating in socialist nations, are subjected to stricter control based on parameters defined by centrally-planned economies. At the same time, it must be noted that "export-import" state corporations of socialist countries have started to operate in the world market, beyond the boundaries of centrally-planned economies. In doing so they have adopted instruments and attitudes prevailing in transnational business at the level of transfer of technology, trade etc.[27]

More scientific research is urgently required into the rôle of the socialist economic systems in the context of the global economy in order to establish the facts, make the necessary distinctions and arrive at assessments. This is necessary not only in view of the primitive anti-communist emotions and arguments so widespread in our churches and sedulously cultivated and mobilized the defence of the *status quo* or to detract attention from our own economic problems, but also and above all because there is a link here between the problems of justice and peace, of North-South and East-West. In a study entitled "Defence Partnership and Peace in Europe", the Theological Study Department of the Federation of Protestant Churches in the GDR has some important things to say on this question:

The present standard of living in Western Europe (average prosperity, health and social services, public institutions, etc.) would be inconceivable without the high rates of profit obtained today by the West European industrial countries, i.e. their economies, in their trade with third-world countries . . . But a gradual and radical change is becoming discernible in this situation. Shifts in the economic and political concentrations of power in the international system and the accompanying gradual changes in world trade structures in favour of third-world countries will lead increasingly to a considerable shrinkage in these possibilities of profit . . .

The socialist countries have a relatively small share in the total world trade (about 10 percent of world exports). Because of this and because of other economic and political conditions in the socialist countries (including a lower average rate of individual consumption), the direct consequences for working and living conditions will be weaker here and so easier to cope with . . .

How Western European countries will cope with the difficult process of adjustment to the new economic conditions resulting from structural changes in world trade will be of great moment for the future of Europe.

Recent history — not least that of Germany in this century — affords plenty of examples where it was not the necessary adaptation processes which carried the day but reactionary developments leading in some cases to fascism and war . . .

There is a real danger of ground being gained by political forces in Western Europe which combine (and disguise) their ideological opposition to necessary changes and adaptations with the revival of reactionary attitudes and the mobilization of forces imbued with them. This mobilization — with national or nationalist slogans, for example — can most easily be achieved and is the most dangerous when no attempt is made to digest and assimilate one's own history or to deal with social conflicts. As recent European history shows, a successful mobilization of this kind can also become a radical threat to the stability of neighbouring Eastern European states. The political solution of the accommodation processes imminent in Western Europe, therefore, is a question of the common defence and security of both parts of Europe.[28]

Over and above the economic system itself, of course, there are other vitally important aspects to be taken into account if the structures are really to be orientated towards justice. The most important of them is the political dimension, both national and international. The ecumenical Advisory Group on Economic Matters (AGEM) presented a study of this aspect to the UNCTAD V conference.[29] Another aspect which has hardly been tackled so far is the question of a new international information order[30] even though the TNCs and the international banks have major instruments of their power within these area. On the other hand, the disastrous growth of the debt mountain of the two-thirds world has meanwhile spurred the Advisory Group to conduct a detailed study of the international finance system.[31] In addition to a historical and analytical study of the problem, concrete proposals for reform are made in this report as well as suggestions for action by the churches on the basis of theological and ethical criteria. It is clear that the TNCs are only one element in a far larger system which must be examined as a whole if the churches are to make their contribution to greater equity and justice.

This is clear also from the conclusions drawn by the Central Committee from the TNC programme for the WCC and its member churches. It was made quite plain that however important the churches' influence might be on individual agents guilty of·an abuse of power, the heart of the matter was the system in its totality:

> The Unit Committee on Justice and Service reaffirmed that any continuing WCC work on TNCs should emphasize the building of awareness, facilitating the exercise of public control over the activities of these organizations. Although strategies for imposing constraints on the behaviour of TNCs may be important in the short term, they are not sufficient to overcome the structures of injustice. Such strategies and the TNCs themselves must be analyzed in the context of the world market system as a whole. This system and TNCs' operations within it are incompatible with our vision of a just, participatory and sustainable society.[32]

With this basic proviso, the Central Committee then recommends various possibilities of action: discussions, codes of conduct, development of a countervailing power by the poor and oppressed and their organizations, and research into radical structural change. The Committee also expressed its appreciation of the work of the churches and WCC sub-units which have actively demonstrated their solidarity with those struggling against oppressive practices of the TNCs.[33]

These recommendations have been before our churches since 1982. In the spring of 1983, prior to the Vancouver Assembly, a second draft of the study was sent to the Assembly delegates of the Evangelical Church in Germany "for their personal information", and with a note to the effect that the final version was to be published immediately following the Assembly. In September 1985, (after the completion of this book) the Board for Church Development Work of the EKiD published a "Contribution to the discussion of the theme: TNCs as a theme of development policy". Compared with the second draft of the WCC study, this "contribution" is radically diluted. It does not even reproduce the precise terms of the WCC Central Committee's recommendations for future work in the churches.

A resolution to continue work on the WCC's recommendations in the Baden provincial church was rejected by the Baden synod after lively discussion. A long drawn-out debate ensued on whether it was permissible to speak of "exploitation" in the present global economic system and whether the church was directly or indirectly implicated in such exploitation. In the background was the fear of a loss of church income from taxes. As one synod member said: "Many of the nominal members of the Baden Church are no longer prepared to listen to what is repeatedly being said today." Another: "The deeper question here is vitally important and affects our whole national church structure, the very basis of our economic existence . . . What is actually at stake is our tax basis, on which our budget depends."[34]

The question for our West German and other European churches, therefore, is when will they be ready, in communion with the one church of Jesus Christ, in obedience to our common Lord, to recognize honestly their direct complicity in the structures of the global economy and draw the necessary conclusions. At its Vancouver Assembly, the World Council of Churches fully confirmed the findings of the TNC study and recommended further study along the lines suggested.[35] The call to discipleship has long been clearly audible.

NOTES

1. Cf. K. H. Dejung, *The Ecumenical Movement in the Development Conflict 1910-1968*, (in German) in *Studien zur Friedensforschung*, Vol. 11, Stuttgart/Munich, 1973; M. Lindqvist, *Economic Growth and the Quality of Life* (Finnish Society for Missiology and Ecumenics), Helsinki, 1975; T. S. Derr, "The Economic Thought of the World Council of Churches", in *This World*, winter/spring 1982, No. 1, pp. 20–33; J. de Santa Ana, "The Economic Debate in the Ecumenical Movement", in *The Ecumenical Review*, 37, 1985, pp. 98–105.

2. *Nairobi to Vancouver 1975–1983*, report of the Central Committee to the Sixth Assembly of the World Council of Churches, p. 160.

3. *Ibid.*

4. Indispensable: J. de Santa Ana, *Good News to the Poor: the Challenge of the Poor in the History of the Church*, CCPD/WCC, Geneva, 1977; idem. *Separation without Hope? Essays on the Relation between the Church and the Poor during the Industrial Revolution and the Western Colonial Expansion*, CCPD/WCC, Geneva, 1978; idem. *Towards a Church of the Poor*, CCPD/WCC, 1979. Cf. also C. Boerma, *The Rich, the Poor — and the Bible*, Westminster Press, Philadelphia, 1979; R. D. N. Dickinson, *Poor, Yet Making Many Rich: the Poor as Agents of Creative Justice*, Geneva, 1983.

5. Cf. the reports of the Bangkok (1973) and Melbourne (1980) missionary conferences.

6. Cf. the summaries in *Nairobi to Vancouver*, pp. 160ff. and pp. 164ff.

7. Cf. report of the working group on TNCs to the WCC Central Committee 1982, *Churches and the Transnational Corporations: an Ecumenical Programme*, Geneva, 1983, pp. 11f.

8. Cf. K. Srisang, *Perspectives on Political Ethics: an Ecumenical Inquiry*, WCC, Geneva, 1983.

9. Published by the CCPD: *TNCs: a Challenge to Churches and Christians*, Geneva, 1982; *Churches and the Transnational Corporations: an Ecumenical Programme*, Geneva, 1983. Cf. also the papers on the international consultation in Bad-Boll, in *epd Development Policy*, Documentation III/1982; the journal *Sharing* and the reports of the Advisory Group in *An Ecumenical Approach to Economics*, parts 1–4; also, J. P. Ramalho (ed.), Signs of Hope and Justice, Geneva, 1980; *"Minangkabau". Stories of People versus TNCs in Asia*, CCA, Hongkong, 1981; G. Grohs, "Transnationale Konzerne und die Kirchen", in *Ökum. Rundschau*, No. 33, 1984, pp. 528–536.

10. *Breaking Barriers. Nairobi 1975*, ed. D. M. Paton, SPCK, London and W. B. Eerdmans, Grand Rapids, 1976, Section VI on "Human Development: Ambiguities of Power, Technology, and Quality of Life", pp. 120ff.

11. Cf. G. Grohs, *art. cit. supra*, p. 528.

12. Cf. R. H. Green, "Die Rationalität Transnationaler Unternehmen und ihr Verhältnis zu Staaten, Arbeitnehmern und Armen", in *epd Development Policy*, Documentation III/1982, pp. 104ff.

13. TNC Working Group, *Churches and the Transnational Corporations*, pp. 9f.

14. *Ibid.*, p. 11.

15. Cited from *ibid.*, p. 14.

16. *Ibid.*, p. 14.

17. *Ibid.*, p. 15.

18. *Ibid.*, p. 17.

19. *Ibid.*, p. 19.

20. Cf. Pascal de Pury, *People's Technologies and People's Participation*, Geneva, 1983; Paul Abrecht (ed.), *Faith, Science and the Future in an Unjust World*, Philadelphia, 1978.
21. TNC Working Group, *Churches and the Transnational Corporations*, p. 26.
22. *Ibid.*, p. 21.
23. *Ibid.*, p. 21.
24. On what follows, cf. *ibid.*, pp. 6ff.
25. *Ibid.*, p. 6.
26. *Ibid.*, p. 7.
27. *Ibid.*, p. 16.
28. In *Sicherheitspartnerschaft und Frieden in Europa* (Aktion Sühnezeichen/Friedensdienst), Berlin, 1983, pp. 16f.
29. *Ecumenism and a New World Order: the Failure of the 1970s and the Challenges of the 1980s* (An Ecumenical Approach to Economics, 1), Geneva, 1980.
30. Cf. C. Hamelink, *Towards a New International Information Order* (CCPD 1978, No. 7), Geneva, 1978.
31. *The International Financial System: an Ecumenical Critique* (An Ecumenical Approach to Economics, No. 4), Geneva, 1985.
32. CCPD, *Churches and the Transnational Corporations*, p. 24.
33. *Ibid.*
34. Proceedings of the Baden Synod, April–May 1984, pp. 7f.
35. Cf. *Gathered For Life*, official report of the Vancouver Assembly, ed. David Gill, WCC, Geneva, 1983, pp. 57, 65, 79, 90.

PART THREE

Finding the way in the wilderness: confession and struggle

When the call to freedom and resistance is heard by individual Christians, groups, congregations and even entire churches, what are they to do about it? Are there criteria for testing and ordering their life and work? This is the question which arises in the time of the "wilderness wanderings and temptations", the time of discouragements, of decisions for (or against) Yahweh. Yahweh gave the pilgrim people signs of cloud and fire to guide them through the desert to the promised land. At Sinai he gave them his life-giving commandments. It was a hard and difficult way, nevertheless.

Translated into terms of the Federal German situation within the total ecumenical context, this is the question of the "conciliar process". How can we learn to be faithful to God's covenant? How can we overcome the nostalgia for the "fleshpots of Egypt"? Resist the temptation to dance around the "golden calf"? To be the church of Jesus Christ less ambiguously? To live in mutual commitment to witnessing and working for justice, peace and the integrity of creation?

Each church's historical experience of these demands for decision is ˉdifferent. The theological language and symbolism for expressing this ecclesial commitment is also different, therefore. Still fresh in the memory of the German church, for example, is the experience of the struggle of the Confessing Church against the "German Christians" who in the 1930s sought to introduce National Socialist ideas into the church in Germany. "Confessing" Christians, congregations and parts of the official church leadership recognized the existence here of a *status confessionis*, i.e. a crisis demanding a clear and costly confession of the faith. The "church struggle" (*Kirchenkampf*) began.

Surprisingly enough, neither in the sixteenth century nor subsequently (until Dietrich Bonhoeffer initiated a new approach) was this term *status confessionis* ever used in connection with a political question of any kind. Yet the explanation is not far to seek. The term in question derives from the *Formula of Concord* (Sol. Decl. X) and the historical context in which it was used was the "adiaphora controversy". *Adiaphora* are matters which are not really vital for faith. The wearing of this or that liturgical vestment in worship is such as *adiaphoron*. Only if pastors were to be required by the state to wear a certain dress to show their abandonment of the Reformation faith would a secondary matter become a matter of conscience calling for clear testimony and, if need be, the endurance of persecution.

In political matters, therefore, a *status confessionis* never arises since, according to Reformation doctrine, politics, economics and the family, far from being *adiaphora* (secondary matters), are always credal matters. For Luther, the doctrine of the three estates — i.e. politics, economics, the church — is an integral part of the confession of faith. We find this reflected in the *Augsburg Confession* (Art. 16) which lays down that God's will is that "everyone, each according to his own calling, (should) manifest Christian love and genuine good works in his (or her) station of life". But it adds: "When commands of the civil authority cannot be obeyed without sin, we must obey God rather than men."

To approach political questions in certain circumstances with the explicit use of the term *status confessionis* made sense, therefore, only when the neo-Lutherans started saying that political and economic matters have their "autonomous" rules and are therefore matters of indifference to the Christian confession of faith, i.e. are *adiaphora* (see Chapter 1 above). This was precisely what happened in 1933 when neo-Lutherans asserted that the handling of the "Jewish question" in state and church was an *adiaphoron*. In opposition to this, Bonhoeffer mobilized the counter-concept of the *status confessionis*, and did so with a double thrust: (1) in face of the interference of the state in the life of the church ("too much" state), and (2) in face of the failure of the state to fulfill its mandate ("too little" state, i.e. its failure to protect its Jewish citizens).

In short, the neo-Lutheran assertion of the "autonomy" (i.e. the "irrelevance") of the political and economic spheres over against the Christian confession of faith, a position explicitly rejected by Barmen II, obliges us to use the term *status confessionis*. In all other cases, however, it is quite sufficient to employ the ordinary confessional terminology of the Bible and the Reformation confessions and quite unnecessary to use this special term. In other words, we should deliberately restrict our use of this term *status confessionis* to the neo-Lutheran heresy and similar ideologies. The term does, however, contain an element reflecting the urgency of church decision. While it is essential that in any question of the church's faith the sifting process should run its course in the form of an ongoing dialogue (which is why I once proposed that we should speak of a *processus confessionis*), this process cannot go on endlessly but demands a decision, just as Bonhoeffer thought in terms of an "ecumenical council". The establishment or declaration of a *status confessionis* contains this element of decision which must not be lost sight of even if we employ other terms.

But in the sort of situation calling for decision denoted by the term *status* or *processus confessionis*, the important question immediately arises as to what all this signifies for church fellowship. What form does the struggle for credal fidelity take? Following Luther and Bonhoeffer, the answer to this question can be summarized as follows:[1]

Within a continuum of temptations within the church, there are clearly three focal points: *the struggle for sanctification — the erring church — the false church*. Differences between theological schools are to be assigned to the struggle for sanctification and not to the whole question of the erring church. In every concrete situation the church has to decide what sort of struggle it has on its hands. The boundaries are not to be established and defined in advance in a theoretical way. A decision has to be made. The same applies to international church organizations. The decisions in question cannot be taken in a book such as this, of course; all we can do is to remind churches where decisions of this sort are imperative.

The struggle is not judgmental in character but is concerned creatively with confessing, praying, interceding, exhorting and questioning. A limit imposed on a church from the outside can be confirmed by that church in a binding decision taken in fellowship with the whole church, even if this means *in extremis* the constitution of itself as a confessing church, as was the case under National Socialism. But under no circumstances can the church make use of secular forms of coercion to combat and even destroy heretics. But to make the abuses amply documented in church history as excuse for no longer posing the question of the true church would be a betrayal of God's love and truth and create a profound insecurity in the congregations.

Part Three accordingly has the following pattern: In *Chapter 5* the present situation of confession and struggle within the global economic system is briefly outlined. The substance of this chapter is derived from my introductory paper to Issue Group 6 at the Vancouver Assembly of the World Council of Churches in 1983. In the following two chapters (*Chapters 6 and 7*) I examine in detail the question whether a *status confessionis* or a credal issue in a broader sense exists today in respect of the global economic system. Since my enquiry is focused specifically on the German context, I use the *Barmen Theological Declaration* as a basic criterion. This confession of faith was adopted in 1934 by the first Confessing Synod of the German Evangelical Church after introductions by Karl Barth and Hans Assmussen. In accordance with the method we have adopted, the analysis is made from two angles: (1) on the basis of the church as the body of Christ (Chapter 6), and (2) in terms of a theological analysis of the economic institutions (Chapter 7). This procedure accords with Bonhoeffer's twofold criterion for testing whether a *status confessionis* exists or not.[2] In the first place, a case of confession exists when the state interferes with the church's mandate ("too much" state). Here, therefore, we have to address ourselves to the perversion of the church in a confessing situation, which was the central problem of Barmen III. On the other hand, the state can signally fail to fulfill its task (the service of justice and peace) ("too little" state). What has to be examined here, therefore, is the structure and mission of the political (or economic) institutions themselves. For, according to Barmen I and II, no secular institution is authorized to absolutize itself nor is the church permitted to recognize the "autonomy" of any area of human life.

NOTES

1. For more details see my book *Conflict over the Ecumenical Movement*, WCC, Geneva, 1981, pp. 16ff.
2. Cf. D. Bonhoeffer, *Die Kirche vor der Judenfrage (1933)*, in *GS* II, pp. 44ff., esp.48f.

5

Jesus Christ the life of the world, and the struggle for justice and human dignity

A personal word to begin with. I am white, male, middle class, and I come from a country whose economy exploits many of you, my brothers and sisters, and from a church which in some measure owes its wealth to this exploitation. That I should nevertheless be permitted to speak to you on the theme "Struggling for Justice and Human Dignity" is therefore a sign of the presence of Christ. For "if we confess our sins, he is faithful and just to forgive us all our sins and to cleanse us from all iniquity" (1 John 1:8–9). Given the background from which I come, the question which must guide my treatment of the theme allotted me is this: How can I, how can my church, be converted to Jesus Christ so that the world may live? Since the 1975 WCC Assembly in Nairobi, how has the situation in the struggle for justice and human dignity and the theological appraisal of this struggle changed? What is new? It is clear from the preparatory materials for the Vancouver Assembly that the different programmes have, in this latest phase, been related to the three concepts: just, participatory and sustainable. These concepts provide biblical criteria for assessing a society. The opposite of a society which can be described as just, participatory and sustainable is one in which power is so misused that it becomes unjust, authoritarian, and even dictatorial and self-destructive. Translated in terms of our special "issue", this means that oppressed races, the exploited poor and likewise oppressed women, struggle for their liberation and that Christians and churches are called to stand alongside them and to share their struggle against the powerful in order to achieve as far as possible a society which is just, participatory and sustainable.

Alongside this central theological starting point, i.e. God's action in politics, economics and society and our own participation in this action, a second approach to our struggle for justice and human dignity comes into view. Here the starting point is the church of Jesus Christ, in its very being as church and not simply in its action. These two approaches are inseparable and complementary, just as Father, Son and Holy Spirit are inseparable and complementary in our Trinitarian faith in God. This second approach has already been adopted in the ecumenical studies on the "church of the poor" and on Jesus Christ as the Messiah of the poor. But there are two reasons why it emerges even more strongly today: firstly, the misuse of power in politics, economics and technology increasingly displays demonic features; secondly, it is becoming ever clearer that the appeal to the precious name of Christ to support such misuse of power is not only sin but also heresy. Let us look more closely at these two reasons:

1. "For we have to struggle not just against flesh and blood human beings but against the principalities and powers, against the world-rulers of this darkness, against the superhuman spirits" (cf.Eph. 6:12). In other words, what we are confronted with in this issue of justice and human dignity, and now also in the weapons of mass destruction and the spoilation of nature, are not just rational economic, political, legal and technological questions or even questions of social ethics. What confronts us when we see the systematic "disappearance", mutilation and torture of human beings, or when we see the machinery of our economic system spewing out year after year millions of victims of starvation or throwing millions of unemployed on to the scrap heap, or when the women of the poor are violated in the interests of mass tourism, or when our forests die for the sake of our economic "growth" and when the superpowers continue their insane arms race — what confronts us here is the twisted face of a "demonic monster" (C. Harper). In short, Revelation 13 and Revelation 18 with their description of the beasts from the abyss provide an increasingly accurate account of our present experience of government, propaganda media and the economic system.

The spiritual response to the demons is exorcism, the expulsion of the demons. The Orthodox contribution to the 1980 Melbourne Conference rightly emphasized, therefore, the twofold rôle of Christians and churches, sent forth into the world in the strength of their communion with Christ in the eucharist: firstly, the healing of the sick in a comprehensive sense; i.e. self-effacing service for the healing of individual, social and political sicknesses, disorders and evils; but also, secondly, the exorcizing of the demons — "the struggle against the idols, racism, money, chauvinism, ideologies, the robotization and exploitation of humanity". In other words, when we set out to bear witness to "Jesus Christ the Life of the World", in the struggle for justice and human dignity, we must and can struggle alongside the poor for the healing of social ills in the political and economic sphere.

But the most incisive weapon in this struggle is the proclamation of Christ's lordship over the demons and over the power of death and injustice.

What does this mean in concrete terms?

Every social system and economic order is endangered by sin and evil. As Christians we believe, however, that in the ordinary way, God has given human beings the intelligence to order and fashion their common life up to a certain point. Sometimes, however, a system can become so totally perverted as to fall, so to speak, into the hands of the demons. Christians and churches must then dissociate themselves clearly by their words and deeds from such a system, either at specific points or even completely. Historical examples of this are the rejection of emperor worship in the ancient church, the resistance offered to tyrants, Luther's complete and conscientious repudiation of the international financial and trading corporations (our present-day "multinationals"!), the struggle for the abolition of slavery in the nineteenth century, the Confessing Church struggle against National Socialism in the thirties of this century, etc. etc. An increasing number of churches today describe apartheid as a perverted system of this sort, or, in theological terms, as a demon-possessed system and therefore not just as a social or political sin.

My question is whether apartheid is not just the tip of the iceberg. We inhabitants of industrialized nations, together with a few tiny élites in the countries of Asia, Africa and Latin America, are exploiting the majority of the world's population just as systematically as the white South Africans exploit the majority of the people in South Africa. The demon of profit for the few at the expense (i.e. the impoverishment) of the many has the whole world economic system firmly in its grip, with all the side-effects in the shape of discrimination and the suppression of human rights. The forty million or more deaths from starvation per year, the direct result of the workings of the present global economic system, require of us just as clear a confession of guilt as did the murder of the six million Jewish men, women and children in Nazi

Germany and as does the deprivation of twenty million people in South Africa of their rights today.

2. But, once again, the question goes still deeper, for the demons seek to rule not only in the world but also in the church. Whenever there is a complete perversion of power in the world, the powers of darkness seek entrance into the church. Sometimes they even start from the church. It is then a question of the antichrist. The "German Christians", for example, sought to undergird the power of death embodied in National Socialism. White "Reformed" Christians have actually developed for themselves the idea of apartheid and divide the Lord's Table on racist lines of white and black.

We even find people defending the cut-throat global economic system in Christ's name. They talk of a "free economy" though it only defends the freedom of the rich and powerful. They affirm, moreover, that this freedom is the basis of religious and civil liberties even though it is these very liberties which are being destroyed in the dependent countries in the interests of the supposedly "free economy". Central and Latin America, South Africa and many Asian countries furnish abundant examples of this. It is no defence of this standpoint to say that the industrial countries of the Eastern block operate on the same lines, as the UNCTAD conferences show, for it is in the West that this gigantic aberration has its origin and driving force.

I hope, therefore, that the Vancouver Assembly will bear witness not only against the apartheid system and weapons of mass destruction but also against the cut-throat economic system of today and its spurious "Christian" justifications. I believe we are called to initiate in our churches a programme of information and decisive action and suggest practical steps for combatting this power of death *as the church*. This is no longer simply an economic question but a question of our faith in God as Lord and of whether as churches we truly live "in Christ" and mediate this life to others.

But what, from a theological standpoint, is the *common root* of apartheid, a cut-throat economic system, weapons of mass destruction and the spoliation of the created world? Sin is the desire "to be as God" (Gen. 3:5). In other words, human beings use the power given them by God not in the service of life as God intends but for violence and therefore in the service of death. To those of us who stand within the Judeo-Christian tradition, the special power God has given to humankind is the faith that we have been created in the likeness of God and that the old and the new people of God have been called to bring this likeness to completion. According to Genesis 1:26–28, being in the image and likeness of God means having dominion over the earth and subduing it. This establishes freedom from the fear of nature. Luther saw our human role as that of God's fellow labourers *(cooperatores Dei)* in the creation.

In modern times this attitude underwent a change. Classic expression was given to this new attitude by the philosopher Descartes who called humanity "maître et possesseur de la nature", *lord and owner of nature*. Firstly, "lord of nature" — cooperation is replaced by operation pure and simple, by manipulation. The working tool of operative humanity to reinforce humanity's power is an objectifying science and technology. Supposedly "value free", it in fact absolutizes our dominion over nature. Secondly, "owner of nature" — humanity's stewardship is replaced by ownership; the accumulation of capital becomes a sign of election. The second idol is money. In combination as love of power, these biblically legitimized idols of modern humanity spawn the following deadly consequences:

— the unrestricted exploitation of nature (destruction of the earth);
— the exploitation of the so-called "primitive peoples" who, from an ethnocentric European standpoint are matter rather than spirit (colonialism, racism);
— the exploitation of manual labour by lords and owners (class domination);
— discrimination against women, who are regarded as creatures of nature and the senses (sexism);
— the use of military force to defend domination and possession.

If it is the case that the specific deadly danger originating in our civilization with its European roots tends to the perversion of the biblical roots and even of specific gifts of the biblical God, then the struggle for justice and human dignity has to begin within the household of God, within the church, since it is not simply a question of a better society but of a choice between Christ and antichrist, between church and anti-church.

In this exorcism of the demons from its own household, the church of Jesus Christ will find itself involved in sharp conflicts; it will in fact be assailed and persecuted by the pseudo-church. It is not only in South Africa, where "Christian" supporters of apartheid persecute confessing Christians, that this happens. Aided by North American finance and secret services, fundamentalist sects

are spreading in South and Central America. Openly or clan-
destinely, they connive at the murder of the poor and persecute
the church of the poor — Rios Montt, the former President of
Guatemala, for example. The same sort of thing can be observed
in Asian countries, such as South Korea and the Philippines. It is
also in this context that we will have to interpret the attacks on
the WCC and the NCCUSA in *Readers Digest* and the CBS, for
example. Even groups which advocate the build-up of weapons of
mass destruction often do so in the name of the "Christian" West.

Sin is the perversion of the power given to all human beings.
Heresy is the perversion of the power of the Holy Spirit bestowed
on all Christians. We have, therefore, to re-learn not only how to
deal with the demons but also how to distinguish the spirits and
to confess Christ faithfully even at the cost of being persecuted by
the pseudo-church.

Learning these things does not mean starting to point the finger
at others, judging them and even using force of one kind or another
to drive them out of the church. On the contrary, a confessing
church will always begin by confessing its own sins. In one way
or another we all of us support the global economic system —
unless we are numbered among the absolutely poor. The only way
to initiate in the church a process whereby God's commandment
becomes known and obeyed is by our own conversion and readiness to suffer. Today this means unambiguously rejecting systems
of exploitation and mass destruction.

Depending on their various traditions, the different churches
choose different theological starting points. In opposition to
Nazism and apartheid, Lutherans have used the term *status
confessionis*. They have recognized, in other words, that here is a
case where clear and costly confession is called for. The reformed
have branded apartheid as heresy. The Baptists gave their covenant
with God and with one another concrete expression in an "abolitionist covenant" for the abolition of slavery. One ecumenical
group in the USA has adopted the same approach in the form of
a "New Abolitionist Covenant", an alliance for the abolition of
nuclear weapons. Other churches call a church which faithfully
follows Christ a "prophetic church". The concept of the "church
of the poor" also means a genuine church of this kind in a situation
where oppression and impoverishment are systemic. In Orthodoxy, the starting point would undoubtedly be the extension of
the sacred liturgy in order to achieve and maintain the clarity and
purity of the church of Jesus Christ.

In cases where there are demonic and heretical perversions of the church and its very being is challenged, it is mostly renewal groups and base communities which are pioneering the answer. These groups are rediscovering the Bible and what is best in their own traditions, and by doing so they challenge the church at all its levels to conversion and discipleship. What results is a conciliar struggle for the truth and a conciliar credal process towards the confession of the Lord Jesus Christ.

In conclusion, therefore, the special character of our situation today in comparison to that which obtained at the time of the Nairobi Assembly in 1975 can be summarized in the following questions:

How are the churches, each in its local context but also in fellowship with one another throughout the world, to reflect and attest Christ as the life of the world in the struggle against the demonic and heretical powers of injustice and death? If our time in Vancouver and in the years to come enables us to become and to remain the church of Jesus Christ in face of these powers, in a living proclamation of Christ, in eucharistic fellowship, in prayer, in the acceptance of suffering, in action and sharing based on solidarity, then we shall have beneath our feet ground firm as a rock in the struggle for justice and human dignity. For the church of Jesus Christ has received the promise that even the gates of hell shall not prevail against it.[1]

NOTE

1. The response of the Vancouver Assembly to the issue of struggling for justice and human dignity is documented in *Gathered for Life*, official report of the Vancouver Assembly 1983, ed. D. Gill, WCC, Geneva, 1983, pp. 83ff.

6

Becoming a confessing church (Barmen III)

"Speaking the truth in love, we are to grow up in every way into him who is the head, into Christ, from whom the whole body is joined and knit together" (Eph. 4:15f.)

The Christian church is the community of brothers in which Jesus Christ acts presently as Lord in word and sacrament by the Holy Spirit. As the church of pardoned sinners, in the midst of a sinful world, it has to witness by its faith and obedience, its message and order, that it is his alone, that it lives and desires to live only by his consolation and by his orders, in expectation of his coming.

We reject the false doctrine that the church is permitted to form its own message or its order according to its own desire or according to prevailing philosphical or political convictions.

(*Barmen Theological Declaration*, Art. 3)

In view of the way the church has approached the problem, as described in the last chapter, it is better not to start right away with the economic question. Historically, the ecumenical learning process has arrived at clearer insights in the issues of apartheid and weapons of mass destruction. This widening of the analysis beyond the economic dimension is also justified by the focusing of the present conciliar process on the triad of justice, peace and the integrity of creation.

In section I, therefore, I shall describe approaches towards a confessing church in respect of several burning issues, and examine these approaches in the light of Barmen III; this will pave the way for section II in which the historical philosophical and theological background will be analyzed in the light of the rejection clause of Barmen III. Then, in section III, we shall consider the process in which the church can and must be engaged today for the confession of its faith in Jesus Christ.[1]

I. Approaches to a confessing church in 1984, in the light of Barmen III

Thesis 1: The general purpose of Article 3 (and Article 4) of the 1934 Barmen Theological Declaration was to ensure the continuing fidelity of the church to Jesus Christ in both its message and its order in face of National Socialist attempts to influence the church via the "German Christians", and to prevent its capitulation to the ideologies and power structures dominant at that given historical moment.

1. IN RESPECT OF APARTHEID

Thesis 2: Throughout the world, apartheid has been rejected as systematic injustice and attempts to defend it branded as heresy. An ecclesiological article today would need to go further than the Barmen Declaration. In virtue of a new sensitivity vis-à-vis both racism and sexism, it would have to speak of the church as a-"community of brothers and sisters" and to affirm and develop the unity of the church as a credal tenet in repudiation of all social, national and confessional ways whereby the body of Christ is rent asunder.

Even the South African police have grasped the point that the issue at stake for the church in this situation is "to be or not to be" a "confessing church". In its evidence to the Eloff Commission it had this to say about the South African Council of Churches (SACC):

> Here is the heart of the SACC's opposition to the present order. In its judgment, certain conditions exist in South Africa which have forced it to adopt the stand of a confessing church. It is obliged, therefore to resist the existing order and (with the aid of foreign funds) to strive for changes to right the wrongs of the present political system.[2]

It is in respect of the system of apartheid that the question of a confessing church has been examined most directly and in the greatest detail. It is a long story,[3] in which the most significant landmarks have been the official declarations of the Lutheran World Federation at its Dar-es-Salaam Assembly in 1977[4] and of the World Alliance of Reformed Churches at its General Council in Ottawa in 1982.[5] The former described apartheid as a perverted social and political system which must be roundly rejected on the basis of the Christian faith and for the sake of the unity of the church. The latter branded the moral and theological defence of apartheid as a doctrinal and theological error (heresy) and suspended the two white Reformed churches in South Africa from membership of the Alliance on the grounds that they were heretical in this sense.[6] In its long struggle against racism, the World Council of Churches has on many occasions endorsed this same theological approach to "confessing the faith today".

But these outstanding declarations and significant decisions can only be understood as part of an intense and widespread church struggle at regional, local and universal levels of the church's life. It is this aspect in particular which interests us in connection with Barmen III.

Within South Africa itself, it was at first only Christian individuals and such groups as the *Broederkring* (now *Beleydende Kring* = confessing community) who within the churches raised the question of the confessing church and were ready to suffer the painful consequences of doing so. Only in the black Lutheran churches in Namibia was the situation somewhat different; because of their majority position and South Africa's illegal presence in Namibia since 1970, these churches adopted a clear and uncompromising stance. Significantly enough, however, the Methodists also acknowledged the existence of a *status confessionis* even though this was not part of their theological tradition in the narrower sense.[7] But the black Reformed and Lutheran churches were in the difficult position of being financially dependent on the white churches and politically dependent on the puppet governments in the so-called "homelands". They nevertheless produced their martyrs.[8] Lacking a comparable base, the SACC is walking a dangerous tightrope course in its efforts to ensure a clear unambiguous confession of God in Christ.

A similar situation is found in the churches in other countries. The initiative is mostly taken by individuals or groups. A typical example is the "Lutheran Coalition for Southern Africa" in the USA. Pursuing a planned strategy, this group first secured the backing of district and regional synods and then of the national Lutheran churches (except the Missouri Synod) for the Dar-es-Salaam decision, with a rider to the effect that church investments should be withdrawn from firms and banks with holdings in South Africa. This was intended as a first step in the concrete response of the churches to the acknowledged *status confessionis* in respect of apartheid. These decisions were taken in the teeth of stubborn opposition on the part of church bureaucracies and at the price of the resignation of some individual church treasurers.

In the Federal Republic of Germany it was the Baden provincial synod which went furthest in the adoption of the Dar-es-Salaam decisions. In 1981, this synod initiated a study process at all levels, including several of the district synods. This process is still going on today. Endorsements of the Dar-es-Salaam decisions were also made in other Lutheran churches, though in many cases these still amount to no more than a verbal assent.[9] On the other hand, attempts to ensure that the slumbers of the national church are not unduly disturbed by such theological approaches as that of the *status confessionis* which call for practical commitment are also clearly observable. Even the Lutheran World Federation lent a helping hand to this retreat by withdrawing its theological study of this problem completely from the churches of the so-called third world and entrusting it once more to safer, exclusively neo-Lutheran (and mainly German) hands.[10]

We now examine this example of ecumenical witness in respect of apartheid in the light of the various components of Barmen III. "The Christian church is *the community of brothers and sisters.*" It is hardly necessary to insist on the relevance of *this* declaration to the confession of Jesus Christ in face of apartheid. According to Eberhard Bethge's excellent analysis of the *status confessionis*, every confession of faith must likewise concentrate wholly on one endangered point vis-à-vis its specific *casus*, in contrast to the attempt to produce a comprehensive credal declaration.[11] He is also right, it seems to me, when he identifies this one point in Barmen in 1934 as the *solus* (Christ alone) but in Dar-es-Salaam in 1977 as the *unum* (unity) — the unity between the races and classes in the body of Christ (Eph.4!). When we turn to the confession of Christ vis-à-vis the economic system, we shall once again encounter this same category of "unity". It is my profound conviction that in any reformulation of Barmen III today, the ecumenical term "unity" would necessarily have its specific place and clarification.

The same applies, of course, to the "sisters" of whom the Barmen Declaration makes no mention. Not in any merely jocular or trivializing form of greater courtesy from predominantly male church committees, of course, but, following the example of the WCC in Vancouver, in recognition of the deep affinity between racism and sexism.[12]

According to Barmen III, it is in this "community of brothers and sisters that *Jesus Christ acts presently as Lord in word and sacrament by the Holy Spirit.* What catches the eye here in this rich and compact affirmation as being especially relevant to the confession of the faith in respect of apartheid is surely the word "sacrament". For if anything in the preparation and reception of the Dar-es-Salaam and Ottawa decisions has persuaded Christians spiritually and theologically — even those still captive to traditional Western prejudices — of the heretical character of "Christian" or "church" support for and practice of apartheid, it has surely been the breach of eucharistic communion even among those who share the same confessional tradition.[13] In other words, in the defence of the unity of the body of Christ, the sacrament assumes even greater significance than it had for Barmen III.

A reformulated ecclesiological article taking the challenge of *apartheid* as its focus would also have one other emphasis. In Barmen III, the present action or active presence of God in the Christian community is limited to the action of Jesus Christ "by the Holy Spirit". In face of apartheid, the Holy Trinity would have a larger part in the formulation of the doctrine of the church. In particular, the faith that God created humanity in God's own image, male and female and as people of all races, and the renewal of this faith will be regarded as an *essential* mark of the true church of Jesus Christ.[14] Is there any connection between this Trinitarian (or cosmological) deficiency (which is all the more surprising in view of the explicit reference to Ephesians 4:1—16[15] in Barmen III) and the failure of the Barmen Confessional Synod in 1934 even to consider an explicit reference to the Jewish question as one of the inescapable political consequences of its own first and second articles?[16]

The advance which Dar-es-Salaam and Ottawa represent over Barmen, it seems to me, is precisely this: that the confession of faith does not just *say* that the witness of the church must be "by its *faith and obedience*" (Barmen III) but spells out in concrete terms what this obedience consists in, here and now. This advance had already been anticipated by Dietrich Bonhoeffer, of course, especially in his essay of 1933 on the church and the Jewish question, and in the Bethel Confession of the same year.[17] As has already been pointed out, Bonhoeffer's test for the *status confessionis* is a twofold one: firstly, whether the state is going beyond its own mandate and trespassing on that of the church ("too much" state) and, secondly, whether the state falls short of its mandate ("too little" state). This latter criterion clearly comes into play when the racist South African government systematically deprives not just a minority but the majority of its citizens of their human rights by a corrupt and indefensible constitution.[18] Not only must Barmen III be read in the light of Barmen I and II but we must also go further than the whole 1934 Declaration and transpose it into the political and economic realities of today. It is precisely here that the rich churches of the West, particularly those imbued with neo-Lutheran ideas, hesitate and stumble, especially when industrialists and business people in their ranks, usually having vested interests in South Africa, begin to protest and even threaten to leave the church.

The question as to whether the church's *order* forms part of the witness and service of the church of Jesus Christ was, of course, at the centre of the debate among Lutherans between 1974 and 1977 on the question of declaring a *status confessionis*.[19]

This comes as no surprise, since the white churches who refused to have visible church fellowship with their oppressed black brothers and sisters based their unwillingness and even inability to do so on the argument that, according to Art. 7 of the Augsburg Confession, all that was necessary for the unity of the church was agreement in word and sacrament, but not "organizational unity" as it was disparagingly called. Dar-es-Salaam rejects this position, affirming that the public and unequivocal rejection of the apartheid system is necessary "to manifest the unity of the church", i.e. to give that unity visible form.

When Barmen III further defines the witnessing and serving community of brothers and sisters as the church of *pardoned sinners, in the midst of a sinful world*, this is important in several ways for the special cases of confession today. For one thing, this definition underlines the fact that the situation of the pilgrim people of God is one of struggle and conflict.[20] It is also a safeguard against the danger of dividing the individuals and groups involved in this conflict into the "good" and the "bad". Every confessing movement or church must guard against usurping the prerogatives of God the Judge or becoming legalistic. And the best defence here is the doctrine of justification.[21] The first thing in the confession of the faith is always the confession of our own guilt or complicity in guilt, and only then the positive declaration of what we believe. Demarcation here is the act not of the confessors but of those who exclude themselves from the community of faith.[22]

On the other hand, the formula "pardoned sinners", based on the doctrine of justification, is often misused in an "antinomian" sense, especially in territorial churches, as carte blanche for inactivity. It is most important, therefore, not to divorce this central utterance of the doctrine of justification from its context in the third Barmen article (and in Barmen II as well). For just as obedience and order have already been recognized as inseparable from faith and message, so now we find clear substantive statements about *what* the community of witness and service is to attest. Firstly, we read, *"it (sc.* the community of brothers and sisters) *is His alone".* This takes up again the theme of the first sentence: "Jesus Christ . . . *as Lord"* acts presently in the church. The question posed here, therefore, is that of loyalty and fidelity; in other words, the question of God or an idol, the question of the first commandment.

Here again we put our fingers on another notorious weakness of neo-Lutheran theology and ecclesial reality in particular. In order to underline the doctrine of justification, such contexts as apartheid are pronounced to be secondary issues, questions of social ethics.

But this overlooks the fact that, in every question of the commandments of the Second Table, decisions are also made about the commandments of the First Table. Why, otherwise, should Luther have begun his exegesis of each commandment of the Second Table with the words: "We should fear and love God, and so we should . . . " do or refrain from doing this or that to our neighbour? So too for the church: its first question is always its being before God and only then, in the second place, the question of its action — which necessarily follows, of course. By legitimizing or tolerating apartheid in church and society, the church is denying, primarily, that Christ is its Lord, that it is his alone. It thereby demonstrates that it has succumbed to idolatry.[23]

Barmen III itself develops this further in the following way. In saying that the church is to attest that *"it lives and desires to live only by his (sc.* Christ's) *consolation and by his orders, in expectation of his coming",* the third Barmen Thesis emphasizes once again that the situation in which the church lives is one of conflict and struggle. Being his witness, it is assailed as he was assailed; it is in need, therefore, of *consolation,* guidance, and a hope which reaches beyond physical death. There is hinted at here that readiness for martyrdom without which there is no confessing church today in South Africa and elsewhere, as we shall see presently. In my own view, in any reformulation of Barmen III today it would be necessary to make explicit reference to the many experiences of individual and church maryrdom in ecclesiastical, economic and political contexts. The phrase *"by his orders"* would also need to be developed so as to bring out their importance as a shield against the deliberate manipulation of information and attitudes in our world, a point to which we shall be returning later.

"In expectation of his coming": this expectation is not only an indispensable aid in the struggle itself but also has a decisive significance beyond that. In the first place, in concentrating on the returning Jesus Christ, the church keeps clearly before it the kingdom of God and the criteria this kingdom furnishes for the church's obedience and order. In southern Africa, this is a defence not only against the pseudo-Reformed heresy of a class society and a class church based on election but also against the pseudo-Lutheran heresy of autonomous political and economic systems and the irrelevance of church organization.

In the second place, this expectation saves the church from the resignation and arrogance of an "all or nothing" attitude and sets it free to take part hopefully and realistically in the difficult task of improving ecclesiastical, economic and political conditions at any given time in obedience to God's will and in the service of the neighbour.

2. Vis-à-vis weapons of mass destruction

Thesis 3: As with apartheid, so with the weapons of mass destruction, we must go beyond Barmen, as Dietrich Bonhoeffer did, and affirm, in accordance with the Confession, the need to repudiate heresy not only in the church's doctrine and order but also in the cooperation of Christians in systematic social or political injustice and the legitimization of such injustice by the church. Under the National Socialist régime that applied to the persecution of the Jews as it applies today to apartheid and also, as is coming increasingly to be recognized in the church today, to weapons of mass destruction. In the light of their experience of the confessional struggle against apartheid, the logical next step for the churches would have been to discover and declare the confessional challenge of the world economic system. For reasons we have still to consider, however, this did not happen. Instead, the spark of recognition and confession leapt over the economic question and lighted first on the question of peace. As early as 1958/59, the church brotherhoods in West Germany produced a theological statement, linking up with the Barmen Theological Declaration, in which they made the following connection:

> "The inclusion of weapons of mass destruction in the coercive resources available to the state for its 'threat and use of force' is possible only at the price of a de facto denial of the God who is faithful to his creation and gracious to his human family. Such conduct is inconceivable on Christian grounds. In respect of this conduct, which we consider sinful, neutrality is incompatible with confession of faith in Jesus Christ. Any attempt to justify such conduct and such neutrality on theological grounds leads to heresy, sows confusion and error, and flouts the will of the Triune God." The ecclesiology behind this position has earlier been defined as follows: "The newness of life brought by the gospel of Jesus Christ includes the active responsibility of both the community and the individual for the maintenance of human life and also, therefore, for the establishment of human orders of justice made possible by the patience of God."[24]

Here already, then, the picture of the Confessing Church was projected to include constitutively and concretely its joint responsibility in the political realm. Here, however, in contrast to the question of apartheid, no broad church base yet existed for recognizing, declaring or responding to a *status confessionis*.

To the best of my knowledge, the first application of this term *status confessionis* to the situation produced by the existence of weapons of mass destruction was when Günther Krusche used it in this sense at the Amsterdam ecumenical hearing in 1980. He himself, moreover, had rediscovered it in company with others as a member of the LWF Study Commission in connection with its theological work on apartheid.[25] Substantively, of course, the credal dimension vis-à-vis weapons of mass destruction had been recognized long before that, in Holland especially, and there too in connection with Barmen.[26]

It is unnecessary to describe in detail here how the question of weapons of mass destruction eventually reached the stage of recognition as a confessional issue.[27] I single out a few points of importance for our present question concerning the reality of the church as church.

We would be ill-advised to insist on this term *status confessionis*. For the strict application of our confessional standards, Article 16 of the Augsburg Confession would itself suffice as ground for roundly rejecting present weapons developments and the strategy of a feasible nuclear war as incompatible with our Christian faith, as the Catholic Bishops in the USA have demonstrated.[28] For the doctrine of the "just war", which is also anchored in this same Article 16 of the Augsburg Confession and which represents the maximum that classical theology ever permitted in the way of Christian participation in public violence, includes such criteria as "proportionality of means", "differentiation between combatants and non-combatants", etc. which are in any case no longer tenable in the conditions of a war waged with weapons of mass destruction. Where the term *status confessionis* is indispensable is where it is affirmed that the question of weapons of mass destruction has nothing to do with the Christian faith and confession but is a matter for private judgment, as neo-Lutherans in particular still heretically assert even today.[29]

We turn now to Barmen III, only selectively here of course, in connection with the question of the church and weapons of mass destruction. Am I right in thinking that, in recent discussions of our confession of Jesus Christ in face of nuclear weapons, the description of the church as the "community of brothers and sisters" has been insufficiently emphasized, if at all? It has not been sufficiently exploited. It could be argued, indeed that because our first loyalty is to Jesus Christ and his body the church, for that reason alone we should as the community of Jesus Christ have to exclude the taking up of arms against one another. On this basis, the argument of the historic peace churches in favour of a complete refusal of military service has consistency and probably even logic on its side. In the case of weapons of mass destruction, at any rate, the argument seems to me unambiguously clear, more so than the argument for absolute pacifism. How can I possibly threaten with mass slaughter my brothers and sisters in the churches of the GDR or the Soviet Union or other East European states?[30] If even the devilish possibility of the unimaginable chaos which would be caused by our waging a nuclear war is an outrage and blasphemy in respect of God's creation, it is also an outrage and a blasphemy, a sin, against the Holy Spirit even to envisage such a rendering of the body of Christ as would automatically ensue when Christians even merely *threaten* other Christians with weapons of mass destruction, let alone actually *use* them.

This gap in the argument permits advocates of the accumulation of weapons of mass destruction to commandeer the church's teaching in their favour. For example, during a campaign conducted by the Baden "evangelical group" of the Christian Democratic Union Party to collect signatures against the Theses of the Reformed Moderamen, the argument deployed was that these Theses threatened the unity of the church! What was meant here by "the unity of the church" was obviously not the unity of the universal church of Christ but that of the sum-total of church-tax contributors within the Baden province of West Germany! It is still necessary, therefore, to deploy the appeal to the unity of the church as an argument in favour of refusing any part in the manufacture, deployment or use of weapons of mass destruction and to translate this argument into practical steps in the peace work of the churches.[31]

Reference should be made here to one other problem. When we join with Barmen III in confessing that Jesus Christ acts presently in the community of brothers and sisters "in word and sacrament", this is naturally to be understood as a reference to the witness of holy scripture. We are confronted here with a hermeneutical problem which is far from simple. The situation of the church in the first three centuries permitted it only an indirect political witness to peace, and this is also the only witness attested in the New Testament. Only as the participation of Christians in the shaping of secular power, including the use of force, increased did it become possible and necessary to develop theological criteria and a code of conduct for Christians occupying responsible public positions, as an answer to the question as to how this form of power could be exercised to the glory of God and as service to the neighbour. The New Testament contains no explicit directives here. Does this mean that the only way the church can influence the shaping of secular structures is by the creation of alternative structures? If not, where do we find the criteria for participation in power in the "word and sacrament" in which Jesus Christ acts presently in the community of brothers and sisters? At the end of the long Constantinian era, we find ourselves still in a state of perplexity. One thing, however, is clear: there is no faith without *obedience*, and no message without an *order* consistent with that message.

When we are confronted with the call to obedience in respect of weapons of mass destruction, the question we raise today is that of civil *disobedience*. Here the church is called to share the risk taken by those who plead for the life of present and future generations by their refusals and symbolic actions. In the matter of a church order consistent with the gospel we have hardly yet even begun to reflect on the consequences. From a practical ecclesiological angle, I am thinking of two problems in particular:

1. If the refusal of military service is becoming a duty today, as

I am convinced it is, in line with the New Testament and the peace church tradition as well as with the Reformation tradition of selective refusal, then this has revolutionary implications for the contemporary form of the church. For this position can only be adopted and proclaimed by a church which is also prepared to accept the economic consequences of this position and this affirmation of faith. This, moreover, in two respects. Firstly, it must reckon with the feared flood of departures from the church, and secondly, it is only entitled to proclaim this position if it is also ready to accept the practical consequences of this position for the soldiers who are members of the "community of brothers and sisters". What I have in mind here, for example, is the "solidarity fund" established by Bishop Matthieson in Amarillo for workers who for reasons of conscience left the Pantex firm where all the nuclear warheads in the USA were assembled.

2. The other problem of conscience is that of the payment of taxes. In the Federal German Republic I have no direct dealings with the state in this matter; I pay my taxes through my employer, i.e. the church. This system makes it impossible for me to divert that portion of my taxes spent on weapons of mass destruction to other, life-enhancing purposes, even though I am ready to accept all the consequences of doing so. In other words, I have first to persuade my employer to engage in civil disobedience, something which in the present mélange of church and state is practically impossible in human terms. The result of such an attempt would be a sterile stalemate between the church authorities and myself rather than concerted action. It would seem that a Catholic archbishop in the USA is freer to obey the gospel than a Protestant pastor in the Federal Republic of Germany. Archbishop Hunthausen first refused to pay his USA defence tax over four years ago, urging his fellow Christians to take a similar course. Despite a number of practical attempts to solve it, this issue continues to be a difficult one in West Germany.

This question of diverting money away from war to justice and life brings us to the *third* urgent challenge to the church to confess its faith today:

3. IN RESPECT OF A GLOBAL ECONOMIC SYSTEM RESPONSIBLE FOR MASS SLAUGHTER

Thesis 4: The GLOBAL ECONOMIC SYSTEM, as the stronghold of huge agglomerations of power, is still the least recognized, the least exposed and answered challenge to the church to confess its faith. It is no longer amenable to control by any political institution for the good of all and at present costs the lives of over thirty million people from starvation annually, not to mention the human rights suppressed and violated in the interest of economic profit. Do thieves, profiteers under this system sit down at the Lord's Table together with their victims? Does the church really carry out its office as watchman here? Is not its financial system locally and globally simply a reflection of the world's class divisions?

Anyone who has taken part in the struggle against apartheid at any stage of the road to the confessing church knows that the most stubborn resistance is encountered where economic interests are at stake. Lutherans in the USA discovered this, for example, when they tried and largely succeeded in reaching and implementing, on the basis of the *status confessionis*, the decision not to cooperate economically or financially with banks and firms investing in South Africa. Still plainer was the case of the Federal German churches which, until recently, showed little interest in the problem of economic investments in South Africa and left the difficult work to their women's movement,[32] whereas, in the Falklands–Malvinas crisis or more recently the Libyan crisis, when the industrial nations overnight organized a boycott and economic sanctions against the countries concerned, there was no opposition at all from the institutional church. All the arguments deployed against the use of sanctions against South Africa were suddenly forgotten ("they wouldn't work", "they wouldn't help the victims", etc.).

Anyone who examines the question of armaments finds the same situation. The considerable part played by the arms lobby in Washington and other capitals in East and West whenever the question of national defence and the armaments industry arises has been highlighted in a whole series of expert studies.[33]

But this is only the tip of the iceberg. As the world economic system emerged from the colonial era and, once the colonies had attained their political independence, developed into neo-colonialism, it has so far proved incapable of solving the problem of distribution even though the production of goods is sufficient to meet the basic needs of humanity.

The impotence of the third world and the arrogance and cynicism of the industrial nations were plain for all to see at the sixth UNCTAD conference in 1983.[34] The mechanisms whereby the rich become steadily richer and the poor steadily poorer (scissors development) are well-known:

> Starvation is the secret mass-murderer of our day. It is avoidable and because it is avoidable it is just as much an accusation against this generation of accomplices as Hitler's mass murder was an accusation against the previous one (Richard Barnet).[35]

The theological and ecclesiological assimilation of these facts and interpretations (the details of which must here be taken as read) has so far been achieved mainly by churches and theologians in the periphery through which they have entered the worldwide ecumenical discussion. I recall here the liberation theology of the Latin American churches,[36] the minjung theology of South Korea (theology of the people),[37] black theology, and third-world theology generally, which has for some years now found a strong echo in a succession of conferences[38] as well as in the ecumenical study programme on "the church of the poor" and "the church in solidarity with the poor".[39]

It must be remembered here, of course, that the published results of all these efforts are simply the precipitates of a real theological struggle against vastly superior forces of oppression, exploitation and destruction. The real habitat of this theology consists of the prisons from which letters are written, the biblical discussions of persecuted *campesinos*, and all the other forms in which the theology of the *ecclesia militans* ("the church militant here on earth") finds expression. Because in our own case the church is not really engaged in a struggle against the powers of oppression, exploitation and destruction, neither is there any theology in Bonhoeffer's sense of a "weapon" or "iron rations" for the church; at least none that really deserves the name of theology in face of the poverty that needs to be eliminated and the guilt that needs to be purged. The main difficulty is that, in contrast to the case of apartheid and weapons of mass destruction, in the case of the world economic system we are still only at the beginning of theological analysis and actual experience in our churches' response to the challenge to confess their faith by their message and their order. In this chapter, remember, we are looking only at the ecclesiological aspect of the problem.[40]

When we ask from this ecclesiological standpoint the possible significance of Barmen III for the confession of the faith in respect of the global economic order, two points strike us at once, as in the case of apartheid: the reference to the *community of brothers and sisters* and the reference to the presence of Christ in the *sacrament*. The indissoluble unity of the Lord's Supper, on the one hand, and universal justice and solidarity within the one body of Christ, on the other, was already stressed by Luther.[41] Not surprisingly, however, it is the Catholics[42] and the Orthodox[43] rather than the Protestants who attach central importance to this aspect. Now would be a good time for *all* the churches to seize on this aspect, since it is given a central place in the Lima convergence documents on "Baptism, Eucharist and Ministry".[44] To pinpoint the issue: Do thieves, profiteers, and the victims of their depredations, all of whom call themselves Christians, continue to share together in the eucharist even if the thieves and profiteers blatantly go on thieving and profiteering and disguising or denying its reality and extent? A Barmen-style theological declaration in a Western industrial society would need to deal explicitly with this guilt and offer encouragement and practical guidance for conversion — not, of course, in any legalistic way but allowing room in our churches for "Christ acting presently as Lord in word and sacrament by the Holy Spirit".

Such a conversion, however, as the work of Jesus Christ himself, would necessarily, in accordance with Barmen III, have concrete consequences in the shape of *obedient conduct* and the reform of our church *order*. Our obedience would need to be related to the concrete monitoring of our national complicity in this death-dealing economic power and, if need by, to resistance to it. Churches in some countries have created institutions and other consultative instruments to enable them to oppose the abuse of economic power.[45] In the churches of Federal Germany, the question of economic power is taboo in official church circles and scarcely any attempt is being made to tackle this "off-bounds" area in our state-financed theological faculties. Merely to produce general criteria and postulates or ideological scenarios of the future is no help whatever. Churches and theologians must here plunge into the details of multinational economics. Obedience, as Bonhoeffer noted, is always concerned with God's concrete command. It is not even enough for ethics to tackle these questions. Nor is it enough to pick up the phrase used by Visser 't Hooft in Uppsala in 1968 — "ethical heresy" — stimulating though this was for the discussion then and since.

For the question here is one of Christian obedience, the obedience of *faith*. This is what is at stake in the question of mammon. It is not only a question of the commandment "You shall not steal!" but also of the commandment "You shall have no gods before or beside Me!" This is what is at stake when we share in the structural theft of the resources of this earth, when we do not behave as *belonging to Christ alone* but exploit and misuse great stretches of the body of Christ and the body of humanity and the earth as if they were our exclusive property.

Once again, this question comes to a focus in the question of the church's *order* and here specifically in the question of the way we handle the church's *material resources*. I can be brief here, since Wolfgang Huber has written a fine essay on this.[46] The integration of the West German churches' financial system in the structures of state and society makes them part and parcel of this state and society. In Luther's view, a church which even accepts interest has already forfeited the right to call itself a church.[47] It is obviously impossible, of course, to transform a church's financial system overnight. In my view, however, the very least we could do would be to introduce uniform material conditions of service in our churches,[48] together with a structural equalization of burdens with third-world churches, and to advocate resolutely and concretely steps towards a new economic world order. All this would inevitably provoke conflict among ourselves as members of churches for we ourselves are the "beneficiaries" of the present unjust world economic system. If our real concern here is for the *esse* of the church and not just with its greater or less comfortable *bene esse*, with its reality rather than its material comfort, then these are the minimum objectives to be striven for.[49]

In the following section I shall develop this argument more fully by looking for 1984 analogies in the light of the rejection clause of Barmen III.

II. The rejection clause of Barmen III and our heresy

Some of the strongest passages in the EKU statement on Barmen III (and in the corresponding synod resolution of 1980) are found in section 5 on the unity of the church. For example:

> "The division of Christendom is the division of the body of Christ" (1 Cor. 1:13). "Church and congregational constitutions must therefore be formulated so as to exclude *racial, national, social and confessional* division of the body of Christ rather than maintaining such division."[50]

The only problem with such statements is that once they have been endorsed, it is back to "business as usual", just as was the case with the statements about the need for uniform conditions of service in the church and its service agencies. Clearly, things are not as urgent as all that. Clearly, the world will still go on turning . . . It is precisely here, however, that the change of climate between when the EKU statement was adopted and our present situation is to be located. For us, the question of a "confessing church" is no longer just a theoretical possibility; it has become an historical "must" which both alarms and exhilarates us.

But this, of course, compels us to take seriously one aspect of Barmen III which is almost completely lost sight of in the EKU statement and in its accompanying essays: namely, the rejection clause of Barmen III:

> We reject the false doctrine that the church is at liberty to form its message or its order according to its own desire or according to prevailing philosophical or political convictions.

In his address to the EKU Theological Commission, Rudolf Weth, at all events, had this to say:

> Already in the time of the church struggle, the rejection clause of the third Barmen Thesis led to a recognition of the connection between ecumenicity and the critique of ideology; in other words, of the summons to the church to "acknowledge its own complicity with such powers and forms as nation, race, class, society, culture and political ideology" (A. Boyens). Weth then continues, very revealingly: "It need not be said, still less can it be explained, what the significance of this complicity is in the present conditions of ideological myopia in which the churches today are implicated — especially in the North-South conflict."[51]

But this is precisely what is at stake today. At the Vancouver Assembly of the WCC, an attempt was made to define two aspects of this new experience. Firstly: despite a growing awareness of the problems, present developments in racism, the violation of human rights, mass deaths from hunger, war and the pollution and destruction of the earth seem to be slipping from our control. We must have done with the collective myopia which has clearly assumed demonic character. Here our faith in the royal sovereignty of Christ over the powers assumes a new and central significance. Secondly: these wrong directions are clearly rooted in an heretical distortion of the Judeo-Christian tradition in modern times and, in addition to this, are being defended and even actively promoted in the churches increasingly by individuals, groups and organizations and lobbies which themselves lay claim to Christ's authority. *As in the case of the "German Christians"* in the time of the church struggle, therefore, *the question is forced on us* of certain groups of self-styled Christians who, by their efforts to establish in the church, with the assistance of economic and political forces, *traditional errors common to us all, are beginning to distance themselves from the community of the church*, or have already done so, and even to persecute the true church of Jesus Christ. In other words, all of us share in the reprehensible traditions in which these errors are reflected. The rejection clauses of the Barmen Declaration, therefore, including that of Barmen III, are in the first instance acknowledgments by the church of its own guilt (B. Klappert). This set of questions is to be developed in two directions: (1) modern heresy: its background in the history of philosophy and social theory; (2) the "German Christians" of today — in ourselves and in our midst.

1. MODERN HERESY IN THE LIGHT OF THE HISTORY OF PHILOSOPHY
AND SOCIAL THEORY

Thesis 5: In the light of the rejection clause of Barmen III, the main question is this: What is it within us and in our midst that in Christ's name promotes and justifies the exploitation of nature and the two-thirds world (racism, neo-colonialism), of manual workers and wage-earners, discrimination against women, and militarism in defence of our domination and our possesssions? We live in a global system of centres and peripheries with an innate tendency to develop FORMS OF FASCISM — brutal forms in the dependent countries, "friendly" forms in the industrial countries — by a coalition of "big business" and "big government" serviced by modern science and technology.

At the Vancouver Assembly, Heino Falcke and I tried to envisage as a unity the confessional questions posed to us today because of the abuse of the growth of power acquired through the Judeo-Christian faith in the creation and the gifts of the Holy Spirit. The Western culture resulting from this is labelled by Falcke a "culture of violence". I, for my part, tried to approach the question more historically by tracing the modern combination of the destruction of nature, racism or colonialism, sexism and militarism, back to its roots in the modern apotheosis of government and possession (Descartes).[52]

In the description of this development, at least one other agent was missing, of course: namely, the institutions of the political community, in short — the state. In the history of Europe since Plato, the political institutions have been interpreted from the standpoint of the common good based on justice. But what happens when these institutions which, in bourgeois society in particular, made possible a hitherto unprecedented measure of legal freedom for a hitherto unprecedented number of people, come increasingly under the control of the economic forces precisely of that same bourgeois society in the interests of an ever-diminishing number of people? Put in concrete terms: how can national political institutions any longer control transnational agglomerates of unimaginable size for the common good?

As has already been said, most radical theory so far advanced to account intelligently for the ever-widening gap and asymmetrical distribution of power within and between the countries in this global system is the theory of dependence. This theory has now been expanded and its focus sharpened by a theory which I would like to call *the theory of global interconnected fascism*. This has been developed in the context of studies of fascism by Bertram Gross in his book *Friendly Fascism: the New Face of Power in America*.[53] In his view, two trends are coming increasingly into conflict: a trend towards a global fascism, and a trend towards true democracy. In the present context I would like to emphasize two points from this fascinating book.

Firstly, Gross advances the thesis that the novelty in the classic fascism of this century was merely the application of the colonial methods of capitalism to the population of Europe itself:

> The essence of the new fascist order was an exploitative combination of imperial expansion, domestic repression, militarism and racism . . . No one of these elements, of course, was either new or unique. None of the "haves" among the capitalist powers, as the fascists pointed out again and again, had built their positions without imperialism, militarism, repression and racism. The new leaders of the three "have-nots", as the fascists pointed out, were merely expanding on the same methods. "Let these 'well-bred' gentry learn", proclaimed Hitler, "that we do with a clear conscience the things they do secretly with a guilty one." . . . *The Nazi war crimes consisted largely of inflicting on white Europeans levels of brutality that had previously been reserved only for Asians, Africans, and the native populations of North, Central, and South America (ibid. p.21f. my italics).*

. . . and levels of brutality reserved for nature by science and technology since the beginning of the modern period . . . we would add. Albert Speer himself stated this clearly enough:

> Hitler's dictatorship was the first dictatorship of an industrial state in this age of technology, a dictatorship which employed to perfection the instruments of technology to dominate its own people (*ibid.* p.25).

Developments following the Second World War clearly reveal the core of fascism, already central in classical fascism but concealed, as Gross demonstrates, namely: *the great coalition of big business and big government* — serviced by modern science and technology. This definition of fascism also permits us to investigate the essential unity of original Western imperial capitalism and its variants in Eastern state capitalism (despite its socialist-humanist tinge), though we cannot pursue this further here. At any rate it should be clearly recognized that "really existing socialism" in the Soviet sphere of power displays the same problems — including the North-South question — in a different form. In the Western imperium, the global connection reveals a double face: one brutal, the other "friendly". In countries which are dependent on the USA and its Western allies,[54] countries like Chile, the Dominican Republic, the Philippines of Marcos, South Korea, etc. it shows a brutal face:

> Most of the governments in these countries are crude military dictatorships with few compunctions about wiping out most domestic freedoms in defence of the freedoms of domestic oligarchies and first-world interests. Sheer brutality, however, . . . does not qualify a régime as fascist; its régime must also be interlocked with concentrated capital. Yet big capital is growing in these countries — albeit in forms that are mainly dependent on first-world support and initiatives. Hence these can best be seen as countries of *"dependent fascism"*. In some of the countries, as the domestic oligarchies become more closely linked with transnational capital, the régimes tend to become more sophisti-cated in drawing velvet gloves over iron fists and in assuming a "friend-lier" face (*ibid.* p.39).

When the brutal puppet régimes are no longer able to cope with the conflicts in "dependent fascism", even the friendlier "central fascism" occasionally drops its mask, of course. The "Watergate affair", for example, finally revealed for all to see the links between the International Telephone and Telegraph Corporation (ITT), the Central Intelligence Agency (CIA), and the Nixon régime (Kissinger). The connections between the interests of Gulf & Western in the Dominican Republic and the many interventions there are familiar and have been presented by the North American Council of Churches in the impressive audiovisual series: "Guess who's coming for breakfast!" But otherwise, this fascist tendency in the USA wears a friendly face, e.g. that of an ageing yet still sprightly film cowboy (Gross, xiii). But it is possible to observe the same phenomenon in all the Western industrial countries.

Excursus

After the manuscript of this book had been complete, I came across an essay composed by Johan Galtung in January 1983 for the science course in Berlin under the title: "Who are the successors of Nazism?" (unpublished). He fully confirms Gross's theory and analysis. His first and main thesis is: *"Nazism is occidental civilization in extremis."* He analyzes the different dimensions of this thesis: (1) space: colonialism; (2) time: tragic orientation of an ideal original state; (3) knowledge: deductive derivation from a dualistic enemy stereotype; (4) humanity-nature: romantic and destructive simultaneously; (5) person-person: centre-periphery structures. (The main points of contact between Gross and Galtung lie here: "All of this can be operated softly as in Northern Europe or very heavily as in South America; the Nazi operation of capitalism is located at the extreme end of that dimension. And this, of course, is consonant with the key hypothesis that *Nazism in particular and fascism in general* is a phenomenon that comes into being *when capitalism is in crisis* and is *no longer* capable of operating (meaning, giving adequate return for investment) *smoothly or softly"* (p. 9).) (6) person-transpersonal: God or an idol destroys the enemy in the end (exterminism).

In a further section, Galtung examines the question as to where and to what extent these different dimensions are operative in East and West Germany.

Gross also analyzes the various dimensions of "friendly fascism": ideology, economics, democratic façade, thought manipulation, "carrot and stick" mechanisms, the syndrome of sex, drugs and new religions, adaptive mechanisms and myths. I choose only the ideological dimension for further comment here.[55]

2. TODAY'S "GERMAN CHRISTIANS" — IN US AND AROUND US

Thesis 6: It is often people who call themselves "Christian" who in the industrial countries support the forces of death by which the confessing church obedient to Christ (in South America and Guatemala, for example) is persecuted. This persecution often starts with the deliberate or unconscious spread of misinformation concerning the church of the poor, the peace movement, etc. The central question, therefore, is: WHERE IS THE NAME OF CHRIST BEING DIRECTLY OR INDIRECTLY MISUSED TODAY TO DEFEND THE POWER OF THE WHITE RACE AND THE PERPETUATION OF THIS POWER, that of the rich and powerful whites in particular, by every possible form of propaganda, economic manipulation and military and other forms of violence?

When Reformed (and other) apartheid Christians in South Africa seek to use the precious name of Christ to justify and cover up their exploitation, racism and militarism and thus come under the ban of the rejection clause of Barmen III, is this just an exceptional case? Consider just one example, that of the Americas. When General Rios Montt was still President of Guatemala, one phenomenon which normally lies beneath the surface was fully exposed to public view: the support of oppression and intimidation by self-styled "Christian" groups. The General proudly announced that there were now two hundred "evangelical" churches in Guatemala.[56] Not only was the wide popular sympathy and ideological backing for the "first evangelical" President from evangelical churches and sects of the most diverse origin given wide publicity in the press but so too the active participation of certain sects in the government's anti-resistance programmes was splashed in prominent headlines. These groups (foremost among them the so-called "church of the word" — *iglesia verbo*) cooperated in the "beans and guns" programme with the army, using foreign financial aid to secure the strategically vital provision of "beans". While thousands of *indios* and, above all, Catholic Christians of the churches of the poor, were victims of the brutal campaigns of a supposedly "Christian" president, members of the sects had special identity cards ensuring immunity from the attention of the security forces.[57] The policy of World Vision in the Honduran refugee camps also made the headlines. By an adroit strategy of divide and rule among the relief and aid organizations, this body finally managed to bring work among the refugees under the control of repressive military forces and people closely connected with them.

In both cases, the trail led back to North America in more than one sense. Most of the so-called "churches" in Guatemala originated from and continued to be financed by fundamentalist groups in the USA. The same applies to World Vision. These specific examples are not haphazard but reflect an entire system. In 1968, Nelson D. Rockefeller, the then Governor of New York, went on a mission to Latin America on behalf of Richard Nixon. In his subsequent report[58] he even mentioned the Catholic Church which at that precise time had come out publicly in support of the poor and the oppressed, in its report of the Medellin conference of Latin American bishops. According to Rockefeller, the Catholic Church was in danger of "infiltration by subversives", i.e. of going counter to USA interests in Latin America.

Reading the recommendations Rockefeller made for the struggle against revolutionary movements, we are not all that far away from the persecutions of the church in Latin America in the seventies. The best-known summary of these recommendations can be found in the *Banzer Plan* of Bolivia which shows exactly what methods governments and secret services are prepared to use in their efforts to divide, manipulate and marginalize a church which begins to identify itself with the poor: for example, Soviet weapons are placed in the hands of murdered priests, calumnies are spread, etc.[59] Here again, the denigration campaigns and attempts to split the church are accompanied by similar activities in the USA itself, indeed in the whole Western world.[60] From the Muldergate publicity scandal in South Africa, the world learned of the methods employed there by the government to pressure public opinion and influence the churches of the Western world in particular. Journals are bought up, publicity agencies are manipulated, etc. etc. Best-known, perhaps, are the *Readers Digest* articles and the TV show *Sixty Minutes*, with their campaign against the World Council of Churches and other ecumenical bodies. In these and other cases, the *media* make use of a whole series of voluntary and university institutes with access to unlimited financial resources from foundations or contributions from industry, which have mushroomed everywhere in recent years. "Major corporations . . . now underwrite at least thirty academic centres and chairs of free enterprise."[61]

The best-known centre of this kind in the purview of the North American churches is the Institute for Religion and Democracy (IRD), a detailed study of which is now available.[62] This Institute is interesting on several counts. In the first place it has, like the *Readers Digest*, a special affinity with the lower middle or "blue collar" class. It is from this class that the Ku Klux Klan recruits its adepts. Fascist or quasi-fascist rulers have always exploited the failures and misfits in society whose aggression it was possible, however, to divert from an attack upwards into an attack downwards and focused on minorities of one sort or other (Jews, foreigners, members of other races, etc.). The new rightist movement in the church — e.g. R. Neuhaus of the IRD — is also recruited from among converted Marxists of the former student movement,[63] who now write books in defence of "democratic capitalism", insert notices in newspapers in support of Reagan's "middle America" and rearmament policies, etc. Finally, there is the phenomenon of the so-called "electronic church", known also as one of the main visible expressions of the "moral majority",

which B. Gross aptly renames the "immoral majority". Its chief
representative is Jerry Falwell and if you are ever in the United
States you should make sure not to miss watching his "Old Time
Gospel Hour" on television. His message is: "Be subject to the
powers that be; be diligent; let the woman be subject to the man!"
He also commends rearmament as a means of fending off the evil
communist adversary who is bent on destroying the existing order.
Much the same thing is also available to us in Germany via cable
television. The control of the media by corporations and banks has
here its most powerful pseudo-Christian and even anti-Christian
expression — at least, if Bonhoeffer was right when he said that
the erring church turns into the false church once it joins in the
persecution of the church.[64]

Why is it that questions of the sort that are plainly arising in
respect of the USA tend to be suppressed by us in West Germany?
My own explanation would be that it is because of the daunting
prospect that we might then find ourselves confronted soon, not
with a run-of-the-mill domestic church controversy but with a
full-blown church struggle. We must nevertheless have the courage
to treat the question of becoming a confessing church today as a
challenge to us to face up to such questions. Need I assure the
reader that in trying to do so now my intention is certainly not to
point an accusing finger at anyone in particular but rather to
encourage all of us to discover our own blind spots in this matter.
In every group, moreover, there are deceivers and deceived. We
lack the means and the mandate to decide which is which.
According to the biblical teaching we are not called to judge individuals but only what we can see of their work. This, however,
we *must* do if we do not wish completely to exclude the question
of God's will (cf. Rom. 12:1–2). The questions we are concerned
with here are in the final analysis concerned with stimulating
progress towards knowledge. They are not apodictic assertions.
But we must make a beginning together.

My first question is this: What are we to make of the fact that
the evangelical press agency *idea* employs a correspondent, Jörg
Wilhelmy, who had been publicly identified, so far without any
challenge in the courts, as a contact person of the South African
secret service? This identification has been made by Gordon
Winter, a former agent of that same secret service.[65] Questioned
about this allegation, *idea* threatened legal proceedings against
anyone repeating it as a statement of fact. (According to German
law, a person is guilty of defamation only if unable to furnish

positive proof that his or her allegation is true. But who can demonstrate that someone is a secret service agent?) But the question which *idea* was interested in, i.e. that of a correspondent's loyalty, is of secondary importance compared with the substantive point that Wilhelmy represented the position of the South African government and that *idea* adopted this position. This point took on ecclesiological significance, in addition to its social ethical aspect, when in the course of the state prosecution of the South African Council of Churches *idea* almost vengefully supported the position of the prosecuting state against the persecuted church.[66] Other examples could be given of the same sort of thing; for example, *idea*'s reportage of events in Guatemala.

It is against this background that we are to see the notorious inability of the Council of the Evangelical Church in Germany to prevent even its own members, not to mention leading personalities of the provincial churches, from visiting South Africa at the South African government's expense, despite the official announcement by the SACC that it would not recognize as representatives of the church persons whose visits were sponsored in this way.[67]

It is clear from these examples that all talk of the *status confessionis* in official West German church circles vis-à-vis apartheid has largely been mere lip-service. If fear of conflict in our own backyard prevents us from recognizing such relatively trivial self-evident considerations, how can we possibly expect to accept consequences of the will of God which are more painful than any conflict which might follow a refusal to accept a ticket paid for by the South African government. (This is not to belittle the sincere efforts being made by some fellow-Christians in positions of leadership in the church; on the contrary, it helps us to cherish them all the more highly.)

The prickliest question in West Germany in this context is that of a *"Christian" political party*, in general, and of the West German CDU/CSU in particular, with its attempt to bring pressure to bear in church matters.

The Eastern branch of the CDU can be left out of account here, since it lies outside the scope of our direct responsibility and is in any case not a governing party. In principle, it is a mirror image of the problem confronting the Western CDU/CSU. I must stress right away that our concern here is with ecclesiological and not party political questions. Obviously, citizens of any political party can adopt the same positions as those taken at present by the CDU/CSU and will have to contend for these positions with political means in the political arena. But the moment a group calling itself "Christian" attaches the label "Christian" to certain political positions and these positions are propagated as such in the Christian church, the question becomes one of explaining the significance of such a procedure for the church of Jesus Christ.

I leave to one side the question of principle, i.e. whether it is compatible at all with Christian doctrine for a political pressure group to appropriate Christ's name for itself. In Luther's view, not to speak of the New Testament, this is excluded in principle. How professors of Protestant theology can teach accordingly in their lectures but do exactly the opposite as citizens has always amazed me from my student days. In the light of the history of the immediate post-war years, there may be some legitimate excuse for the interconfessional alliance in the CDU/CSU, but the question and conflicts increasingly confronting us today urgently call for a new round of intense interconfessional theological discussions. The same question is also to be put to the idea of a "Christian Peace Movement" (as against a peace movement of both Christians and non-Christians).

I confine myself here to the concrete question of what the Western CDU/CSU actually says and does in Christ's name in the credal issues already referred to. It should be noted that there is a more open version of this position within the CSU, especially among its leaders, and a more evasive version within the CDU. Herr Strauss's attitude to apartheid in South Africa and Namibia is well-known. Only recently he asserted bluntly that equality for blacks in South Africa is not Christian and would only lead to chaos.[68] He clearly favours the continued domination of the whites with barely concealed racist terminology and by avoiding any reference to apartheid as such. Surely the Bavarian delegates to Dar-es-Salaam who endorsed the LWF Assembly's decision on the *status confessionis* should have initiated a thorough church discussion on the compatibility between belief in and demonstration of church unity and support of a political party like the CSU which persists in opposing the Lutheran position as made explicit at Dar-es-Salaam and in calling this opposition "Christian"? Such a procedure would surely have required them to become a confessing church in the years since 1977. What were the thoughts of the Bavarian delegates at the LWF Assembly in Budapest in 1984 when the question was put to them: What have you done concretely in Bavaria to support the joint Lutheran declaration of a *status confessionis* in respect of apartheid?

Mutatis mutandis, the same question could be put to the churches in other parts of the Federal Republic where, instead of the CSU, it is the Western CDU which advocates similar positions, as is clear from its statement of general principles.[69] It needs to be emphasized once again that some individual fellow-Christians who belong to this party resolutely oppose apartheid. But it became very clear in the debate in the Federal Parliament on 10 February 1984 that the position of the coalition government, already luke-warm in the sense of excluding any pressure or sanctions against the régime in South Africa, had been still further watered down under the influence of the Western CDU/CSU so that even the constitutional changes which in the last analysis only help reinforce the apartheid régime are now welcomed as an advance in the direction of reform. This is of a piece with the West German government's Central American policy which likewise either mini-mizes or openly approves the Reagan administration's repressive policy in that region and supports the military dictatorships in place there. And all this in Christ's name! Another area requiring investigation from this angle is West German policy towards non-Germans and asylum seekers.

We turn next to the challenge to confess our faith in respect of *weapons of mass destruction*. This is not yet recognized as a credal issue by all the churches, of course. An intensive dialogue is going on and must be continued in order to sift truth from error. Considering, however, all the efforts already made in this field by churches and theologians, synods and church leadership bodies, it is strange that the one party which calls itself "Christian" should have failed to brief even a single member to stand up in the parliamentary debate in November 1983 and state the conscientious grounds, shared by millions of Christians and propounded by certain churches even officially, against the so-called "moderniz-ation" of weapons, and to vote against another step in the continu-ation of the arms race.

In respect of the *question of the global economy*, which of course is even less recognized officially by the churches as a credal question than the issues already mentioned, the Western CDU/CSU is well to the fore in promoting national economic interests and supporting a development aid where investments produce the maximum financial returns. It is also committed to unconditional support of Western vested interests.[70] Also of considerable import-ance in this connection is the campaign conducted by the Western CDU/CSU to transfer the public media to the control of private enterprise monopolies. In the question of the *treatment of the natural environment*, too, a similar picture emerges: here again, it is industrial interests in the main which are promoted by an appeal to Jesus Christ.

All these issues need to be re-examined in the light of the gospel and, in the first place, in terms of social ethics. Are the institutions being rightly used in accordance with God's will and in the direction pointed by Jesus Christ? But our main interest here is in the *ecclesiological dimension* of these questions. Special interest attaches, therefore, to the way in which the Western CDU/CSU tries to influence congregations and churches, both through individual party members and through party organizations, in the direction of its own political answers to these credal issues. The avowed aim of the "Protestant Working Group" of the CDU is to enlist the support of Protestant citizens for the political options of the CDU. What exactly this means will be made clearer by a few examples. A systematic theological analysis and interpretation of these questions is still awaited.

In one congregation I know, the question of apartheid was due to be raised following the Dar-es-Salaam decision. It was decided to explore and decide the matter in direct partnership with South African Christians and churches. Whereupon two CDU members of the church board of the congregation pressured their fellow board members and the pastor into eliminating this question *de facto* from the agenda. If it was not excluded, they would split the congregation. One of the two CDU members is also a member of the "Emergency Fellowship of Evangelical Germans", whose groups in South Africa and Namibia publicly support the apartheid system. It is well-known that this "Emergency Fellowship" is also a member of an association of right-wing German evangelicals whose organ (once again!) happens to be *idea*.

The Protestant Working Group of the Western CDU in Baden launched a campaign to collect signatures in opposition to the Reformed Theses.[71] In this serious case of conscience, no heed was paid to any substantive theological arguments. Two arguments only were deployed: (1) this was a matter for the experts (i.e. the neo-Lutheran heresy repudiated by Barmen II); (2) the adoption of a clear position on this question would endanger the unity of the church (i.e. once again the veiled threat of schism).

Furthermore, a growing tendency is observable in the Western CDU not only to palm off a policy of economic self-interest as "development aid" but also to promote charitable development projects which studiously avoid tackling the problems of power and structures at both ends of the line. We also need here a study of the Konrad Adenauer and Hanns Seidel Foundations. Both these foundations also support movements and influential people in other countries who oppose the cause of human rights and often even our fellow Christians and partner churches in these countries. Similar questions arise in the matter of ecology. Attempts are made to ensure that in discussion processes within the churches loyalty to economic interests is given priority over theological and ecclesiological clarification.

The importance of these questions comes even more sharply into focus when the Western CDU/CSU deploys political pressure in respect of them. Here again, we can only raise the ecclesiological question inherent in these questions; in other words, the question of how this political party uses its power in relation to the church. Firstly, what is the significance of the fact that, in pursuit of this party's policy, support is given to forces which hinder our fellow-Christians and churches in their struggle to follow Christ in faithful and obedient discipleship or even persecute them? In face of the credal issues touched on, all of which are ecumenical, i.e. global, in dimension, too little serious attention has been given to the fact that the danger of an erring and pseudo-church arises not only when the persecution of Christians is assisted in our own country but also when actions are performed or positions adopted *in Christ's name* which increase the sufferings and add to the deadly toll taken of sections of the one body of Christ in other countries (as well, of course, to the one body of the humanity and earth created by the one God).

It is also mainly in groups close to or even belonging to the Western CDU/CSU that we once again find the political and ecclesiastical pacemakers in the *opposition to and even sometimes the slandering of the ecumenical movement*. This again is symptomatic of a "Christianity" whose primary concern is to strengthen its own interests and its own power. If the heresy of the "German Christians" in the time of the Nazi Third Reich was their blasphemous misuse of Christ's name to extend the power of the German Aryan "master race", the question put to us today by the rejection clause of Barmen III is the following: *Where is Christ's name being directly or indirectly (mis-)used today to justify and maintain the power of the white race, especially that of its wealthy and powerful representatives, by every available kind of propaganda, economic manipulation, and military and other forms of violence?*

In other words, if the questions raised are the correct ones and if the tendencies identified are real, what we are witnessing today is the development of a global heresy which amounts, in the last analysis, to the recognition, alongside Jesus Christ the one word of God, of a second quasi-religious claim; not "German-ness" as in 1934, but "Western-ness",[72] which is also defended and spread imperialistically by every available coercive means as a supreme value.

Once again it should be noted that our purpose here is not to look aghast at other people, not to condemn and excommunicate. The point being made is that, whichever group we may adhere to, we are all entering into a process in which a decision will eventually have to be made. For it is clear that all of us, as individual congregations, synods and church leadership bodies, are deeply imbued with these traditions of our Western "cult of violence" (Falcke); so much so, indeed, that we can easily allow ourselves to be dismayed, divided, paralyzed by the strength of economic, political or communication pressure groups, and even coerced and driven in the same direction. The vital question, then, is how can we promote in our own church at all levels processes in which we learn to test and practise the decisions required of us in the light of holy scripture and the Christian creed, in fellowship with the one Christian family and, above all, in solidarity with the poor.

III. Confessing the faith: a conciliar process in the life of the people of God

Thesis 7: The starting point for a confessing church is its own repentance, not the exclusion of others. It confesses its faith in Jesus Christ affirmatively in a specific situation and in doing so promotes the confessing process in all the social forms of the one church. This process of confessing the faith includes, of course, as a final possibility, the transformation of an erring church into a pseudo-church and its exclusion — perhaps only temporarily — from the community of the true church.

In the global confessional process, apartheid has already been declared a *status confessionis*. The weapons of mass destruction are well on the way to being declared a *status confessionis* and this will assuredly provoke still greater tensions to test us, since here the decision-making bodies cannot rest content with mere rhetoric as they often have been in the case of apartheid. The greatest backlog to be made up is in the case of the global economic system and its recognition as a challenge to the unambiguous confession of our faith in Jesus Christ as the Prince of Peace. Patient work is imperative here to end the taboo imposed on analysis and discussion and above all, on action in this field. Here the life of millions of human beings is at stake.

The dangerous questions I have raised will have been badly formulated if it is not clearly understood that their challenge to repentance, costly discipleship and a visible confessing community of faith in Jesus Christ is addressed to us all individually, author and readers alike. As Bonhoeffer put it, writing of ecclesial communion,[73] the confession of faith becomes legalistic if it begins, on the contrary, by defining the boundaries of the church, who is within and who is without. If boundaries are drawn, they are drawn by those who exclude themselves. Even then, the confessing church will continue to signal the hope and desire for renewed unity in the truth. The important thing, in any case, is the careful ordering of the confessional process.

The use here of the terms "conciliar" and "people of God" connects the theological terminology of the German Reformation tradition (*Bekenntnis*, confession) with other theological traditions in the ecumenical movement. The terms "people of God" and "covenant" remind us of our solidarity as Christians with the Jewish people. The point here is simply to ensure that we do not lose sight of this wider complex, so closely connected with our main theme, even though we cannot dwell long on it here. If it be true that our present critical situation with its dangerous and potentially disastrous currents derives from the dynamic released by the Judeo-Christian tradition, then the continuation of the Jewish-Christian dialogue with renewed intensity is a must.

The connection with ecumenical theology can be illustrated by reference to the summons of the Vancouver Assembly of the World Council of Churches to join in a conciliar process (covenant) for justice, peace and the integrity of creation.[74] The use of the term "conciliar fellowship" or "conciliar process" in this connection is not new.[75] Following up Barmen III, the 1980 synod of the Evangelical Church of the Union (EKU) urged "especially in face of a torn and divided humanity, a renewal of efforts towards the conciliar fellowship of the churches".[76]

To speak of a conciliar process towards confession of the faith implies, of course, the determination to arrive at decisions, in the same sense that Bonhoeffer had decisions in mind when he urged the holding of an "evangelical council". The GDR delegation in

Vancouver also proposed a genuine council, a proposal taken up in Group 6 which formulated it as follows: "that the WCC should convoke an ecumenical council for life, justice and peace as culmination of the urgently required process in churches and Christian network groups".[77]

But apart altogether from the process towards concrete decisions, the concept of "conciliar fellowship" necessarily includes the element of binding mutual commitment within the body of Christ because this conciliar fellowship has grown out of and is to be understood in terms of the eucharistic fellowship.[78] In other words, a confessing church in a Christian tradition of conciliarity, especially in the Orthodox tradition, would mean a church practising eucharistic fellowship. The Christ of the poor (Matt. 25) and the Christ of the breaking of bread would then be one and the same Christ.[79]

My *hypothesis*, therefore, is this: in order to formulate the theme "confessing church" in ecumenical terms, we must in any given situation identify where in a specific church tradition we are confronted with an historical experience and a theological assimilation of this experience which, in face of a real threat, maintains the church's visibility, identity and reality as the body of Christ.

This is the case in certain Anglo-Saxon traditions where the term "covenant" has been used.[80] The "Alliance (= covenant) for the Abolition of Slavery" is echoed today in the "new alliance for the abolition of weapons of mass destruction". Another advantage of using the concept of "covenant" to complement the concepts of "confessing" and "conciliar fellowship" is that it not only includes the dimensions of commitment and active engagement but also reminds us of the frequently recurring biblical covenants made by God with God's people, with humanity. In other words, the use of this term excludes the erroneous notion that what should and could happen here is something concerning us human beings alone. All action by human beings and the churches, from congregation to congregation, from group to group, and the sum total of all such action throughout the entire inhabited earth, is enclosed within, made possible, filled with spirit and life, given a plenitude of hope which more than compensates for all our failures, sufferings and martyrdoms, by the God who in Jesus Christ has established a covenant with creation, a covenant of fidelity and new creation with us and with the earth.

On this basis (which would need to be made explicit in a new ecumenical "Barmen III"), we turn in this third and final section of chapter 6 to the following question: If certain rudiments of a confessing church are discernible today in various situations and in various quarters in the ecumenical movement (as we have suggested, in section I of this chapter, is the case in respect of apartheid, weapons of mass destruction and the global economic system), and if, on the other hand, as we have suggested in section II, certain global forces, disguised in various forms as authorized agents of Jesus Christ, have made it their business to hinder, thwart and even attack this process of confessing Christ and keeping the covenant, the question is how we can and should play our part concretely in this total ecumenical struggle, i.e. how are *we* to become a confessing church, in the Federal German Republic and in other rich countries?

At this point let me interject a personal assessment of our situation. When I look back over the last five and a half years of my life and work dealing with this question in congregations, groups, provincial church, ecumenical working groups, and so on, in Baden, I am conscious of a real tension. Starting from the New Testament axiom that we rich can only see or enter the kingdom of God by a miracle of the Holy Spirit, I am amazed at all the miracles I have seen for myself in so many individuals, groups, congregations and even institutions.[81] Anyone who compares these recent years with earlier years has to admit that the learning process, the advance in understanding which has actually been achieved over so broad a base, exceeds anything we could have hoped for. On the other hand, I have the feeling that hardly anything of this human growth in understanding at all levels — in the question of peace it was even "majority learning" (to use Ernst Lange's hopeful term) — has so far rubbed off, so to speak, on the institutions. Indeed, the institutions are wholly geared to the defence of property. The very same synod which in 1981 was able to speak so generously in favour of our fellowship in the ecumenical movement, in autumn 1983 cut the allocation for church development aid by 8 percent and refused to examine the question of the transnational economy and our complicity in it concretely in the light of faith and love in the one church.

The lesson I learn from this experience is that we must become gentler in manner and more resolute in action, as the old Latin tag puts it, even if the resultant conflict is all the harder and the price to be paid in our own lives all the higher. "The reality of the act of confessing our faith will be proved by our willingness to make decisions which are costly to ourselves" (W. Lienemann).[82] What does that mean specifically?

As already indicated,[83] I identify *four social forms* of the life of the church: local congregation, discipleship groups, regional church, universal church. We become a confessing church when all these social forms become a confessing church in a conciliar process. For obvious reasons, present challenges to confess the faith, recognize the covenant obligation and live as a genuine eucharistic conciliar fellowship, are usually first taken up by discipleship groups or the global ecumenical fellowship, or both. In the very nature of the case, discipleship groups have the mobility and the economic independence to respond to the call of the Spirit while the ecumenical fellowship of the church is the first to feel it when one member suffers. The danger is that these groups and the ecumenical fellowship should keep to themselves instead of leavening the local congregations and the regional churches.

As I see it, the *top priority* is the initiation of theological processes in the organized church — in congregations, district and provincial churches — at the decision-making level and with the decision-making bodies in view, processes which press for *a decision as to where our primary loyalty lies*: the white race or the Christ who transcends race? The maintenance of existing economic and property conditions, or sharing — firstly within the body of Christ itself? A security and defence based on mass murder, or a security and defence based on measures which create trust and establish justice?

These questions need to be faced not only in this conciliar process within the organized churches but also in the camp of the conservative evangelicals and conservative political parties in the rich countries. Our fellow-Christians in these groups need to be given every opportunity to shake off their vested economic and political interests and loyalties and to understand and feel for their fellow-Christians and fellow human beings who are increasingly bearing the burden of our economic and defence interests. The chances of achieving this understanding and sensitivity are particularly bright in conservative evangelical groups which, on the basis of their traditional pietism, already have all they need for an integral vision of the Christian life of justice and peace and already include among them a growing band of credible exponents of the confessing church.

To give just one example: the Sojourners Community in Washington which publishes a monthly journal; and its namesake

"Unterwegs" in West Germany.[84] Members of the Sojourners Community furnish an impressive example of a contemporary confessing covenant church with the "human shield" they are creating in company with other Christians on the Nicaraguan frontier so that if the USA attacks Nicaragua it will have to do so over the dead bodies of Christians from the USA. The Sojourners are also leading co-founders of the "New Covenant for the Abolition of Weapons of Mass Destruction".

Why do I attach such importance at this particular juncture to this challenging dialogue with Christians in conservative political parties and evangelical groups? Because the questions calling for decision should at least be clearly understood in all groups, however the total church process works out in detail, which is not in our hands. We must face up to the difficult questions together while at the same time leaving no stone unturned to prevent a schism based on ignorance.

In all these processes within the church and within the voluntary groups bearing the Christian label it is vital to recognize the precise *stage or phase of the confessing process* a credal issue has reached. In my observation, when a credal issue emerges the learning process in the church veers between two poles: on the one hand, there is a developing theological consensus and, on the other hand, there is the pole of concrete action as consequence of the act of confession. Overemphasis on either pole endangers the learning process. In West Germany, for example, when an attempt was made to learn how to conduct the struggle against apartheid at first exclusively in terms of the PCR Special Fund or the boycott of South African goods, the debate soon settled down into a discussion of the political and economic pros and cons. On the other hand, when people are content simply to note the existence of a *status confessionis* but unwilling to draw any concrete conclusions from this declaration, "they abolish Christ by preaching him", as Luther said of the antinomian exponents of cheap grace who failed to follow their faith with acts of obedience.[85]

That makes it all the more important to note once again the three dimensions of the confessing process as proposed by E. Wolf and E. Bethge: (1) recognition, (2) declaration, and (3) response to the *status confessionis*. In the question of apartheid, we are clearly at the second dimension, the declaration of the *status confessionis*. In this case, therefore, our efforts should be in the direction of deliberate steps towards a concrete response on the part of the churches: for example, the token refusal to cooperate with banks and firms which invest in South Africa. If such steps, based on the obedience of faith, are not accepted, then individuals or groups must, in all Christian love and patience but with the directness and firmness of Paul at the Jerusalem council of the apostles (Acts 15), urge them at a synod or conference of church leaders and not let up until the issue has been discussed and decided canonically and in a Christian spirit in the appropriate bodies, even if conflicts should arise. We seem to have too little confidence in the principles of conflict management based on the New Testament, canon law and ecumenical experience. The revision of the decision leading to support of the WCC's Programme to Combat Racism by the Rhineland Synod is a good example of the required persistence. Only in this way can it be determined whether a church or one of its social forms is in church fellowship with all confessing churches and Christians in the issue in question.

The issue of weapons of mass destruction has been declared by the Vancouver Assembly of the World Council of Churches to be ripe for decision and some churches have already taken the next step. In the Federal Republic of Germany, however, the process towards a binding declaration has for the most part still to be initiated. We were just at the point of doing so when a new situation arose as a result of the Federal Parliament's decision in 1983 on the stationing of middle range missiles in West Germany. The mood in the Federal Republic is now one of "Thank God! It's all quiet again!" The opposite response would be more appropriate. On the one hand, the process of intensifying theological awareness needs to be intensified and in many cases even initiated at the congregational level. Only in Westphalia does there appear to have been a grassroots movement of the same intensity as that in Holland and among the Catholics in the USA.

Possible lines of action here include signature collection campaigns to stimulate the discussion of the issue at congregational meetings and in district synods. Petitions to provincial synods requesting position papers on such questions as whether it is permissible in the light of the New Testament and the Augsburg Confession (Art. 16) for a Christian to choose a political party which burks even at the criteria for a "just war" could also lead to debate on the central issues. In other words, the process of theological clarification is by no means over and confessing Christians and groups should lobby for continued reflection and eventual decision.

Turning finally to the "response" dimension of the *status*

confessionis, this embraces such points as the following: No one is entitled at this stage to present a specific universal demand as obligatory; for example, one requiring all members of the church to refuse military service and payment of the defence tax. Some Christians, of course, will feel obliged to take this course and to give their specific theological grounds for so doing as an act of concrete Christian obedience today — though always in such a way as to show their acceptance of the consequence and cost of such action. The institutional church should certainly in any case already be practising the "fellowship of risk" (J. Garstecki) as illustrated earlier in this book by the example of Bishop Matthiesen.

In the issue of the *global economy* as a *status confessionis*, we have still a good deal of ground to cover in study and reflection. Here we are hardly at the first stage, that of recognition, let alone the second and third stages of declaration and response. Ecclesiologically, the following list of priorities would appear to be in order here:

1. Continued patient work in groups and congregations, by means of "partnerships", i.e. personal experiences in cooperation with the "two-thirds" world and the poor "at home", and biblical studies directed to the identification of idols and taboos.
2. Self-supporting regional research and advisory groups which will observe and critically monitor the TNCs in their own neighbourhood and, when appropriate, notify the church of specific injustices committed in their own or in other countries in respect of the churches' own complicity with such firms and banks.
3. In discipleship groups, on the basis of the Lord's Supper, the discovery of the joy of sharing within "the community of brothers and sisters", combined with the development of networks of mutual support among such groups.
4. Advocacy of a uniform system of conditions of service within the church.

Every opportunity should be taken of confronting the church as a whole with the basic theological questions in the light of this work at the grassroots.

To conclude, let me stress a point already clearly stated by Dietrich Bonhoeffer in his first study of the problem of the *status confessionis*.[86] The moment the church — or even a handful of Christians or Christian groups — recognize, declare and then respond to the *status confessionis* in face of the state or, as in our case, in face of the economy too, it is sometimes assumed that this recognition or the action taken in consequence is in some sense hostile to the state or to the economy. But the truth is that when it really is a case of Christian knowledge based on Christian obedience, the *institutions* (in Bonhoeffer's terminology, the "mandates") *are on the point of destroying themselves* whenever they despise God's will and, along with it, their fellow-creatures as well.

If we in our relationship to the two-thirds world develop in the same way as white South Africa is developing in relationship to the overwhelming majority of the population of that country, we shall destroy ourselves as white South Africa is destroying itself. The distant thunderclaps were already audible when Brazil, once the land of the "economic miracle", a land exploited to the full at the expense of human rights, almost went bankrupt because of debt. A state which reckons on mass murder and suicide in its "defence" plans can not only destroy itself physically when war comes but is also already destroying itself morally now, in the sense that its legitimacy and its acceptance by many of its citizens are already at risk.

In other words, the practice of constitutional resistance and possibly even civil disobedience in respect of credal issues is in reality a defence of the state when it is tempted to set foot on the slippery slope towards its own destruction. In a credal situation, therefore, even the church's resistance to institutions is really vital assistance in the interest of these institutions themselves and therefore witness to the contemporary presence of Jesus Christ — the life of the world.

At the Vancouver Assembly, Aruna Gnanadason told us of the poor women of North India who, when the contractors came to fell the trees on which the very livelihood of the women and their community depended, each clung to a tree as if in defiance of the contractors' saws. Gnanadason sees here the women's struggle to defend their life against the beast from the abyss with its many faces. "Sisters and brothers . . . let us commit ourselves to be a healing community in a broken world!"

NOTES

1. See below, Chapter 10.
2. Cf. *Bekenntnis und Widerstand. Kirchen Südafrikas im Konflikt mit dem Staat*, ed.

Ev. Missionswerk, Hamburg, 1983, pp. 101ff. here p. 106.

3. From the growing body of literature, cf. Duchrow, *Conflict over the Ecumenical Movement*, WCC, Geneva, 1981, pp. 271ff.; E. Bethge, " 'Status Confessionis' — was ist das?", in *epd Dokumentation* 46/82; J. de Gruchy and Ch. Villa-Vicenzio (eds), *Apartheid is a Heresy*, Lutterworth Press, Guildford, UK, 1983. W. Lienemann has pointed out to me that the term *status confessionis* was first applied to apartheid by W. A. Visser 't Hooft in 1964.

4. *In Christ — A New Community*. Proceedings of the Sixth Assembly of the LWF, Geneva, 1977, p. 179.

5. In de Gruchy & Villa-Vicenzio eds, *op. cit.*, pp. 168ff.

6. Meanwhile, the LWF Assembly in Budapest in 1984 made a comparable decision in respect of the white Lutheran churches in Southern Africa. Cf. *Budapest 1984*, proceedings of the Seventh Assembly, LWF, 1985, p.162f., pp. 179f.

7. Cf. *Lutheran World Information* 46/82.

8. The best known being the cases of Dean Farisani and others in Vendaland.

9. Cf. *epd* 26-27/83.

10. Cf. E. Lorenz, *Politik als Glaubenssache?*, Erlangen, 1983.

11. E. Bethge, *art.cit. supra*, n. 3, p. 23.

12. Cf. *Gathered for Life*, ed. D. Gill, *op. cit.*, pp. 84ff.

13. Cf. *epd* 26—27/83, 60f.

14. Cf. M. Buthelezei, "Ansätze Afrikanischer Theologie im Kontext von Kirche in Südafrika", in I. Tödt (ed.), *Theologie im Konfliktfeld Südafrika. Dialog mit Manas Buthelezi* (Stud.z. Friedensforschung, Vol.15), Stuttgart/Munich, 1976, pp. 50ff.

15. Cf. on the contrary the introductory section of the Ottawa decision of the World Alliance of Reformed Churches; cf. E. Käsemann, *Versuche und Besinnungen*, Göttingen, 1960[2], pp. 284ff.

16. Cf. H. Prolingheuer, *Der ungekämpfte Kirchenkampf 1933-1945 — das politische Versagen der Bekennenden Kirche*, Neue Stimme, Special No. 6, 1983; E. Bethge, *art.cit.*; Eberhard Busch, *Juden und Christen im Schatten des Dritten Reiches*, Chr. Kaiser Verlag, Munich, 1979.

17. *GS* II, 44f. (48f.) and 115ff.; cf. also E. Bethge, "Dietrich Bonhoeffer und die Juden", in *Konsequenzen. Dietrich Bonhoeffers Kirchenverständnis heute*, Chr. Kaiser Verlag, Munich, 1980, pp. 171ff.

18. Cf. EMW, *op. cit.* and in particular "Südafrika — Bekenntnis und Widerstand. Ein Memorandum".

19. Cf. M. Buthelezi and W. Kistner, "The Proclamation of the Gospel and Other Marks of the Church", in *Lutheran World*, 23, 1976, pp. 21–32.

20. Cf. Duchrow, *Conflict over the Ecumenical Movement*, Chapter 1.

21. The best account of this is still Bonhoeffer's essay on "The Question of Church Fellowship" in *GS* II, pp. 217ff.

22. See below in section III of this chapter.

23. Cf. the Ottawa statement.

24. *Theologische Existenz heute* No. 70, 2nd ed. pp. 15f.

25. Cf. also his as yet unpublished dissertation, *Bekenntnis und Weltverantwortung. Die Ekklesiologiestudie des LWB — ein Beitrag zur ökumenischen Sozialethik*, Leipzig, 1983, esp. Chapter II.

26. Cf. H. U. Kirchhoff (ed.), *Wort an die Gemeinden zur Kernbewaffnung*, Neukirchen, 1982, XI.

27. Very useful here is U. Möller, "On the problem of the *status confessionis*" (in

German) in R. Wischnath (ed.), *Frieden als Bekenntnisfrage*, Gütersloh, 1984, pp. 236–271; cf. also B. Klappert and U. Weidner (eds), *Schritte zum Frieden*, Neukirchen, 1983.

28. Cf. pastoral letter of the Catholic Bishops' Conference of the USA.

29. See introduction to Part III.

30. A similar view has recently been expressed by Heino Falcke from the standpoint of the Christians in the German Democratic Republic.

31. One interesting move in this direction is the proposal of peace groups from churches of the GDR that individuals should enter into peace contracts. This proposal has been approved and adopted by the Synod of the GDR Church Federation.

32. Cf. E. Stelck, *Politik mit dem Einkaufskorb*, Wuppertal, 1980; Baldwin Sjollema, *Isolating Apartheid*, WCC, Geneva, 1982, pp. 69ff.; U. Duchrow and M. Stöhr, "Boycott als legitime christliche Aktion?" in *EMW Information* No. 34, Hamburg, 1982. Cf. also *EMW Information* No. 62, 1985. At its Synod in November 1985, the EKD cautiously abandoned its refusal of economic pressure.

33. Cf. for example, Mary Kaldor, "The Role of Arms in Capitalist Economy", in D. Carlton & C. Schaerf eds, *Arms Control and Technological Innovation*, London, 1977, pp. 322ff.

34. Cf. *epd Entwicklungspolitik* No. 12, 13 (1983).

35. *"Brot für die Welt"*, *Arbeitsheft* 1982/83, p. 20.

36. Cf. authors like CI. and L. Boff, G. Gutiérrez, J. Sobrino, J. M. Bonino, C. Mesters, J. de Santa Ana.

37. Cf. Kim, Yong-Bock ed., *Minjung Theology; People as the Subjects of History*, CCA publication, 1981.

38. Cf. A. Boesak, *Farewell to Innocence*, J. H. Kok, Kampen, 1976. Reports of the EATWOT meetings published by Orbis Books, Maryknoll, USA.

39. Cf. Julio de Santa Ana, *Good News to the Poor: the Challenge of the Poor in the History of the Church*, CCPD, WCC, Geneva, 1977.

40. For a theological analysis of the economic institutions themselves, cf. above, in Chapter 3 and below in Chapter 7. Cf. also "The Church and the Powers: a Study Document of the French Protestant Federation", 1970, in *Study Encounter* III, 3, 1972.

41. See Chapter 3 below.

42. Cf. N. Greinacher, *Im Angesicht meiner Feinde — Mahl des Friedens* (GTB 1051), Gütersloh, 1982.

43. Cf. the paper presented by Protopresbyter V. M. Borovoy at the WCC Vancouver Assembly 1983 (see *Gathered for Life, op. cit.,* pp. 25f.).

44. *Baptism, Eucharist and Ministry* (Faith and Order Paper No. 11, 1982).

45. Cf. for example, the work of the Interfaith Center for Corporate Responsibility in New York.

46. W. Huber, "Zeugnisauftrag und Materielle Struktur. Gibt es theologische Kriterien kirchlicher Ökonomie?" in *idem, Folgen christlicher Freiheit* (NBSTh. Vol.4), Neukirchen, 1983, pp. 219ff.

47. M. Luther, *Von Kaufshandlung und Wucher*, WA 6, 50ff., esp, 59.

48. Cf. the decision of the EKU Synod (15 June 1980): "We affirm the character of church law as witness to the gospel. This challenges the church to make greater and better use of the latitude allowed it in the fashioning of its order and its law. This applies also to the development of a uniform structure of service for all employees of the church and its diaconal ministries." In A.

Burgsmüller ed., *Kirche als "Gemeinde von Brüdern"*, Barmen III, Bd. 2, Gütersloh, 1981, p. 18.

49. Cf. Ernst Lange, *And Yet It Moves . . . Dream and Reality of the Ecumenical Movement*, Christian Journals Limited and World Council of Churches, Geneva, 1978, pp. 99ff. Cf. also Duchrow, *Conflict over the Ecumenical Movement*, pp. 338ff.

50. A. Burgsmüller (ed.), *op. cit.*, Vol. 2, pp. 45 and 55.

51. A. Burgsmüller (ed.), *op. cit.*, Vol. 1, p. 221.

52. See Chapters 3 and 5 above and, for Heino Falcke, cf. *epd Dokumentation 46/ 83*, pp. 37ff. Cf. also L. Newbigin, *Foolishness to the Greeks: the Gospel and Western Culture*, WCC, Geneva, 1986.

53. South End Press, Boston, 1980.

54. See Gross, *op. cit.*, pp. 35f. for a list of the ways in which the centres are able to bring pressure to bear on the peripheries.

55. Cf. in addition to the works by Gross and Galtung, J. P. Miranda, *Von der Unmoral gegenwärtiger Strukturen. Dargestellt am Beispiel Mexiko* (Judie-Taschenbuch No.7), Wuppertal, 1973 and more recently F. J. Hinkelammert, "Die Politik des 'totalen Marktes'. Ihre Theologisierung und unsere Antwort", in Ev. Studentengemeinde (ed.), *Kirche und Kapitalismus*, Stuttgart, 1984, pp. 58ff.

56. Cf. *epd ZA* 43, of 2 March 1983.

57. Cf. *Latin America Weekly Report*, 7 January 1983 and the many publications of the Mexican journalist Gregorio Selser in *El Dia*, 1983, *passim*.

58. *The Rockefeller Report on the Americas* (Quadrangle Books), Chicago, 1969.

59. See below, pp. 229ff., Appendix II. A more recent example: the US Information Service finances lecture and information tours by a former nun expelled from the Maryknoll Order because of her marriage, in order to conduct propaganda against the work of the order with the poor and against the government of Nicaragua.

60. From the extensive literature, cf. especially P. Lernoux, *Cry of the People: United States Involvement in the Rise of Fascism, Torture and Murder, and the Persecution of the Catholic Church in Latin America*, Doubleday, New York, 1980 (reprinted by Penguin Books 1982 under the title: *Cry of the People: the Struggle for Human Rights in Latin America — the Catholic Church in Conflict with US Policy*). For us in Germany, the section on "The German Alliance" is especially important, since it points out the use of West German church funds to support right-wing organizations. A special rôle is played here by "Adveniat", the Catholic Bishops' Conference, the Conrad Adenauer Foundation and multinational enterprises. German funding has here in part replaced CIA money without this being realized by the parties concerned. On the whole question, cf. also G. Neuberger & M. Opperskalski, *CIA in Mittelamerika* (Lamuv), Bornheum-Merten, 1983.

61. Gross, *op. cit.*, p. 200. Quotation is from *Newsweek*, 30 April 1979. Cf. also Neuberger and M. Opperskalski, *op. cit.*

62. E. Hochstein and R. O'Rourke, "A Report on the Institute on Religion and Democracy", in IDOC International (ed.), *An American Dream: Neo-conservatism and New Religious Right in the USA*. The Institute on Religion and Democracy (IDOC Bulletin Nos. 8–9), Rome, 1982. Cf. P. Steinfels, "Neoconservative Theology", in *Democracy*, April 1982, pp. 18–27.

63. Gross, *op. cit.*, p. 200.

64. *GS* II, pp. 227f. On the control of international communication by firms and banks, cf. Cees Hamelink, "A Key to the Exercise of Power. Transnational

Corporations and International Communication Structures", in *Überblick* 4/ 1976, pp. 29–32; *idem. The Corporate Village*, IDOC, Rome, 1977; *idem. Finance and Information*, Ablex Publ., Norwood N.J., 1983; *idem.* Cultural Autonomy in Global Communications, Longman, New York and London, 1983.

65. Gordon Winter, *Inside Boss*, Penguin Press, 1981, p. 516.
66. Cf. the *idea* announcement No. 22/83 of 17 March 1983 and the response of the EKD Church Office in *idea* No. 23/83 of 21 March 1983.
67. Cf. the visits of Council members A. V. Campenhausen and E. Kimmich.
68. Cf. *FR* of 25 February 1984. In May 1987 he congratulated P.W. Botha after re-election.
69. Cf. *FR* of 30 March 1983, pp. 10f. and cf. also the frequent declarations of Graf Huyn in this sense.
70. Cf. for example, the statements of Minister Warnke on 23 December 1982 in favour of a development aid of benefit to our German economy (*FR* of 24 December 1982).
71. Cf. *Aufbruch* (Evangelical Church paper in Baden) No. 15/83 of 10 April 1983.
72. Cf. Roman Herzog in a letter addressed to all pastors in August 1982 in his capacity as Federal President of the Protestant Working Group of the CDU/ CSU: "Our concern — defined in general terms — is to be able to maintain and freely develop our western style of life" (p. 2). It is also clear here that just as it was possible in 1933 to latch on to quite normal "German national" ideas, we must today keep in view the way in which all sorts of quite "normal" western values can develop even among ourselves. South Africa and the fascist countries of Asia and Latin America already provide us with a mirror to recognize ourselves in.
73. *GS* II, pp. 217ff.
74. Cf. *Gathered for Life*, official report of the Vancouver Assembly 1983, pp. 83ff.
75. Cf. Duchrow, *Conflict over the Ecumenical Movement*, Chapter 5.
76. A. Burgsmüller (ed.), *op. cit.*, Vol. 2, p. 19.
77. *epd Dokumentation* 46/83, p. 2.
78. Cf. esp. J. D. Zizioulas, "The Development of Conciliar Structures down to the Time of the first Ecumenical Council", in *Councils and the Ecumenical Movement*, WCC, Geneva, 1980.
79. Cf. note 49 above.
80. Cf. U. Duchrow, "New Peace Movement in the USA — Theological Roots and Perspectives", *Pastoraltheologie*, 72. 1983, pp. 33ff.) and H. Falcke, "Church in God's Covenant of Peace" (in German in *Ev. Theol.*, August 1985, pp. 348–366).
81. Cf. my letter on "Through the Eye of a Needle", in German in *EK*, 3/83, pp. 151ff.
82. In an unpublished paper read to an open seminar in Heidelberg in the winter term 1983/84.
83. See Chapter 3, Part III.
84. Cf. the journal *Sojourners*, Washington, and the books by its editor, Jim Wallis; in the Federal German Republic, the journal *Unterwegs*.
85. WA 50, 627.
86. *GS* II, pp. 48f.

7

Choosing life: resistance to idolatry and "autonomy" in the economic field (Barmen I and II)

1. *"I am the way, and the truth, and the life; no one comes to the Father but by me" (John 14:6). "Truly, truly, I say to you, he who does not enter the sheepfold by the door but climbs in by another way, that man is a thief and a robber. I am the door; if anyone enters by me, he will be saved" (John 10:1, 9).*

Jesus Christ, as he is testified to us in holy scripture, is the One Word of God, which we have to hear and which we have to trust and obey in life and in death.

We reject the false doctrine that the church can and must acknowledge as sources of its proclamation, except and beside this one world of God, other events and powers, forms and truths, as God's revelation.

2. *"Christ Jesus, whom God made our wisdom, our righteousness and sanctification and redemption" (1 Cor. 1:30).*

As Jesus Christ is God's declaration of the forgiveness of all our sins, so, in the same way and with the same seriousness, He is God's mighty claim upon our whole life. Through him we obtain joyful deliverance from the godless bondage of this world for the free, grateful service of his creatures.

We reject the false doctrine that there are areas of our life in which we do not belong to Jesus Christ, but to other masters, realms where we do not need to be justified and sanctified by him."

(Barmen Theological Declaration, Articles I and II)

No treatment of world reality or even of a single aspect of that reality at any given time can possibly be complete if it starts

• Parts of this chapter were originally presented in address form: first, at the annual conference of the Community Service of the Evangelical Missionary Agency in South West Germany in April 1985 in Schmie; second, at the Barth Conference in Leuenberg, Switzerland, July 1985. Various insights derive from a seminar at the University of Heidelberg which the economist Dr H. Diefenbacher and I organized together in 1984/85.

exclusively from the question as to how the church's "message and order" are affected by that reality and to be what Jesus meant them to be (Barmen III and IV).[1]

Faith in the Triune God as revealed in Jesus Christ seeks to understand the world, its structures and history, in the light of God's judgment and promise in order to help organize the world responsibly or at least to behave responsibly towards it. So we find Luther reflecting on the "estates" and Bonhoeffer on the "mandates" as the context of responsible human cooperation in God's creation and as the frame of reference for the church as the body of Christ. So, too, the ecumenical movement not only seeks to foster a church in solidarity with the poor but also to grasp in theory and promote in practice "a just, participatory and sustainable society".[2]

We seek in vain in the *Barmen Theological Declaration* for criteria or explicit directives as to how a confessing church is to deal with economic institutions. In conflict with the totalitarian state, the Barmen Declaration restricts itself to this specific institutional issue (Barmen V). Indirectly, of course, Barmen I and Barmen II also provide firm footholds for our question concerning the present global economic system:

— they reject as false the view that, alongside the one word of God in Jesus Christ, other events and powers, forms and truths, can have the character of revelation;
— they also reject as false the view that there are any autonomous areas of life where we belong to and would have to obey other lords than Jesus Christ, areas where we would not need to be justified and sanctified by him.

Today, however, the idea that economics is an autonomous area is widely held, even and especially in the church. More important still, the assertion of this autonomy of the economic field is a dangerous threat to the life of the vast majority of the world's population. What are we to make of this state of affairs and what consequences must the church draw from it? I shall tackle this question in two stages: I. The myth of the "autonomous market"; II. Theological models to assist the church in dealing with the present global economy.

I. The myth of the "autonomous market"

1. WHO IS RESPONSIBLE FOR EXPLOITATION?

Thesis 1: Only in cases of notorious economic injustice can individuals or firms be called to account. The general trend in the present global economic system is for the rich to grow richer and the poor to become poorer. This trend results from the interaction of various agents. The key feature of this situation is that the economic forces either escape effective control by public institutions or else coopt them and that, in the final analysis, none of the agents involved appear to be free-agents since whatever happens in the so-called "free market" obeys rules which it is taboo to examine more closely.

When six million Jewish men, women and children are "liquidated" by a political régime and this same National Socialist state provokes a war in which more than forty million people lose their lives, the question of responsibility is not difficult to answer. The same applies to the apartheid régime in South Africa which robs the majority of the population of their civil and human rights and employs brutality and violence to defend and entrench its tyranny. Some share of responsibility must be apportioned, of course, to those sections of the population which support this tyranny, as well as to those foreign powers which support such régimes or make their continued existence possible. Yet it is relatively clear who the primary agent is: namely, the national régime and its government in particular. The same applies to direct colonialism, whereby a colonial power actively subjugates and exploits another country.

Serious attempts have been made over the centuries in the history of the church and of the nations to develop and enforce rules of conduct for both external and internal state relationships. One typical example of the efforts of Western states in this direction has been the introduction of "power sharing" as in a way of checking and balancing political power and guaranteeing constitutional rights at least in domestic national life.

In the case of the present global economic system, it is a very different story. It is by no means clear who is chiefly responsible for the death of more than forty million people from starvation each year while a tiny minority of the world's inhabitants in the industrial countries and in the élites of the so-called "developing countries" live in real or relative luxury. Who are the agents responsible for this obscene annual human sacrifice? How are they to be called to account?

As a first approximation, the following institutions may be listed as having some rôle in this matter:

1. Political institutions which are responsible for economic policy and justic (nation states represented by their governments, regional institutions such as those in Europe, international governmental bodies such as the United Nations Organization).

2. Multilateral and bilateral economic organizations and treaty systems within which the industrialized countries exercise a more or less preponderant influence:
   a) such institutions as UNCTAD directly created by UNO;
   b) treaty systems in the field of world trade, such as:
      — GATT (General Agreement on Tariffs and Trade);
      — the Lomé Agreements (I and II);
      — various forms of South-South cooperation, etc.
   c) financial institutions such as:
      — IMF (International Monetary Fund);
      — World Bank.

3. Transnational institutions in the private sector:
   a) in the field of production: transnational corporations (TNCs);
   b) in the field of finance: transnational banks.

4. Small and medium enterprises:
   a) in industry;
   b) in agriculture;
   c) in the service sector.

5. Social organizations such as:
   a) labour organizations (unions);
   b) farming organizations;
   c) medical associations;
   d) churches, etc.

6. Science and technology

7. Communication media

8. Consumers and savers/borrowers

With this list of agents in mind, we turn to concrete economic processes, taking a quite simple case to begin with. A few years ago, the Henkel Company in Düsseldorf dismissed all the black employees in its South African subsidiary for having organized an approach to the company with claims which in any case fell short of the requirements of the EEC's minimum code for firms in South Africa. The dismissed black workers enlisted the aid of journalists to publicize their case; the journalists in turn took up the case with the Rhineland Church and trade unions in Germany. Heinz Oskar

Vetter, then general secretary of the German Trade Union Association, visited South Africa and eventually the Henkel Company reinstated the dismissed workers.

The responsible agent in this particular case was easily identifiable: the directorate of the Henkel Company. There was no government or legal authority, of course, which could have compelled the company to behave differently, since the codes of conduct are not legally binding and therefore cannot be enforced. Other agents, however, journalists, trade unions and the church, were able to call those responsible to account and to help the dismissed workers.

Another fairly straightforward and well-known example is that of the Swiss firm of Nestlé. By its aggressive advertising campaign in the two-thirds world, this firm was selling babyfood products in conditions which led to the death of or serious damage to many infants. In this case, it was Kenyan doctors and nurses who mobilized "third-world" groups in Switzerland who in turn organized a consumers' boycott. In this way a considerable improvement was effected in this firm's publicity methods. For the moment, the boycott has been lifted though the development of the situation continues to be carefully monitored. This case showed that the courts (though able to pass only a moral condemnation on the firm), as well as associations, voluntary groups and customers, are able to bring some direct pressure to bear so as to curtail a firm's destructive practices. At this level, too, Christians undoubtedly have a direct responsibility and concrete opportunities to bring influence to bear on industrialists.

The question gets more complicated if we consider, for example, the matter of seed-supplies in particular and "agro-business" in general. What is happening here is rather alarming. Multinational chemical firms, especially in the USA and the Netherlands, are buying up small seed-supply firms.[3] The avowed purpose of the chemical firms is to develop highly productive strains of seed. As a result, strains requiring a lavish use of artificial fertilizers and pesticides have been promoted most, which is profitable, of course, for the chemical industry. In the process, however, not only is a wide range of different seeds eliminated but the use of such quantities of artificial fertilizers and pesticides also has incalculable ecological consequences. Small farmers both in our own country and in the two-thirds world become even more completely dependent on industrial products which they can less and less afford to pay for because of the increasingly unfavourable exchange conditions between these industrial products and their own agricultural products. This trend is reinforced by the development of hybrid seed strains whose harvest cannot be used by the farmers themselves for further sowing, so that they have always to buy seed from the firm concerned. Then, banks only give a farmer a loan if he trades with this firm (and only on condition that the credit is used for the purchase of the recognized seed-strain!). This procedure also tends to encourage monocultures and the export-oriented farming of the large landowners, which are in turn backed by International Monetary Fund policy. If we ask who is responsible for this problem, which in any case is only a tiny fraction of the whole "agro-business" question, and how they can be called to account and perhaps persuaded to behave differently, the complex network of agents involved makes it difficult to offer a satisfactory answer. Let me quote one attempt to describe the different interests intertwined here:

> Modern agrarian technology is based on agricultural inputs (seed strains, fertilizers, water, pesticides, machines) which are easily monopolized and come within the marketing area of *multinational concerns*. The independent *foundations* (Rockefeller, Ford) have not only had a decisive say in determining the strategy in the developing lands . . . but have also controlled agronomic research in these same developing lands . . . The provision of the necessary financial resources is to a large extent channelled via the *World Bank*, which itself is linked with the Food and Agriculture Organization (FAO) in the "FAO/ World Bank Cooperative Programme" . . . The World Bank is in league with the *multinational concerns* not only because it finances the inputs which come within the marketing area of these concerns but also via the "International Finance Corporation" which gives loans to these concerns . . . For a considerable period of time, the multinational concerns have had a direct influence on the FAO, via the "Industry Cooperative Programme" . . . On the interaction between the multinational concerns, *governments in the industrial lands*, and *international organizations*, cf. the Berne Declaration of 1978 (The Undermining of the UNO System by the Multinational Concerns, Ropress, Zürich). On the interaction between *governments in developing countries, universities and research institutes*, cf. Myrdal 1970 (Political Manifesto on Poverty in the World, Frankfurt-on-the-Main) . . . Two further phenomena should be noted in connection with this complex structure of "vested interests": the manipulation of concepts and the opportunistic use of statistics . . . [4]

The TNCs can certainly be recognized as powerfully influential factors in this interplay of forces but, even if we can go some way towards identifying those responsible for specific infringements on the part of individual firms and calling them to account, it is practically impossible to do this in respect of their activities as a whole, precisely because the network of other agents involved is so complex.

The problem becomes impossibly difficult when we try to present a survey of the combined effect of the eight identified agents on the present global economic system, even a survey reduced to the bare essentials.[5] The only thing that is clear about the global economic system resulting from the combined actions of these and other agents is that the rich are growing richer and the poor becoming poorer, and this not just within the individual countries but also between the industrialized countries and the "developing" countries. What is known as the "scissors movement" is also a feature of relationships between industrialized countries in the area of "really existing socialism" with their state-capitalist structure and the "developing" countries in the communist camp, even if in a modified and less crude form. Even the destruction of the environment is not a purely "Western" problem (Chernobyl!). In what follows, however, I shall confine my attention to the area under Western jurisdiction. Who or what here is responsible for this catastrophic development? Does exploitation come into the picture? We still await agreed answers to these questions.

We run through the eight indentified agents:

1. *Political institutions.* The role of these in the global economic process reveals the main difference between colonialism and neo-colonialism. In colonialism, the colonial powers exercised direct political and military control in order to promote and protect their own economic interests in the colonialized land. The disintegration of the indigenous economic patterns, the exploitation of the mineral and other resources of the colonialized land as well as of the labour force available there, the reorganization of agriculture into export-oriented monocultures, the recruitment and training of an élite favourably disposed towards the colonial power and its culture, etc. etc. — these all date back to this colonial period. This is the period when the exploitation was blatant. In this period the decisive steps were taken in the direction of the "development of underdevelopment".[6]

In the meanwhile, the colonial lands, almost without exception, have attained political independence. In the meanwhile, too, the firms and banks have acquired a transnational organization and are therefore no longer subject to the direct and decisive influence of one nation state alone — and not at all to that of the government of a weak developing country, very little to that of a strong industrial country, even supposing the will to exert such influence existed. On the other hand, the United Nations Organization, the most important international political organization, has no executive power and is deliberately kept in a weak position by the strong countries. That bars the road to the traditional theological way of influencing the economy, i.e. by the reminder to the government of its rôle as servant of the good of the whole community. For there is no political machinery for carrying out the necessary equalization of burdens.

2. *UNO's multilateral economic organization,* UNCTAD. For the same reason, it is also impossible for this global body to get beyond discussions and proposals. The more powerful countries block anything conflicting with their (short term) interests. The only really powerful multilateral economic organizations are GATT, the IMF and the World Bank, and these are controlled by the industrial countries. A central issue in the debate on development policy in the seventies was the negative effect of existing conditions of trade and tariffs for the products of the "developing" countries.[7] Now it is the monetary aspect of the handicap to which the "developing" countries are subject that is coming increasingly to centre-stage: i.e. the "debt crisis". From 1955 to 1983, the total debt of the developing countries rose from 7 to 812 milliard dollars! Above all, the inevitable result of high interest rates on the international credit market (provoked among other things by the massive capital demand of the USA in connection with, for example, the present rearmament programme), in combination with a radical deterioration in the terms of trade for many developing countries, is an external trading account in which debt-servicing payments exceed income from exports.[8]

Faced with this situation, the IMF imposes on developing countries conditions which can only drive them even deeper into the impoverishment of the majority of their populations: mainly, lowering of real wages, budget economies in welfare and education, gearing of economic policy towards exports (in other words, conditions which favour the industrial countries and the indigenous élites) and pressure to reduce government expenditure (which mainly affects development programmes of benefit to the general public).[9]

3. and 4. *National and transnational firms and banks.* Here the main feature is a powerful concentration. Turnover and volume of trade in the case of the largest firms exceeds the GNP of small and medium-sized states.[10] But even strong industrial countries cannot escape the *de facto* influence of the industrial lobby. The Lockheed and Flick scandals (where politicians and political parties were bribed by big firms) are only the tip of the iceberg. The main purpose of the TNCs and banks is increased profits for owners of capital, as well as to stay in existence, maintain their relative position in the market, long-term diversification, etc. They therefore tend to invest their money where there is a supply of cheap labour, minimal trade union organization, tax concessions, no problems over the transfer of profits. There is some conflict between these aims and the concern for good market outlets, since the steady impoverishment of the majority of the population means a corresponding decline in a country's purchasing power. The small and medium sized enterprises, in the developing countries especially, are either bought up by the large firms or else develop in some cases into cells of an alternative economy.

5. Among the *social organizations*, the trade unions play a central rôle. Strengthened by their long and hard struggles in the industrialized countries and having thereby secured for the workers of these countries a certain share in industrial profits, the trade unions now face the difficult question of dealing with the TNCs and their transnational operations while they themselves are mostly organized only at the national level and internationally have only a loose federative structure. Believing in the international solidarity of the workers on moral grounds, they face the dilemma of sharing themselves in profits accruing to industrial countries from the increasing gap between poor and rich while their own position is steadily weakened by the increasing suppression of jobs and the resultant structural unemployment in which the unemployed themselves are left with no bargaining power whatever.

6. *Science and technology.* Modern science, geared as it is in its extrovert form to reproduction and feasibility, is essentially an economic factor. Up to the present, we have failed to find ways of regulating the scientific extension of human power and directing it into channels which will benefit humanity. More and more money is poured into weapons research (over 50 percent of the American centres of research into the natural sciences and technology are financed by the Pentagon) and the research itself is made to conform with economic criteria, not least the maximizing

of profit. The question of scientific responsibility remains unanswered.

7. The rôle of the *communication media* is usually omitted completely in this context or, if mentioned, only to be minimized. On the one hand, the leading banks in collaboration with the computer industry have established a complete parallel communication system alongside the public systems, one which can process economic and political information days faster than these public systems and make use of this information in the interest of capital owners.[11] The Swedish government has already legislated to prohibit and penalize the furnishing of vital public data to this parallel system. On the other hand, a smaller and smaller group of firms and banks owns what is called the "consciousness industry".[12] The public consciousness is infiltrated and manipulated by hidden publicity in favour of the consumer system in general and the products of certain firms in particular, in a whole range of material from children's comics to pornographic literature.

8. *Consumers, savers/borrowers*. Without these, the last of the main agents listed, without their investments and consumption, the entire system would collapse. Influence is brought to bear on them, therefore, to convince them that the existing system is the best possible or, at any rate, one which objective forces make it impossible to change. In actual fact, consumers and savers/borrowers have considerable power even if they are only seldom aware of it.

What conclusions follow from this brief summary for the question of *responsibility and accountability* in the present global economic system? One such conclusion, of course, is that all the agents should be held responsible and called to account in every possible way when they commit palpable injustice, i.e. above all, in particularly serious cases. Individual Christians and churches also have a rôle to play here and could certainly do far more than they are at present, especially in view of the fewness of those now willing to perform this rôle. But is this enough? Economic experts in the Western industrial countries are on the whole ready to agree when it comes to correcting particularly flagrant cases of economic misconduct. For the rest, however, they defend the so-called "free market system" as such and present it as the best of all known systems.

We cannot restrict our enquiry, therefore, to the agents in the world economy but must also focus on the rules by which they act separately and in conjunction, i.e. on the system itself, the capitalist world market.

2. RULES OF THE "FREE MARKET"

Thesis 2: The "autonomy" of the capitalist market, however, is not at all an inherent truth either of nature or reason but an assumption with a particular historical pedigree. It springs from the modern method and world-view with its decision to take account only of the objectifiable and manipulable aspects of reality and to consider these aspects (i.e. to absolutize them) as the whole of reality. The result is a mechanistic distortion of reality which, in the case of economics, is possible only by an increasing neglect of the basic needs of real human beings and a disregard for the integrity of the earth on which we live. This essentially manipulative and exploitative classic and neo-classic approach, which increasingly employs brutal violence to defend itself in its advanced stage of "national security capitalism", conceals its true nature as manipulation and exploitation under the cloak of a supposed "autonomy" based on nature and reason. The theological question, however, is whether the manifest failure of the economy to fulfill its true rôle, i.e. its God-given "mandate" to meet the basic needs of concrete human beings, does not confront the church with a clear "case of confession".

The clearest account of the problem was given by Max Weber long ago:

In virtue of its "impersonal" character, the capitalist economic system cannot be regulated by ethics, unlike all other forms of government. Even externally it mostly appears in so "indirect" a form that it is impossible to tell who the "ruler" really is or to confront him with ethical demands. In the relationship of householder and servant, teacher and pupil, landowner and staff, master and slave, patriarchal prince and subjects, it is possible to present ethical postulates and to insist on adherence to concrete norms, since these are personal relationships and the services to be performed are a product and integral part of the relationship . . . *The factors determining conduct at the decisive points* are the "competitive capacity" of the market (labour market, money market, production market), i.e. "objective" considerations, factors which *are neither ethical nor unethical but simply an-ethical, ethically neutral, at a level where ethics are irrelevant* (my underlining U.D.), "where impersonal authorities come between the human beings engaged. This 'slavery without slaveowners' into which capitalism ensnares workers or borrowers *can be discussed in ethical terms only as an institution"* (my underlining, U.D.) but this is certainly not — in principle — the personal behaviour of an individual — either among rulers or ruled —

behaviour which has been prescribed for him in all essentials on pain of punishment by objective situations and (this is the decisive point) having the character of "service" in respect of an impersonal *material goal* (M.W's underlining).[13]

It should be noted that these are the words not of a critic of the capitalist market principle but of one who defended it as an "autonomous" principle. In other words: within this system, once it is accepted, there is, in the final analysis, no ethical responsibility. Only as an institution can it be discussed, if need be, in ethical terms. Weber, of course, advances this only as a theoretical possibility, one which he himself has to reject in terms of his own approach, since the known rules have to be recognized as a law of logic which rules out any further questioning.

In Weber's view, beyond this modern mechanistic market logic there are only irrational value judgments. Like the gods of antiquity, the value systems are condemned to a struggle presided over, in the last analysis, by an impersonal fate. Certainly this also means that Weber recognized the capitalist system as one which developed from a value-judgment in the historical past, a development to whose understanding Weber himself made an outstanding contribution by his studies of the connection between Protestantism and capitalism. Now, however, in virtue of its own dynamic and historical force, this system with its impersonal logic has to be accepted as an "autonomous" entity.

Are we entitled or even compelled to resign ourselves to this mental veto today? Barmen II encourages us not to do so. The vast majority of economists, of course, still tread the traditional road of classic modern economics and their neo-classical "stars" in the Chicago monetarist school, Milton Friedmann to the fore, still enjoy a massive political following today, especially in the USA, Great Britain and Chile. But the actual consequences of this traditional approach for those who suffer them in these countries and, via them, in the global economic field and also the theoretical critique of this approach which has since been developed help us to recognize its fatal weaknesses and to discern possible alternatives. These can be developed here only in broad outline, of course.

Mention should be made of two currents in economic theory which can contribute to the critical eclipse of classic and neo-classic economics: the theories of dependence[14] and *"institutional economics"*. Among the better known major exponents of the latter are economists like Veblen, Kapp, Myrdal and Galbraith.[15] From the Weber quotation above it is already clear that the capitalist version of the market leaves the concrete human being out of account. This is the main starting point for the critique developed by the "institutional economists". The human being on which the capitalist market and its theoretical apologies are based is an abstraction. The factors which motivate this human being are reduced to the "striving for wealth" (J. S. Mill) or the "acquisitive instinct": *homo oeconomicus* (economic man). This abstraction is permissible on methodological grounds as an abstract model on which to base partial scientifically measurable statements about certain aspects of economic behaviour. But absolutize this isolated aspect and treat it as the only or the decisive aspect of human economic activity and it becomes a dangerous ideological distortion of reality. This is precisely what happens in the classic and neo-classic theories and in the economic systems based on them. Abstract *concepts* of the market are based on modern mechanistic reasoning. The historical philosophical and epistemological relativity and limited relevance of such concepts are no longer recognized. The concept is taken — mistaken — for the whole of economic reality. This, however, is a complete distortion of real life in this specific area of human activity. This area cannot be reduced to a set of objective data and laws. The market is no longer treated as a place of exchange where basic human needs are met in accord with rules of comparable benefit, but is turned into a hunting field where all are hunters "serving" the impersonal "material" purpose of "striving for wealth"!

The *second critical approach* broadens the economic horizon beyond the individual by including the social and natural contexts of economic activity. In the classic and neo-classic economic theory and practice, these contexts are deliberately ignored, excluded from the "real" analysis and regarded, if at all, only as marginal data. Institutional economics is so-called because its analysis includes not only the informal institutions (such as culturally informed behaviour patterns of the individual human being) but also the formal social, political and ecological institutions.

We must examine this twofold critique more closely, beginning with that directed against the absolutizing of the behaviour patterns of "economic man".

Firstly: If we regard the individual pursuit of economic self-interest as not only "natural" but also "morally justified" (A. Smith) or as logically and rationally necessary (M. Weber), we are tacitly assuming "that each individual is in a position to define what is in his or her own self-interest and then able to pursue it in society".[16] Yet this assumption was never warranted and becomes even less so as freedom of choice sinks to zero or below zero for the majority of the world's population. In classic and neo-classic economic theory and practice, the questions of power, domination and injustice are simply ignored.

Secondly: So, too, when *homo oeconomicus* is abstracted from history and absolutized, insufficient heed is paid to the effects of the pursuit of individual economic interests on the total wellbeing of individuals (quality of life in respect of the social and natural environment).[17]

Thirdly: The striving for maximum utility is usually equated with the striving for maximum consumption. This means the absolutization of *one* of the needs of the human being. Moreover, the definition of the goal of economic activity as consumption turns out to be, in the way the economy actually works, at the same time an ideological cloak to hide the fact that the real dynamic of economic development is the desire and intention of the entrepreneur to make a satisfactory profit. In order to ensure that markets actually achieve this profit for production, consumer needs are largely created by advertizing campaigns.[18]

Fourthly: The absolutizing of the market model based on acceptance of the abstraction of *homo oeconomicus* leads ultimately to the evacuation of the economic process of much of its substance by ignoring all its concrete cultural, social and political dimensions. Everything is reduced to the single concrete form of a financially quantifiable unit, as for example in the financial code term "national product".

The question of human *needs* in this connection has a special importance for our later theological reflections. Without giving the matter much further thought, classic and neo-classic economic theories assume that the human being who strives rationally for his own advantage has *preferences*.[19] In this approach, however, there is no mention of the basic human needs (food, clothing, shelter, health, education), nor of his social and political needs (participation) nor of the human being's relationship to the creaturely world which constitutes his environment — and even less of all these things in their concrete historical form. On the contrary, all these things are subordinated to the logic of the market as a process geared to the advantage and profit of the individual.

Above all, however, the society organized in principle on the market economy ignores the needs of the human being by taking them into account exclusively as "demand" in the sense of a basis for marketing industrial products.

> By relating money or monetary value (purchasing power) to needs, we arrive at the total "demand" realizable in the market . . . Firms therefore produce not to meet concrete needs but with the abstract goal of selling their products on the market. Moreover, whereas the original goal of all economic activity was to provide human beings with the basic material necessities of life, money-making has become the goal of the "derivative" industries . . . Money can be endlessly accumulated; my need for money is unlimited. When the securing of goods to satisfy my needs is tied to money, money, though only a means of obtaining goods, suddenly becomes the all-important component . . . [20]

The behaviour pattern which follows from this is a constant "desire for more" on the part of some and a failure to meet the basic needs of others, and this in no accidental way but as the inevitable outcome of the system itself. One institutional economist, K. W. Kapp, analyzed the inherent weaknesses of the market in this respect over half a century ago:

> In the first place, the market cannot respond to needs but only to purchasing power, i.e. the only needs taken into account are those which can be reflected in effective demand. In the second place, élitist and monopolist markets distort the relative shortages and this in turn raises the question of consumer sovereignty. In the third place, the market machinery is incapable of taking into account the distribution of resources over several generations . . . In the fourth place, the market machinery ignores the problem of social costs . . . [21]

As a consequence, the satisfaction of the needs of individuals who are able to pay has priority over the satisfaction of communal and social needs even if this means "public squalor" (Galbraith) and, above all, the neglect of the elementary needs of the poor:

> While, on the one hand, the most elementary needs of that section of the population with relatively low incomes remain unsatisfied, the method of evaluation in terms of market prices in itself already permits and even enforces the production of goods to satisfy less basic needs, i.e. the luxury needs of that section of the population with relatively high incomes. [22]

If we relate this basic principle of the capitalist absolute market system to the general question of feeding the world and to the particular question of agriculture in the dependent countries, the conclusion is:

> Given the lack of purchasing power of large sections of the population, the market machinery inevitably results in a transfer from the production of basic foodstuffs to the production of goods in high demand.[23]

The deadly effects of the global economic system, therefore, are not accidental but, given the modern mechanistic approach, an inevitable consequence of assigning priority systematically to abstract market "laws" which automatically result in advantaging the strong and the rich and in ignoring the real basic needs of human beings.

Attempts to meet real crises or the criticisms levelled at the modern "market logic" (for example, those of J. M. Keynes) by adapting this market model have been designed exclusively to ensure that economic activities continue to conform to market principles. The state is assigned the task of keeping the symptoms of a crisis in check, in the "centre countries" at all events, by absorbing the costs of the market economy ("privatization of profits, nationalization of social costs").[24] Centre countries were thus given a few decades of welfare capitalism. This time is now over and increasingly giving place to a period of "national defence capitalism" in which social achievements are being dismantled in favour of larger defence systems designed to defend by force the privileges of those who are the beneficiaries of the market economy.[25]

A Latin American economist and theologian, Franz J. Hinkelammert, described this process as follows at the Barmen Jubilee:

> The present world economic crisis has put an end to the economic policy known as Keynsianism. The more the logic of this economic policy threatened to produce socialist economic forms in response to the growing crisis, the more an economic policy calling itself "liberal" or "anti-interventionist" gained ground. The logic of this policy is the ruthless application of the logic of capital accumulation to all government and social policy. This policy, far from being "anti-interventionist", is in reality a new form of interventionism directed against the welfare state elements in Keynesianism. In the USA in particular, fiscal deficits and subventions, supposedly inacceptable elements consequent on a Keynsian policy, have increased to an extent that would have been quite inconceivable even ten years ago. Only their orientation has shifted in a definite direction. Instead of social deficits, it is now a case of military deficits; instead of social subventions, it is now a case of subventions for the international financial and banking system. These, moreover, reach unprecedented levels and are enforced by the International Monetary Fund which compels debtor countries to give

state guarantees for bankrupt private debts and in this way converts these into public debts. In Mexico alone, subventions of this kind amount to around forty milliard dollars, i.e. half of the total debt.

This new interventionism is directed against the welfare state and can therefore seek its security and legitimacy only in a progressive development of the police and the military apparatus. The latter becomes increasingly prominent, therefore, while the welfare state rôles are dismantled and in many cases completely eliminated by privatization. A myth emerges, that of a supposed anarcho-capitalism with its illusion of a complete transfer of all state rôles to private competitive enterprises. Under cover of this myth, the police and the military become the real centres of political power . . . In the third world especially, the civil democratic processes no longer produce sovereign parliaments but elected civil governments exercising a political power which is only delegated to them by the police and the military. A new slogan would aptly describe this situation: "Welfare state enslaves! Police state sets free!" The ideology of the total market which underlies this development is an ideology of struggle. Since society as a whole is viewed and treated in terms of development in the direction of the total market, the mysticism of the total market becomes the mysticism of the market struggle to which all areas of society are to be subjected. Within this totalitarian approach there then emerges the mysticism of a struggle to be waged against all who resist this subjection of all areas of life to the market struggle ("the enemy within!").

From this there comes the image of an adversary, an image which itself is the creation of this mysticism of the market struggle. This adversary is not a competitor in the market struggle but an adversary of the total market struggle as such and all its works. The adversary is anyone who resists acceptance of the market struggle as the organizing principle of society. This explains the totalitarian view of subversion. Anything expressive of value concepts which conflict with or are a potential threat to the total market and the unrestricted accumulation of capital is interpreted and treated as subversion.

This concept of subversion is synthesized in the term "utopian" and in political terms becomes "socialist" or "communist". As a form of criminalization, it becomes "terrorist".[26]

When the question of responsibility and accountability is raised against this background, it finally becomes clear that a mechanism also exists for disguising the patterns of responsibility within this whole system. The key form of the division of labour in the market process is the commodity relationship, the purpose of which is "to render invisible the effects of the division of labour on the life or death of the individual human being":

These commodity relationships make human relationships seem

independent of the result of the division of labour for human survival. They appear as game rules whereas in reality they are the rules of a life and death struggle between human beings, with no holds barred, or as nature itself apportioning life and death according to its own laws and leaving no room for human protest. In reality, they are a human artefact which must be held responsible for its results . . . The fact that we are confronted here with the rules of a life and death struggle and therefore with a conflict between human beings, is denied. The ideology, instead, makes these rules seem like the rules of a game in which the dead are treated as the victims of natural accidents.[27]

According to Weber and Hinkelammert, therefore, exploitation in this sense can only be discussed as a question of the entire system, the system we are dealing with here being one which makes hunger and death appear to be the natural and unalterable consequences of material forces and not deeds for which we are humanly responsible.

Talk of a "free market", therefore, is pure ideology, in the sense that this term rationalizes and disguises the interests of the more powerful participants in this life and death struggle. Even from a historical standpoint, the global market structure in the colonial period was imposed by force: by armed might, by slavery, by protectionist tariffs, and so on. (In India, for example, the indigenous textile industry was destroyed by, among other means, the amputation of the little finger of Indian weavers to prevent them from practising their craft.) Once established in this way, the market structure has been maintained and developed in present-day neo-colonialism by an international division of labour which keeps the weaker participants in a state of tutelage by mechanisms for which no personal responsibility is accepted and which operate according to rules which the agents of the industrial countries, consciously or unconsciously, maintain to their own advantage.

To grasp this point is to clear away a common misunderstanding. Talk of exploitation seems to imply an attack on a particular person or firm. The view is also frequently expressed that if only the individuals could be converted, an industrialist, for example, then the structures would automatically be changed as well. This is belied *not only* by the experienced fact that in spite of all the undeniable efforts of individuals in recent times, the existing system of market relationships, which (as Weber insists, on principle and not out of personal malevolence) accepts no moral responsibility, has deepened the gulf between poor and rich, *but also* by the fact that, in the final analysis, none of the institutions engaged in the market process is ready to accept responsibility for something which affects countless human beings in the most devastating and painful way.

The only solution, therefore, is for *all* the agents to begin to accept responsibility for changing the system as a whole.[28]

Summarizing the results thus far: The present global economic system is based on the same ideological assumptions as classical physics and technology. The centre of economic activity, therefore, is occupied not by the concrete human being, one's elementary needs and the creaturely world around one, but by an abstract mechanistic way of thinking based on models which disregard everything indeterminate and non-manipulable and which thus increases the power of the owners of the means of control and production. So far, the disastrous consequences of this approach, increasingly evident to a growing number of people, have not been seen as a spur to conversion but rather as occasion for defending the system by force. What little there remains of political control is outmanoeuvred or else the political institutions as a whole are enlisted in support of the system.

This also explains why the neo-Lutheran "two kingdoms doctrine" in particular is so readily invoked in defence of the "autonomy" of the economic process. Historically this stems from the same approach on which the still dominant logic of the rational market is based, namely, the modern approach from Descartes onwards, as formulated in economic terms above all by Max Weber. A church which endorses the logic of this doctrine theologically and which defends the modern classic or neo-classic economics and the market economy based on the abstract *homo oeconomicus* not only falls foul of the anathema of Barmen II but also sets a law invented by man and misused in order to gain power over human beings, a law which by its inherent logic leads to the death of millions of human beings, above the elementary needs of the concrete human being and of the earth (cf. Mark 2:27).

If Bonhoeffer is right in affirming that one criteria for the existence of a *casus confessionis* is the notorious failure adequately to fulfill a "mandate" (in the field of human responsibility in institutions and in the service of God) and if the "mandate" of economy and trade is to help meet the basic needs of humanity, surely this means that a specific case of confession exists for the church in respect of the entire system of abstract market logic (and not simply in respect of isolated actions within this system)?[29]

This is *not* to say that anything in the nature of a market is to be rejected as one dimension of the economy. Paradoxical though it may sound, the truth is that the market needs to be delivered from its absolutization in order to become truly to become a "free market". It needs to be replaced within a broader context and become once more an instrument in the service of humanity. In the view of institutional economic theory, how is this liberation to be achieved? What would be the shape of a quite different paradigm for the economy?

3. ALTERNATIVES

Thesis 3: It is false to say there are no alternatives. There are new economic approaches which make the meeting of the basic needs of concrete human beings and ecological sustainability the starting point for the economic system.

Criticism of the existing global economic system is often repudiated by the assertion that, apart from the state capitalism of "really existing socialism", there is no alternative. Quite apart from the fact that it is permissible to criticize an existing system even if one does not already have a complete alternative blue-print, providing this criticism is called for in the interests of concrete human beings and in obedience to the will of God, the affirmation that there is no alternative is in any case unwarranted. In addition to the institutional economics and the dependence theory already referred to, along with the solutions they propose, there is also a wide variety of new approaches which make similar assumptions. These include the *Bariloche* model which is a full-scale global model.[30] All these alternatives have a new paradigm as their basis; i.e. a basic new pattern over against the classic and neo-classic theory and practice. The following *basic new elements* are included in this new approach:

Firstly: This new approach is based on a view of humanity in which the economically engaged human being is seen to be inseparable from his or her cultural and natural environment.[31]

Secondly: This new approach proceeds from the existential problems of our time (dependency, failure to meet the basic needs of most of the human race, threat to the ecological cycles which sustain life, etc.) and not from an abstract model. It develops social and environmental indicators.[32]

Thirdly: Problems of distribution are viewed from the angle of present victims and with a deliberate value-judgment. The values presupposed in this approach are: "the meeting of existing basic needs", "self-reliance" and "durability" (in the sense of capacity for survival). In other words, its values are precisely the three criteria of justice, participation and sustainability which have come to the fore in ecumenical social ethics. Another name for this alternative economic concept is "eco-development".[33]

Fourthly: In view of the failure of the neo-classic and Keynsian measures in conformity with the traditional system, the institutional economists call for fundamental institutional reforms making use of criteria which are problem-oriented rather than market-oriented. This implies not a complete rejection of the market mechanism but a reduction in its range of influence.[34]

Combining these four elements to construct a new paradigm, i.e. a basic new model of economic theory, we arrive at the following *fundamental characteristics:*

1. Neo-classic Keynsian economics works with closed models. "These closed models are obtained by a process of abstraction which differentiates between 'economic' and 'non-economic' factors and thereby separates the economy from its social and natural environment." It defines the subject matter of the discipline by the theory.[35] Institutional economists, on the contrary, see the national economy as an *open-ended system* and this in three ways: (a) in respect of the social environment; (b) in respect of the natural environment; and (c) in respect of international economic relationships. From this results the following basic model of a national economy open in three directions by the inclusion of the dependence theory in the context of international economic relationships:[36]

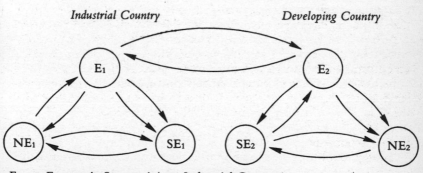

E$_1$ = Economic System 1 (e.g. Industrial Country)
E$_2$ = Economic System 2 (e.g. Developing Country)
SE = Social Environmental Conditions
NE = Natural Environmental Conditions

"Institutional economic theory starts from the problems identified in our present situation (threat to the basic conditions of human existence from underdevelopment, destruction of the environment, etc.) and identifies the relevant economic, social and ecological factors in the nexus of factors which produce the problems under investigation."[37]

2. "There is a circular interdependence between all the basic elements defining relationships within the system."[38]

> Institutional economists identify the following six factors as basic elements in the social system as a whole. Further differentiations depend on the questions under investigation.
> 1. *Population* (subdivided into demographic groups, classes, castes, etc. according to the question being studied)
> 2. *Patterns of thought and behaviour* (including value concepts, i.e. culturally determined human responses to "problematic situations" in which the behavioural response in question is deemed probable)
> 3. *Technology* (understood as a society's "know-how")
> 4. *Resources* (natural and produced, i.e. including labour and capital goods)
> 5. *Institutions* (in the sense of formalized or non-formalized social establishments, including property relationships)
> 6. *Output* (goods and services produced, including in the special case the social product or national income)

Steppacher examines these basic elements and their interactions in respect of three open relationship areas:
— the systems of decision-making in the social system (i.e. not just the price system of the market but also the political and autonomous systems of decision-making);
— the basic elements of the natural environment;
— international economic relationships.
From this follows:
3. Recognition of the asymmetrical nature of social relationships,[39] including economic relationships. This asymmetry is rooted in:
— asymmetry in the power of the different sections of the population;
— asymmetries in the decision-making systems;
— asymmetries in the adaptability of various basic elements in the social system (institutions which are quite indispensable for human life can endanger the life-process by their inertia, i.e. when sheltered by their ruling élite and the sub-sectors it manipulates from new and imperative needs).[40]

"Institutional economists call, therefore, for an analysis of institutional conditions and their interaction with other basic elements in the social system, and a search for substantially defined concepts of rationality required in a changing cultural context on the basis of explicit fundamental values."[41]

To meet this methodological requirement, Steppacher takes the example of the problems of agricultural development in third-world countries, analyzing these problems in the light of their social, cultural, ecological and global economic ramifications. This cannot be discussed in detail here.[42] Our purpose here is simply to show the existence of economic approaches which have taken the first steps towards overcoming the segregation and absolutizing of the market principle as "autonomous" and seek to relate economic activity once again to the concrete human being and the concrete earth and therefore to the questions of life and survival actually posed by contemporary history. Such approaches have long existed here and there, and have multiplied in quite recent times.

All this, it may be said, while theoretically illuminating is not much use in practice. At all events, not a single viable alternative is in sight. But this objection does not hold good in respect of the "two-thirds" world. Whereas not one of the countries in that world which depend on capitalism can be cited as meeting the basic economic needs of all its inhabitants, this requirement is in fact met in at least two socialist countries: China and Cuba.[43] And China accounts for a fifth of the world's population. Here there is no starvation, no lack of clothing, shelter or medical care, which can be put down to the economic system. Targets in some areas such as housing may still be far from being met but at least no one has to live on the street, under cardboard or in rubbish dumps.

Jesus warns us not to be taken in by those who say "Lord! Lord!" but to heed only those who do the will of his heavenly Father. The fact that the Marxists in China or Cuba call themselves atheists is unimportant, therefore. "By their fruits you shall know them!" And in respect of basic economic needs, which Jesus put first among his demands, these two countries certainly match his command in the conditions of the two-thirds world more faithfully than any of the corresponding capitalist countries. Just as Jesus once held up the despised "pagan" Samaritan as an example in stark contrast to the two devout and respectable Jewish travellers on the Jericho road (Luke 10:25–37), so too today we are invited by Jesus to heed the challenge of these socialist countries in the economic field, despite the primitive anti-communist propaganda in our churches and even all the more because of it.

Only when that has been recognized are we also obliged to examine in detail, and in the relevant hisorical context, what is germane in the reproaches levelled at "really existing socialism" and the abuses of power identifiable here too: Soviet expansionism; the handicaps imposed on individual Christians, churches and church groups (where the ground for such discrimination is not simply a class-conditioned option in favour of capitalism); dogmatic errors in the economic field; the needless lack of basic human and political rights. It is certainly quite inept to use the fact that "socialism" as it now exists in Eastern Europe was not introduced and is not maintained voluntarily as an argument against socialist elements in the economic system. The problem of the distribution of the products of the economy is better solved in socialism than under capitalism, which fails completely in this respect.

The weaknesses in the systems of "really existing socialism" also make it impossible, of course, to set up "socialism" as an alternative to capitalism and to strive for it accordingly. It is all the more necessary, therefore, to establish criteria, as the institutional economists are doing, which can also help to improve these existing socialist systems. We obviously need to give much more thought to the broadening of our concept of basic human needs to embrace more than purely economic needs, just as Jesus did in his parable in Matt 25:36 (human dignity, political participation, freedom of conscience — as indicated in the keyword "prison").

A full discussion of the theme "church, theology, Marxism" would take us beyond the limits of the present study and I shall confine myself here to asking: What constructive models are available today for church and theology to help them to respond to the challenge of the global economic system on which the "West" has so deeply imprinted its mark?

II. Theological models for the church's approach to the global economy today

When we tackle the question of the church and the global economy from the standpoint of the church as the body of Christ, as we did in Chapter 6, the eucharistic fellowship with Christ is the most obvious place to start. Recent Orthodox studies, in particular, adopt this approach.[44] We could define this *model* of the church-world relationship as *the liturgical and, above all, eucharistic representation of the love of the Triune God.* (No real clarification is offered here of the attitude to power in the history of Orthodoxy, ranging all the way from "Caesaro-papism", which accommodates itself to power, to the church of the martyrs with its refusal of power and its consequent sufferings.)

If, on the other hand, we begin not only from the question of the church's reality as church but also, alongside it, from a theological analysis of the economic structures, as we do in the present chapter, three further models in particular can be distinguished.

1. CONSTANTINIAN MODEL: THE DOMESTICATION OF POWER

Thesis 4: The aim which this first theological approach, that of the Constantinian type of majority church, sets itself is the domestication of power by a critical but constructive participation in it. The Catholic bishops in the USA have adopted this classical approach, which is also that of Luther and the German Protestant confessional documents, and applied it in an impressive way to the present situation of the USA in a world context. The basic needs of all, i.e. of the poor in particular, provide the criterion in accord with which the state is to establish the common good over against the private pursuit of profit. Respect for these basic needs is rooted in the dignity of the human being, which is theologically fundamental and can only be guaranteed in a community which practises solidarity. This approach, however, remains largely exhortatory.

We are in the fortunate position here of being able to refer to a remarkable recent document in which the questions posed by the capitalist economic system are examined in the light of the classic Catholic tradition, which largely coincides with the classic Reformation approach. I refer to the third draft of the US Bishops' Economy Pastoral: *Economic Justice for All: Catholic Social Teaching and the U.S. Economy*.[45] Addressed primarily to the Christian community, this document is biblical and theological in its argument but, seeking as it does to influence the agents of economic activity, this argument is also based on rational criteria. Its key questions are: "What does the economy do *for* people? What does it do *to* people? And how do people *participate* in it?" (p. 33, Ch. 1, §1). According to the bishops: "The fundamental moral criterion for all economic decisions, policies and institutions is this: They must be at the service of *all people, especially the poor*" (Ch.1, §24). This approach shows that the bishops are determined to view economics not just in an abstract form concerned only with institutions and regulations but with direct reference to concrete human beings.

After an initial chapter on "The Church and the Future of the U.S. Economy", chapter 2 deals with the "Christian Vision of Economic Life", making use of the three basic categories of creation, covenant and community (between God and humanity and between human beings themselves) — the focal points of Israel's faith (§30). These categories apply to all human beings and not just to a few elect. "The justice of a community is measured by its treatment of the powerless in society" (§38). Many of the values of an increasingly materialistic society stand in direct conflict with the gospel, therefore. According to the bishops, the ethical norms for economic life indicate that economic institutions are not to be evaluated simply by their productive efficiency or by the amount of goods and services they make available, important as these surely are. We must also ask whether these institutions allow that measure of active social and economic participation which befits their common membership in the human community (Draft 1, §73). Testing the situation against these ethical norms, the bishops believe that the level of inequality in income and wealth in American society and even more, the inequality on the world scale today must be judged morally inacceptable (Draft 1, §100). "Does our economic system", they ask, "distribute its benefits equitably or does it concentrate power and resources in the hands of a few? Does it promote excessive materialism and individualism? Does it direct too many scarce resources to military purposes?" (Draft 3, §129). On the basis of standards of justice, priorities are to be established as follows: fulfilment of the basic needs of the poor, increased economic participation of the marginalized, the direction of investments of wealth, talents and energy primarily to the satisfaction of basic human needs and the extension of participation (Draft 1, §§105–106). The bishops examine in detail four subjects: employment, poverty, food and agriculture, and the role of the USA in the global economy. A fourth chapter is headed "A New American Experiment: Partnership for the Public Good", in which cooperation within firms and industries, local and regional participation, partnership in the development of national policies, and cooperation at the international level are examined and principles established and actions proposed. Chapter 5 is entitled "A Commitment to the Future" and looks at the Christian vocation in the contemporary world, the challenges to the church in respect of education, the family and economic life, and the commitment of the church to a kingdom of love and justice. On cooperation at the international level, the bishops affirm that "economic policy can no longer be governed by national goals alone". "The fact that 'the social question has become worldwide' challenges us to broaden our horizons and enhance our collaboration and sense of solidarity on the global level. The cause of democracy is closely tied to the cause of economic justice . . . Whatever the difficulty, the need to help poor people in developing countries is undeniable, and the cost of not providing such help can be counted in human lives lost or stunted, talents wasted, opportunities foregone, misery and suffering prolonged and injustice condoned" (Draft 3, §§318 and 320). This moving document concludes with an appeal to personal conversion: "While we have discussed institutions, structures, relationships, concepts, in this pastoral letter, all of these must be grasped, deepened and employed by *people*. All of us must move from observation and analysis, through judgment and exhortation, to action. We have to move from our devotion to independence, through an understanding of interdependence, to a commitment to human solidarity."

It is much to be hoped that the churches in Europe will undertake a similar effort to reach an independent church position over against the ideology and pressure groups of the supposedly "free market economy" by serious Bible study and thorough examination of their own theological tradition.[46] Our Protestant tradition does in fact include the Augsburg Confession with its Article 16 as well as Luther's exegesis of the commandment "You shall not steal" and draws on traditions very similar to those which nourish the USA bishops' pastoral letter, in particular the medieval social doctrine. For Luther, too, the primary criterion for his interpretation of God's will is "the need of the neighbour".

The weakness of this approach, however, is that it remains exhortatory and omits any reference to the first commandment, i.e. to the question of idolatry. It rests on the assumption that by constructive criticism the powerful can be persuaded to change their attitudes and behaviour and effect a transformation of the institutions. Luther at all events thinks in terms of refusal strategies when the laws of faith and love are flagrantly violated. Another large gap in the USA bishops' analysis is an examination of the neo-colonialist system with its indirect violence, building on the old colonialist system with its direct violence. Nor do they analyze the question as to which social agents would be prepared to work for change should the powerful not listen to constructive criticisms and proposals or whether they can even "listen" at all if *a priori* it is a case of anonymous rules and forces.[47] The second theological approach takes up the story here though, historically speaking, it is even older and more original than the approach we have just considered.

2. The "peace church" model: refusal and alternative community

Thesis 5: The early Christian and "peace church" approach assumes THAT THE STRUCTURES OF THIS world have radically succumbed to the powers of sin and death and therefore to violence and oppression (cf. Matt. 20:25). Its response to this situation is to refuse to participate in the structures of injustice and to seek to construct an alternative community as a sign of the coming kingdom of God (Matt. 20:26). In both these ways, this approach has a powerful political significance indirectly while at the same time it does not presuppose any participation in the power structures.

"But Jesus called his disciples to him and said: You know that the rulers of the Gentiles lord it over them and their great ones make them feel the weight of their authority" (Matt. 20:25). "It shall *not* be so among you!" This is the realistic starting point of Jesus, early Christianity, and, later on, of the historic "peace churches" (e.g. Mennonites, Quakers, Brethren Church, etc.). The response here is a refusal to participate in unjust structures and an effort to create an alternative community excluding violence and exploitation. "Whoever would be great among you must be your servant and whoever would be first among you must be your slave!" (Matt. 20:26f.).

The sayings of Jesus about being a servant and the last (Mark 9:35; 10:41–45; Matt. 18:4; 20:25–28; 23:11; Luke 9:48; 22:24–27) have been examined in detail by P. Hoffmann and V. Eid.[48] All three synoptic evangelists relate Jesus' words directly to the order which is to govern the group of disciples, i.e. to the church community. But, indirectly at least, Jesus is also calling in question the ordinary human attitude to precedence, power and prestige. In these sayings, Jesus turns this normal attitude upside down.[49] The basis of the call to renounce lordship is the eschatological overthrow of the earthly order of things by the kingdom or lordship of God. The hope of this overthrow is based on "faith in Yahweh, who in His action in history secures justice for the poor and oppressed".[50] The presence of the kingdom of God in Jesus makes signs of this overthrow already possible here and now. This approach is also clearly illustrated in the early Christian community orders[51] as well as in the sharp distinctiveness of social groups which follow Jesus and appeal to him as Lord.[52] G. Theissen speaks of Jesus as having effected a "revolution in values" in anticipation of and in preparation for the "revolution in power" by which God will utterly overthrow the existing structures and conditions of power in the final fulfilment of God's lordship.

At this point a word must be said about an objection which is based on one of the biblical "proof texts" popular with the "throne and altar" ideologues as well as with proponents of the neo-Lutheran "two kingdoms doctrine". When Jesus told his disciples to "give to Caesar what is Caesar's" (Matt. 22:21), was he not expressly requiring them *not* to interfere with the secular structures of power before the final coming of God's kingdom? As has been demonstrated, this exegesis rests on a misunderstanding of this passage and on a mistranslation.[53] By his initial words, "Fetch me a denarius that I may see it!", Jesus already shows in fact that he has nothing to do with this idolatrous coinage with the cult-image of Caesar imprinted on it. This is also why he says *"render* (i.e. give *back*) to Caesar what is Caesar's" i.e. have nothing to do with it! But rather, pay God what belongs to God, i.e. God's image, i.e. you yourselves.[54]

In other words, while Jesus makes no direct attempt to influence the machinery of power, he does nevertheless influence them indirectly in two ways: he rejects for himself the ideology and practice of the political and economic power structures and, within the circle of his own disciples, overthrows the structures of domination. As can be seen from the story of Zacchaeus (Luke 19:1–10) as well as from the story of how "material possessions" were shared in the first Christian community (Acts 2:43–47), this also has direct economic implications.

This is the tradition in which the historic "peace churches" stand. Among the theologians who have in our time sought to develop both the theory and practice of this way of life are André Trocmé, John Howard Yoder, Ronald Sider and Jim Wallis.[55] Since the first appearance of Trocmé's book on *Jesus and the Nonviolent Revolution* in French in 1961, the appeal to the Old Testament theme of the "Sabbath Year" has played an important part in the discussion. Not only in his first sermon in Nazareth (Luke 4:16ff.) but also on many other occasions, Jesus regarded four elements as signs of the dawning of the kingdom of God in his (Jesus') own presence in the world: (1) the earth is periodically left fallow; (2) debts are cancelled; (3) slaves are set free; and (4) each extended family has its original family portion of the land restored to it as an economic basis of life. To be sure, this was to happen only periodically, every seven years, but at the same time it was also a signpost for the daily life of the alternative community.

The importance of the "peace church" position for the economic question was developed in particular by R. Sider. Not only does he give examples of an alternative life-style for the individual but he also describes how house communities offer a way of life in which Christian nonconformity and community of possessions are possible. In this tradition we also find projects for cooperatives of both production and sharing.

The third theological approach to be mentioned here combines to some extent the strengths of both the traditional approaches: namely, combining the Constantinian tradition of intervention in the power relationships on behalf of the neighbour with the creation of alternative communities, but also expanded to include the question of ideology.

3. THE POST-CONSTANTINIAN "LIBERATION CHURCH" MODEL: CRITIQUE OF THE IDEOLOGY OF DESTRUCTIVE POWER SYSTEMS AND A CONFESSING ECUMENICAL CHURCH CHAMPIONING THE LIFE OF ALL HUMAN BEINGS AND OF THE WHOLE CREATION

Thesis 6: There is an affinity between the liberation church approach and that of the confessing church. This approach contests the "autonomy" of the capitalist market (with Barmen II), regarding it as a form of idolatry and heresy when the church and its theologians seek to justify the present global economic system (e.g. the "Counter Pastoral Letter" of Catholic laity in the USA) when it is in fact a system which causes oppression and death (cf. Barmen I). The keypoint in this approach is whether the church sides with the underprivileged in order to promote life for all human beings or, on the contrary, with the powerful, thereby ensuring the death of many. The social form of the church which is the driving force for the movement of the whole church towards life is the base community identified with the poor.

a) Barmen I and the idolatrous character of capital

It was already pointed out in Chapter 6 that whenever theology is used in the Western world to justify the oppression of the church of the poor we are confronted not simply with false action but increasingly also with false doctrine and perhaps even with a "pseudo-church". We turn therefore to the question whether and where, in the context of the global economy, "*other events and powers, forms and truths*" are being set alongside "*the one word of God*" and acknowledged "*as God's revelation*". We now have to add to the traditional critique of the present global economic system based on the dependency theory two books by Franz J. Hinkelammert and a team of theologians and social scientists from the Ecumenical Studies Department of Costa Rica (San José), in

which a further clarification of the issues from a theological standpoint is provided: (1) the already cited book *The Ideological Weapons
of Death: the Metaphysics of Capitalism*, and (2) *The Idols of Oppression
and the Liberating God.*[56]

In addition to these positive contributions, we also have now
the "counter pastoral letter" recently published by a group of
Catholic laity which is critical of the document produced by the
bishops. Entitled *Towards the Future — Catholic Social Thought and
the US Economy*, this document is a good example of the ideological
misuse of the Bible and theology to legitimize the present global
capitalist system. We shall try to evaluate these documents and see
what light they shed on our theme.

Firstly the USA Catholic "Lay Letter".[57]

The purpose of this document is to offer a biblical and theological
apologia for the capitalist economic system as, in principle, a "good
society", to prove that this system is an essential basis for democracy,
to portray its opponents as supporters of communist tyranny, to miti-
gate failures in this system as regrettable exceptions to the general
rule and, very emphatically, to repudiate the thesis that the system
automatically enriches the rich at the expense of the poor.

The starting point is the motto found on every US dollar bill: "In
God we trust", and the concordance of the church's principles with
the interests of the republic. The limits of the state are set by private
property as a law of nature and as a right which is in turn legitimized
by the commandment "You shall not steal!" According to G. K Ches-
terton, "property is merely the art of the democracy". "It means that
every man should have something that he can shape in his own image,
as he is shaped in the image of Heaven." Americans think in terms of
"creation theology", as understood by the Archbishop of Ireland at
the end of the last century, who declared it impossible not to believe
that "a singular mission is assigned to America" and that "with our
hopes are bound up the hopes of the millions of the earth . . . The
world is in throes; a new age is to be born . . . "

The word "capitalism" "comes from *caput*, head." "The cause of
the wealth of nations is inventive intellect, the creativity of the human
intelligence seeking to decipher the wealth hidden in creation by the
Creator himself . . . Skills, knowledge, drive and ambition are forms
of capital." Speaking of "competition", it is frankly admitted that "the
graveyard of defunct corporations and business enterprises is many
times larger than the list of the living" . . . "The path of a free
economy is marked, like that of God's creation itself, with what
Schumpeter has called 'creative destruction'." The principle of genuine
self-interest can be derived from the golden rule, "Love your neighbour
as yourself". The "Lay Letter" quotes Lippmann: "It was not until the

industrial revolution had altered the traditional mode of life that the vista was opened at the end of which men could see the possibility of the Good Society on this earth. At last the ancient schism between the world and the spirit, between self-interest and disinterestedness, was potentially closed."

Under appeal to Genesis 1:26 and John Paul II, it is stated: the market system is "the only system built upon the liberty of its participants". "Only a market system respects the free creativity of every human person, and *for this reason* respects private property, incentives (rather than coercion), freedom of choice, and the other institutions of a free economy."

The vital thing, therefore, is the spirit of enterprise. "Among the poor, it (sc. enterprise) inspires imagination and adventure, rather than resignation" (one might almost say a "Get on your bike!" spirit). "In short, the relation is triadic: not only labor and capital but also creative intellect. The entrepreneur who supplied the intellectual vision putting labor and capital together is a co-creator." "Economic activism is a direct participation in the work of the Creator himself." According to Matthew 25:14–30, economic talents are not meant to be buried. "Preserving capital is not enough — it must be made to grow." Then it will be possible to feed the hungry, clothe the naked, educate the unlearned and assist the millions of all nations. The "Lay Letter" endorses Cardinal Ratzinger's opposition to the theology of liberation and his assertion that "no one can localize evil principally or uniquely in bad social political or economic 'structures' ". "Profit serves the common good by allocating resources creatively and stimulating entre- preneurial activity." "The Christian scriptures themselves borrow abundantly from the language of profit in many elementary metaphors. The concept of incentive and reward is by no means foreign to Chris- tianity. The fundamental justification for profit rests upon a social decision to confer rewards on those who have resources if they abstain from consuming them on luxuries for themselves in order to invest them in the creation of new industries, new goods and services, and new wealth." Critics of the profit-motive live for the most part off the profits of others, as indeed does the church itself. The critics also overlook the fact that "a free economy allows for the fullest possible range of motivation. In economic activities the practice of Christian virtue has full and wide scope, the more so where liberties are full and dynamic growth makes opportunities flower."

"The market is a *social* institution, expressing the social nature of humankind. It respects the liberty of each participant, while tying each through a social device to every other. Further, a market teaches all who participate in it to be alert to the needs and wants of others. No one can succeed in markets without a considerable degree of other- regardingness . . . A market system is a system of service to others." Catholics who emigrated to America "have experienced here — under the torch of the Statue of Liberty — a 'liberation theology' that works . . . US 'liberation theology' — perhaps better described as 'creation theology' — has been both amazingly productive and amazingly liberating. Its work is incomplete, but it has been well begun."

"Multinational corporations arose out of both moral and material necessity." The only alternative to them would be "economic isolation". If there are poor countries, this is only because they do not have the right "system". "Those few societies on this planet based on private property, market systems, incentives, and the discipline of profit succeed with astonishing speed in raising up the living standards of their poor." In Matthew 25 "Christ does not speak about the distance between rich and poor but about the real needs of the poor which must be met. Such systematic needs can only be met by systems designed to conquer scarcity. This is the problem for which the political economy of democratic capitalism has been expressly designed."

Moreover "poverty is not primarily a problem for the state. It is a *personal* and a *community* problem which each of us and all our appropriate associations, not only the state, ought to address." Conclusion: "We judge markets to be by far the most successful social device ever discovered . . . 'By their fruits ye shall know them' (Matt. 7:20)".

It is not enough just to wax indignant at statements of this kind or to dismiss them as cynical in face of the actual "fruits" of the economic system for which an apologia is offered here. The real problem is that these statements are quite seriously made and reflect an ideology which is widespread not only among the ruling classes but also among ordinary people in the USA and other capitalist countries. One of the co-authors of the "Lay Letter" is a former foreign secretary of the USA — namely, Alexander Haig. A detailed examination of the theological dimensions of this position is called for but all I have room for here are a few pointers. The basic point, in my view, is that this document sets a "creation theology" alongside the total biblical position. In this "creation theology", the entrepreneurial intelligence (in the sense of Descartes' *ratio*) is posited as the *imago Dei* and regarded as at liberty to shape the world ("matter") according to this image, i.e. in accord with the logic of the market.

The two *Latin American books* mentioned above set out to demonstrate that this approach is based on idolatry.

The title of Hinkelammert's essay in *The Idols of Oppression and the Liberating God* is "The economic roots of idolatry. The metaphysics of the entrepreneur". He defines this metaphysics as "a metaphysics of merchandise, money, the market and capital". It derives from Thomas Hobbes who described bourgeois society as "Leviathan" having money for its blood. Since then, "the mechanism of bourgeois society has become the cult object of the bourgeois social sciences". "Bourgeois thought derives its ethics and morality from this cult object; the values and norms of the market turn out then to be the ways of virtue; if the cult object is disregarded or despised, on the contrary, they are the ways of sin." The cardinal virtue is "humility towards the (market) processes; its supreme reward is the "economic miracle". Obedience to the market indicators is "natural" or, since Max Weber, "rational". "The human being is free so long as the dollar is free." Nature being the work of God, the enemy of the market is the enemy of nature, i.e. a rebel against God. Against this enemy the use of force is always justified.

The real subject in this world is merchandise. The enterprises, of which the particular entrepreneur is merely the servant, comply with whatever demands merchandise may make. If the merchandise is to be free, the price must be free. Money is the hyphen connecting merchandise and the enterprise, the blood which flows in the veins of "Leviathan". The purpose of the accumulation of capital is the progress of humanity, but what it achieves, in fact, is the destruction of humanity and the earth. The global struggle against inflation with the assistance of the International Monetary Fund is waged by means which include the destruction of social services and trade union rights and the reinforcement of military and police forces.

In metaphysical fashion, responsibility for economic history and the economic process is transferred to "nature", the logic of the market, rational thought. "There is no longer any such thing as exploitation any more than a storm can be said to exploit anyone. The law of gravity simply operates; so too, the law of market." When flesh and blood human beings, with their right to work, food and shelter, defend themselves from the metaphysical "nature" of the world of merchandise, entrepreneurial metaphysics brands them as materialistic, arrogant, utopian and violent.

"In the entrepreneurial metaphysics, anyone who rebels against the conditions governing the exchange of money and capital, anyone who therefore sides with the flesh and blood human being and his or her right to work, food and shelter, is a rebel against God Himself. On the one side, is God and capital; on the other side, the concrete needy human being and the devil. This is the summit of the entrepreneurial metaphysic."

"To everyone else, if not to the entrepreneurial metaphysics, it is clear that this is a monstrous form of idolatry in precisely the sense in which this term is used in the biblical tradition. With incidental reference to this biblical tradition, Marx's term for this was 'fetishism'. It means the enslavement of the human being and his or her concrete daily life to the product of his or her own hands, and the consequent destruction of the human being as such in virtue of this relationship entered into with the idol. In this sense, every idol is a Moloch who devours human beings. The idol is a 'God' in league with oppression . . . But in the biblical tradition, the true God is the God whose will is to set the flesh and blood human being with his or her concrete needs at the centre of society and history. By becoming a rival of the human being, the idol is in rivalry with God."

The biblical evidence in support of this thesis is summarized by *Pablo Richard* in a thorough exegetical study included in this same volume. Richard distinguishes between the problem of the cult-images of Yahweh ("Yahweh idols") and the worship of strange or false gods. Both these forms of idolatry are antithetical to the liberating and life-saving activity of Yahweh — as classically formulated in the opening words of the Decalogue: "I am the Lord your God who brought you out of the land of Egypt, out of the house of bondage. You shall have no other gods before me" (i.e. no alien or false gods). "You shall not make for yourselves a graven image" (Ex. 20:2-4; Deut. 5:6-8).

1. The best-known instance of Yahweh idols is the story of the "Golden Calf" (Ex. 32). "The sin against the transcendence of God lies in the people's refusal of its own liberation and its preference for a pseudo-liberation via an alienating worship of an idol who only comforts but does not liberate." To worship such a comforter-god is idolatry; the throne from which he reigns, i.e. from which his presence among men is represented, is gold; gold in turn is the symbol of sovereignty. Later, the use of images in the worship of Yahweh was rigorously excluded.

The theological justification for this prohibition was that the human being alone is the image of God (Gen. 1:27). "Taken together, these passages permit the conclusion that, since God reveals himself in the Bible as the *liberating God*, then only the image of the *liberating human being* reveals the transcendence of the one true God. Both oppressor and enslaved are idolaters who distort and pervert the revelation of the liberating transcendence of God."

2. There were two stages in the worship of "strange" gods: "In the first stage people believe that these strange gods really exist and possess power in their territory." Yahweh then becomes the supreme god among the many gods. "To become subject to a strange people automatically meant recognizing also the superiority of its god." "The best-known examples of this kind of idolatry in the historical books of the Old Testament are connected with the kings of Israel. In these instances, *wealth*, *power* and *idolatry* always go hand in hand and the consequence is always *injustice* towards the poor" (Solomon, Ahab, Manasseh). From the Exile onwards (sixth century BC) idolatry takes on a new significance. In the strict monotheistic faith in Yahweh, the idol is explicitly identified as a human construction, an expression of the human manipulation of power. Jeremiah 10:1–16 and Isaiah 44:9–20

(Second Isaiah) are especially clear examples and attestations of this view.

Richard distinguishes between talisman, fetish and idol: "The talisman is a material object with miraculous power. The fetish is a material object inhabited by a spirit which gives it power. The idol, too, is a fetish though with this difference, that the material object here seeks to reproduce symbolically and perhaps even directly the form and mode of action of the spirit or god who inhabits the fetish." The power of the idol is neither fictitious nor illusory; it is real power but has its origin in the power of the human being. The human being has the power to transform nature and is therefore able to satisfy his needs; but with the same power and the same work he can also create fetishes and idols. In the actual circumstances of their time, the idolatry with which Jeremiah and Second Isaiah were concerned was that of the Babylonians, Israel's oppressors at that time. "The prophet is concerned to show that the power of the Babylonian idols is the political, military and cultural power of the Babylonians and not the power of the idols they worshipped." The false prophet Gedaliah demands Israel's capitulation to the Chaldaeans (2 Kings 25:24) but the message of Jeremiah is: "Be not afraid of the king of Babylon!" (Jer. 42:11). "Faith in the liberating God is always subversive in relation to power and subversion is always directed against idolatry. When we seek deliverance in power, power becomes a fetish, is deified, passes over into a transcendent world."

The later book of Wisdom connects the devising of idols with the corruption of life and a threat to life (*Wisdom of Solomon*, 14:12 and 21). "The yoke of power engenders idolatry and idolatry destroys life. Idolatry is a fall; i.e. it allows the oppressing power to become a 'spiritual' and 'transcendent' world which in this way veils and legitimizes the oppression. This fall prevents both oppressor and oppressed from becoming aware of the oppression and is also, at the same time, an obstacle to the knowledge of God: 'Afterwards it was not enough for them to go astray as touching the knowledge of God; but also, while they live in sore conflict through ignorance of him, that multitude of evils they call peace' (*Wisdom of Solomon*, 14:22)."

In the *New Testament*, Richard identifies four theological arguments against idolatry:

1. *Idolatry destroys human beings, nature and history* (Acts 17:16–34; Col. 1:15). The argument here is that the human being or Christ is the image of the invisible God.

2. *The idolatry of money* (1 Cor. 5:9–13; 6:9–11; 10:14–17; Gal. 5:19–21; Col. 3:5; 1 Pet. 4:3; Matt. 6:24). Along with sex, money is the determined ally of idolatry. The following equations should be noted:

"Idolater = greedy person = robber = thief.
Idolatry = enmity = quarrelling = jealousy = dissension = envy.

Like all other vices and perversions, idolatry proves a disturbing factor in human relationships and community life." Greed is "a mania to possess or to want to possess more than others". "Money would then be the idol, not money as a reality in itself but *money as the possession of power* in order to desire or take still more money from others; an idolatry which produces hostilities and dissensions. Idolatry is the subjection of the human being to this power of money". Paul excludes idolaters from the congregation and from the eucharist. Jesus himself is quite explicit: "You cannot serve God and mammon!" (Matt. 6:24), where "serve" is equivalent to "be the slave of". Money is a substitute for God and, as such, an idol. To turn money into a fetish is also to turn all human, social and political relationships into a fetish. In other words, we are faced here with a clear choice.

3. *Idolatry of the law* (Gal. 4:8–11; 4:21–5:1; Mark 2:1–3:6). Here again the contrast is between either destruction or liberation. "The fetishism of the law oppresses and destroys the human being even more so than other forms of idolatry, for here it is an ethical and religious fetishism which leads the human conscience itself into error." "The person who has been liberated by Christ can confess, communicate and celebrate his or her faith only as a practical commitment in the constant struggle against the false gods, against false deifications and a false transcendent or supernatural spiritualization in all its forms whereby money and law are turned into instruments of domination. 'For freedom has Christ set us free; stand fast, therefore, and be not entangled again in the yoke of bondage' (Gal. 5:1)."

4. *Idolatry of oppressive political power* (Rev. 13:11–18; 14:9–13; 15:1–4; 16:2; 19:20).

The "beast" of the Apocalypse at that time was the oppressive power of the Roman Empire. The idol has real power because the "beast" has power. "The Christian witnesses to his or her complete liberation in Christ. This does not necessarily mean overt political opposition to the Emperor but simply the denial of his legitimacy and the rejection of all claims to a transcendent, supernatural or divine dimension which the Emperor manipulates in order to dominate and oppress. The message of the Book of Revelation with its opposition to idolatry was thus a message of hope and deliverance for Christians persecuted and oppressed by the Roman imperium."

In conclusion, Richard shows the hermeneutical difference between the Bible and today; Christians at the earlier time had no possibility whatever of deliberately changing the system.

Jon Sobrino's contribution to the book provides a positive counterpoint to Richard's essay. His theme is "The God of life made visible in Jesus of Nazareth". His concern is with the life of flesh and blood human beings rather than with the death-dealing idols.

It may be objected at this point that the biblical evidence

concerning the nature of idolatry in general and money as usurped power in particular is directed against individual persons or actions but is irrelevant to the critique of an economic system. This makes it all the more important for us to realize that *Luther*, under Constantinian conditions, did precisely what liberation theologians do today; namely, applied the biblical theology to the early capitalist system of his own day and came to the conclusion that it was idolatrous. In a richly documented essay, F. W. Marquardt has demonstrated that in Luther "economics becomes one among many other problems in the area of theology or talk about God; it is no longer simply an ethical problem but is now a dogmatic problem."[58]

> In his exposition of the first commandment in his *Large Catechism*, Luther deals with Mammon as the first of his list of "common examples of failure to obey this commandment". "Mammon is in fact seen as a totality, as a system of reality" (Marquardt). According to Luther, "not only is mammon their god, therefore, but they themselves also want, through mammon, to be god of the whole world and to make themselves worshipped as such. But the poor, though they neither can nor want to have mammon as their god, are also required nevertheless to worship mammon's divinity in his idols, or, rather, in his gods, or else die of starvation" (*An die Pfarrherren, wider den Wucher zu predigen*, 1540, cited in Marquardt, p. 189). "Profiteering is a huge and horrible monster, like a werewolf." In other words, capital invested to gain more money by interest "eats" human beings and "estates" up to and including the Emperor. Luther, too, was familiar with the ability of certain people to find pseudo-Christian arguments in defence of profiteering. "Fifteen years ago I wrote against profiteering at a time when it was already so deeply ingrained that I could entertain little hope of any improvement. Meanwhile, however, it has grown so bold that it now refuses to regard itself as something criminal, sinful and scandalous but even claims praise as a glorious and virtuous thing, as if it demonstrated great love and Christian service to people. If scandal has now become a boast and crime a virtue, what can help and counsel us now?!" "With the use of their intelligence alone, the heathen could recognize a profiteer as fourfold a thief and murderer. But we Christians hold them in such honour that we worship them simply in virtue of their wealth." Luther had a name for theologians who lent their support to such a legitimization of the accumulation of capital by interest; he called them the "plutologians" (*plutologi*)!

But what do these reflections of Luther and the liberation theologians signify for us today as we wrestle with the question of the confession and practical witness of the church of Jesus Christ within the present global economic system? What Luther regarded as the systematic tendency of capital to impoverish an increasing number of human beings and to make a few increasingly rich has today become a worldwide and universal tendency. In other words, we are faced not simply with a question of ethics but with the choice between God and false god, between true worship and idolatry.

In the light of this, what is the significance of the fact that some of our church members vehemently defend the so-called "free market economy" despite its same tendency to produce a widening gap between rich and poor and to destroy social counterbalances, as a taboo which we are forbidden to examine more closely, whereas others feel obliged or free to withdraw into their sense of impotence in face of this tendency? Does this not mean that the global economic system has become an article of faith, an idol, one which is moreover defended by "Christian" arguments?

It is just here that Barmen I and II enter the picture with their references to "other events and powers" and to "other lords". Barmen I bars the way, in particular, to any positive justification of the global economic system as an absolute and divinely ordered institution, whether by the use of arguments based on a supposedly "impartial reason" or by appealing to isolated biblical passages wrenched out of their context, or even by oppressing the church of the poor. All these "justifications" come within the Bonhoefferian category of "too much", where secular institutions trespass on the mandate of the church and by doing so go beyond their own mandate. Barmen II bars the way, in particular, to any attempt to declare the mechanisms of merchandise, money, market and capital "autonomous", as if we were, after all, the servants here of lords other than Jesus Christ, the subjects of laws and idols that kill. Barmen II is directed, above all, against any passive justification of an abstract capitalist "autonomous market" in the sense of the neo-Lutheran "two kingdoms doctrine".

The link between the "liberation church" approach and that of the Barmen Theological Declaration is not simply a verbal one, therefore, but one of substance and content, one, moreover, which is especially helpful to us in the recognition of the global economic system as a mission field for the confessing church today.

b) Liberating church promoting life for all

The "liberation church" approach does not rest content with a general economic and theological critique of the present global economic system and its ideology of justification. It also seeks to define in positive terms the confession of faith, the form and action, of a church which would obey Jesus Christ in this situation. Franz Hinkelammert concluded his paper on the "total market" policy at the Barmen jubilee conference in 1984 with the following statement:

> To confess our faith in the God of life means confessing our solidarity with the actual life lived by the human being, i.e. the life of all men and women. It means rejecting the deification of any market and any state, institutionalization in any form. There is no way to God which does not pass via the relationship between flesh and blood human beings who recognize each other as people with needs. These include their basic material necessities, which we are not at liberty to fob off on to imaginary and illusory automatic future effects of the market or any other supposedly autonomous institutional rules.
>
> On the other hand, neither are we thereby compelled to invert the process and transform the market or the state of other institutions into demonic forces. Concrete life can only be secured within such institutional forms. Their existence is part of the way in which life is secured. In them, too, God is present to the extent that they serve this concrete life, but not as a result of their uncontrolled autonomy. Only on this basis does the confession of faith in the God of the fullness of life lead to the acceptance of responsibility to God for the politics of social justice, peace, the environment and development. On this basis, the God of life is the God of the poor. Liberation theology says this out loud. But there is more to it than this. We also have to confess this God. Let me also say, in conclusion, that what we need is a new church, an ecumenical church, a church interested in the life of all human beings and of all nations, a confessing church.

Hinkelammert's words contain two theological perspectives which are important for our theme:

Firstly: Eberhard Bethge has more than once pointed out that, in a specific confessional situation, while the confession of the whole faith is always at stake, this nevertheless crystallizes at a quite specific point. In the case of the total state and its pseudo-Christian defenders, it was the *"solus Christus"*, the "Christ alone" attested in holy scripture, which epitomized the confessional question (Barmen I). In the case of apartheid (i.e. "separation") it is the *"unum"* which is at the centre of the required confession.[59] What then is the salient point, theologically speaking, in the question of the supposedly autonomous "total world market"?

If the first priority of the global economic system is no longer the satisfaction of the basic needs of *all* human beings, as the World

Council of Churches, the Catholic bishops of the USA, and the alternative economists properly insist it should be, and if this global economic system takes for granted the death of millions of poor people as the price to be paid to ensure a "better" life for the few, then the salient point would seem to be this: does the church champion *the life of all human beings and of the whole earth*, or does it side with the global economic system which at least tolerates and even automatically causes the mass death of so many and the destruction of the earth by the mechanisms so structured? If this *is* the salient question, it would also identify for us the theological crossroads where such questions as the following intersect: arming for death/peace, economic death/justice, destruction of the earth/ preserving the integrity of creation. But much more intensive theological work is required on the problems of "life for all" as the salient point in the question of the global world market.[60]

Secondly: The concept of an ecumenical confessing church championing *the life of all people and the whole earth on which they dwell* is by no means as abstract as might first appear. The keyword "all" also points, it is true, to the universal dimension, the catholicity, of the church, which it is difficult to grasp in concrete terms. In a situation in which a large part of the world's population is hungry and dying and the creation is in danger of being destroyed, it is certainly no longer idle to ask whether the church of Jesus Christ is ecumenical, i.e. a church related to the whole inhabited earth. But when we speak of the life of *all*, this is not just a reference to the universal worldwide dimension but an emphatic insistence on our need to assign top priority to those who are being deprived of their opportunities and possibilities of life. The basic question for the church — the question of its *reality* as church — then becomes the question whether it is siding with the poor, i.e. with the classes discriminated against by the structures, or with the powerful, i.e. with the classes which dominate and control the structures. This is precisely the distinction examined by L. Boff in his essay on the "marks of the church" in a class society.[61] In this essay he identifies fifteen marks of a church on the side of the underprivileged classes:

1) church as the people of God;
2) church of the poor and powerless (at the bottom of the heap);
3) church of the exploited (those denied their human dignity);
4) church of the laity;
5) church as koinonia of power (power-sharing);
6) church whose members are all charged with ministries;

7) church of the diaspora;
8) liberating church;
9) church which gives a sacramental form to concrete steps of liberation;
10) church continuing the central tradition;
11) church in communion with the institutional church;
12) church which develops unity on the basis of its liberating mission;
13) church which embodies catholicity in a concrete new way;
14) church which is apostolic in its totality;
15) church with a new style of holiness.

In practice, this means that wherever the church is found, it must live, work, worship and struggle in concrete solidarity with the underprivileged — locally and worldwide. Precisely because in the present market system transactions are anonymous and kept that way, the key starting point for this church are the concrete personal relationships in small base communities — championing the life of all in the particular local situation but also in worldwide solidarity with all human beings.

As Hinkelammert says, this is not to proceed in an anti-institutional way but, on the contrary, to make every effort to persuade the institutions in both church and state to fulfill their God-given function of promoting and protecting life. In some of the Latin American countries, at all events, in striking contrast to what happened under the Nazi régime in Germany in the thirties, the institutional church has heard this summons, sided with the poor, and so made superfluous there the development of an independently organized "confessing church". Will this also be possible for the churches in the rich industrial countries?

NOTES

1. See Chapter 6 above.
2. See Chapters 3 and 4 above.
3. Cf. P. R. Mooney, *Seeds of the Earth — A Private or Public Resource* (Coalition for Development Action), London, 1979; H. Diefenbacher, "Feeding a Human Race Endangered by Progress. How the Agromultinationals Represent a Threat to the Variety of Seed Strains", in German in *Orientierung*, 30 September 1980, pp. 192ff.; S. Bertolami, *Für wen die Saat aufgeht. Pflanzenzucht im Dienste der Konzerne*, Z Verlag, Basle, 1981; cf. also J. Collins and F. Lappé, *Vom Mythos des Hungers*, Frankfurt, 1978; Susan George, *How the Other Half Dies*, Penguin, London, 1977. In his novel, *L'empereur de la faim*, Flammarion, 1986, Jacques

Lamalle gives a fictional account of the worldwide struggle between the large-scale agro-food enterprises based on an intimate knowledge of the facts of life in this area.

4. R. Steppacher, "Basic Characteristics of Institutional Economy (Part I) Illustrated by Problems of Agricultural Development in the Third World", in German in Chr. Leipert (ed.), *Konzepte einer humanen Wirtschaftslehre. Beiträge zur institutionellen Ökonomie und zur Integration der Sozialwissenschaften* (Arnoldshain Documents on Interdisciplinary Economics, Vol. 2), Frankfurt, 1982, pp. 229f.

5. Brief examples of such summary surveys can be found in the President of Tanzania Julius Nyerere's address during a visit to West Germany in August 1985 entitled, "The Poor are Still Making the Rich Richer", published in German in the papers of the Third World Information Centre, No. 127, August 1985; also Nigel Twose, *Cultivating Hunger: an Oxfam Study of Food, Power and Poverty*, Oxfam, UK, 1984; W. Gern, article on third world, in German in EKL[3], Vol. 1, pp. 923–935; a more detailed account is available in the Brandt Commission's Strategy for Survival, 1980.

6. Cf. for example, W. Rodney, *How Europe Underdeveloped Africa*, London and Dar-es-Salaam, 1972, 1973[2]. A clear and helpful survey and discussion of the different theories can be found in W. Ochel, *Die Entwicklungsländer in der Weltwirtschaft*, Cologne, 1982, pp. 65ff.

7 Cf. P. J. Opitz (ed.), *Die Dritte Welt in der Krise*, Munich, 1984; A. Datta, *Welthandel und Welthunger* (dto. 10317), 1984; R. H. Strahm, *Warum sie so arm sind*, Wuppertal, 1985.

8. On the debt crisis, cf. R. Gerster, *Fallstricke der Verschuldung*, Basle, 1982; Peter Körner, Bero Maass and others, *Im Teufelskreis der Verschuldung*, Junius, Hamburg 1984; *epd — Entwicklungspolitik* No. 17, 1984, *Schwerpunkt Verschuldung*, with articles by Körner and Maass, Diefenbacher and others; R. H. Strahm, *op. cit.* Cf. also Charles Elliott, *Inflation and the Compromised Church*, Belfast, 1975.

9. Cf. the special issue on "Debt and the IMF" of the papers of the Third World Information Centre, No. 121, Freiburg, November 1984, pp. 28ff.

10. Thus the GNP of Pakistan, Egypt or Chile in 1977 was less than the annual turnover of Chrysler, a firm which in that year was only 10th in the USA list. With the exception of Brazil, Nigeria, Algeria and Libya, the national reserves of all African and South American states at the end of 1976 were less, for example, than the assets of the St. Gall cantonal bank (cf. Kidron/Segal, *Hunger und Waffen*, rororo, Reinbek, 1982[3]). On the whole of this section, see also Chapter 4 above and especially R. H. Green, "The Rationality of Transnational Corporations and their Relationship to States, Employees and the Poor", in German in *epd-Entwicklungspolitik, Materialien* III/82, pp. 104ff.

11. Cf. Cees Hamelink, *Finance and Information: a Study of Converging Interests*, Arblex, Norwood N.J., 07648, 1983.

12. Cf. Cees Hamelink, *The Corporate Village: the Role of Transnational Corporations in International Communication*, IDOC, Rome, 1977.

13. M. Weber, *Wirtschaft und Gesellschaft*, Tübingen, 1972[5], pp. 708f.

14. See Chapter 3 above and W. Ochel, *op. cit.*, n. 6 above.

15. In what follows I keep close especially to Chr. Leipert's article on "Social Environment and Human Needs . . . " and R. Steppacher's article on "Basic Characteristics of Institutional Economy . . . " in Chr. Leipert (ed.) *op. cit.* note 4 above, pp. 133ff. and 161ff. See also Karl Polanyi, *The Great Transform-*

ation, 1944. Similar approaches can be seen in ecological studies of the economy, see note 20 below. A. Rich, *Wirtschaftsethik. Grundlagen in theologischer Perspektive*, Gütersloh, 1984, also takes the same direction in his study of the question of "criteria of human rights".

16. Leipert, *op. cit.*, pp. 138ff.
17. *Ibid.*, pp. 141f.
18. *Ibid.*, pp. 142ff.
19. *Ibid.*, pp. 145ff. and also F. J Hinkelammert, *The Ideological Weapons of Death: on the Metaphysics of Capitalism* (in German, Münster and Freiburg, Switzerland, 1985, pp. 70ff.).
20. Cf. I. Schöne, "The Assumption of Society Organized on the Market Economy Principle that Human Needs are Unlimited", in German in Öko-Institute Project Group on Ecological Economy (ed.), *Arbeiten im Einklang mit der Natur. Bausteine für ein ökologische Wirtschaft*, Freiburg im Breisgau, 1985, pp. 89f.
21. K. W. Kapp, *Planwirtschaft und Aussenhandel*, Georg, Geneva, 1936, as summarized by Steppacher, *op. cit.*, p. 214.
22. Kapp, *op. cit.*, p. 37.
23. Steppacher, *op. cit.*, pp. 224f.
24. *Ibid.*, p. 232.
25. J. Holland and P. Henriot S.J. (in *Social Analysis: Linking Faith and Justice*, Center of Concern, Washington, 1985[2], 64ff.) have described how this development of modern industrial capitalism took place in three phases which indicate, of course, only the main tendencies and for which regional differences must be allowed in each case: (1) laissez-faire industrial capitalism (nineteenth century); (2) welfare capitalism (at least for the centre countries in the period following the world economic crisis); (3) the capitalism of national security (1968 . . .).
26. F. J Hinkelammert, "The Politics of the 'Total Market': its Transformation into Theology and Our Response" (in German in ESG (ed.), *Kirche im Kapitalismus*, Stuttgart, 1984, pp. 59f.
27. F. J. Hinkelammert, *The Ideological Weapons of Death . . .* , in German, *op. cit.*, p. 14.
28. See also and especially H. Gollwitzer, *Die kapitalistische Revolution*, Münich, 1974; J. P. Miranda, *The Immorality of Present Structures* (in German, Wuppertal, 1973); A. Th. van Leeuwen, *De nacht van het kapitaal. Door het oerwoud van de economie naar de bronnen van de burgerlijke religie*, SUN, Nijmegen, 184, 1985[2]; R. de Almeida, art. on poverty in P. Eicher (ed.), *Neues Handb. theol. Grundbegriffe*, Vol. 1, pp. 25–61.
29. For what also must be said on the basis of Barmen I about the claim to revelation, i.e. about the "too much" of the ideology of the autonomous market, see section II of this chapter and Chapter 6 above.
30. A. O. Herrera, H. D. Scolnik and others, *Grenzen des Elends. The BARILOCHE Model: So kann die Menscheit überleben*, Frankfurt, 1977 (Fundación Bariloche Argentina).
31. Cf. Leipert, *op. cit.*, pp. 153ff; Steppacher, pp. 163f.
32. Steppacher, *op. cit.*, p. 164.
33. *Ibid.*, p. 165.
34. *Ibid.*, pp. 165f.
35. *Ibid.*, p.172.
36. *Ibid.*, p.171.
37. *Ibid.*, p. 172.
38. *Ibid.*, pp. 175ff.

39. *Ibid.*, pp. 202ff.
40. *Ibid.*, pp. 235ff.
41. *Ibid.*, p. 243.
42. In a planned second part of the study of basic characteristics other individual persons will be investigated; cf. the summary, *Ibid.*, pp. 166ff.
43. Cf. LWF Studies Department (ed.), "Christian Faith and the Encounter with China", *epd Documentation* 2/75; idem, "Theological Reflection on the Encounter of the Church with Marxism in Various Cultural Contexts", in *Junge Kirche* 1977, pp. 483–504; Frei Betto, *Fidel·e a religião*, São Paulo, 1985.
44. See Chapters 3 and 5 above, and V. M. Borovoy, "Life in Unity", in *Vancouver Assembly* 1983.
45. National Catholic Reporter No. 9, 23 November 1984.
46. Meanwhile, the Church of England has also produced a 400-page report on "Faith in the City" in which it severely criticizes the UK government and sees the "new poverty" as a consequence of our economic system (cf. *Newsweek*, 16 December 1985, p. 10).
47. For a constructive criticism of the Bishops' letter cf. also Center of Concern, "For a Clear Alternative", in German, in *Public Forum Documentation*, Frankfurt, 1985.
48. P. Hoffmann and V. Eid, *Jesus von Nazareth und eine christliche Moral* (Quaestiones Disputatae 66), Freiburg, Basle, Vienna, 1975, 1976², pp. 186ff.
49. *Ibid.*, pp. 194ff.
50. *Ibid.*, (201ff.), 203.
51. *Ibid.*, pp. 214ff.
52. *Ibid.*, pp. 231ff.
53. On what follows, cf. P. Lapide, *Er predigte in ihren Synagogen* (GTB Siebenstern 1400) Gütersloh, 1980, pp. 34ff.
54. Although Paul in Romans 13:1–7 takes a positive attitude to the lawful public institutions of the Roman Empire, he is not here canvassing an uncritical conformity but rather a strict assessment of what Christians can and cannot go along with in this world (Rom. 12:1–2). Cf. Duchrow, *Christenheit und Weltverantwortung*, Stuttgart, 1980², pp. 109f, pp. 137ff.
55. A. Trocmé, *Jésus Christ et la révolution non-violente*, Geneva, 1961; John H. Yoder, *The Politics of Jesus*, Eerdmans, Grand Rapids; R. Sider, *Rich Christians in an Age of Hunger*, Intervarsity Christian Fellowship of the USA, 1977; C. Sugden, *Radical Discipleship*, Marshall Morgan and Scott, London, 1981; J. Wallis, *The Call to Conversion*, Sojourners, Washington DC, 1981. On Trocmé, cf. Philip Hallie, *Lest Innocent Blood be Shed*, Harper, 1979.
56. H. Assmann *et al.*, *Die Götzen der Unterdrückung und der befreiende Gott*, Münster, 1984. Cf. *Texte und Kontexte. Exegetische Zeitschrift* No. 24, Berlin, 1984, pp. 5ff. and T. Veerkamp, *Die Vernichtung des Baal*, Stuttgart, 1983.
57. The following quotes are a retranslation of the text as published together with the pastoral letter of the Bishops in Publik-Forum-Dokumentation, Frankfurt, 1985, pp. 150–216.
58. F. W. Marquardt, "God *or* Mammon, but theology *and* economics, in Martin Luther", in *Einwürfe I*, Munich, 1983 (pp. 176ff.), p. 183. Cf. Chapter 3 above and on the question itself, Almeida, *op. cit.*, p. 59: "The central and essential question of theology from the perspective of the poor is . . . the denial of God by economic rationality, by power, technology and accumulation."
59. Cf. E. Bethge, "Status confessionis — what's that?" (in German in *epd Documentation*, 46/82).

60. The statement of D. Conrad in his essay on "The Human Right to Basic Necessities" is interesting: "The right to life in the full sense of self-maintenance is the first and basic right" (in N. Wagner and H. C. Rieger, eds *Grundbedürfnisse als Gegenstand der Entwicklungspolitik. Interdisziplinäre Aspekte der Grundbedarfstheorie, Beitr.zur Südasienforschung*, Vol.70, Wiesbaden, 1982, p. 123).
61. Published on several occasions, most recently in *Kirche, Charisma und Macht*, Düsseldorf, 1985, pp. 195ff.

PART FOUR

Renewing the covenant

On our route so far, an attempt has been made to identify possible ways whereby even Christians, congregations and churches from the rich countries can become an ecumenical covenant people of God and a church confessing its faith in face of the life and death issue of the global economy. We analyzed first the ideological and institutional fetters which bind them. We then probed our own tradition for resources to help us along the way to liberation and justice. Next we examined the present situation of our church and the global economic system in the light of the criteria furnished us in the *Barmen Theological Declaration* of 1934. In this fourth and final part, we turn to the question of the practical implications of all this; to the question as to how our church in all its forms can in practice travel the way of liberation, confession and obedience in fellowship with the whole world Christian family.

After the tribes of Israel, liberated from Egypt, had received the divine law in the wilderness to guide them towards the promised land and, after many trials, had arrived at the borders of that land, their captain Joshua (Jesus!), according to the biblical narrative (Josh. 24), organizes a festival in which the divine covenant is renewed. In an exposition of this Old Testament passage, Heino Falcke identifies four elements in this renewal of the covenant (cf. *The Ecumenical Review*, July 1986).

1. Anamnesis: Joshua reminds the people of God's mighty acts of deliverance.
2. He proclaims the will of God to the people.
3. The abjuring of the false gods: here Joshua makes it clear to the people that hitherto they have not proved themselves capable of really repudiating the idols and serving Yahweh alone. He also conjures up for them the disastrous consequences should they repeat or continue their apostasy from God in the promised land.
4. All this takes the form of the Jewish festival of renewing the covenant; in other words, it has liturgical celebratory dimensions.

A fifth element can also be identified: namely, the personal commitment which necessarily accompanies the abjuration of the idols and the imperative claim of God's justice. Joshua confronts the people with an inescapable decision when he tells them: "But I and my family, we will worship the Lord" (24:15).

This fourth and final part of our book is structured in accordance with these elements:

Chapter 8 reminds us that the only possibility for Christians and churches in the rich countries to serve the Triune God, to confess God and to walk in God's ways, is in accepting the forgiveness of all their sins in the new covenant in Christ's blood and justification by God's grace. Not, of course, by "cheap grace"; only in such a way that their liberation is concretely demonstrated in sanctification, in a life based on God's will, in the abjuration of the false gods which claim their worship in the present global economic system. Chapter 9 provides an example of how Christian discipleship and action groups in Baden (and increasingly also in other parts of the Federal German Republic) are trying to say: "But I and my family, we will worship the Lord". They hope that they can, in this way, stimulate the conciliar credal process in all the other forms of the church, in the congregations and synods.

Above all, it is hoped that, by means of the conciliar process for justice, peace and the integrity of creation which the World Council of Churches is now promoting, these efforts will be coordinated with similar efforts in all the Christian churches. Chapter 10 reports on the position at present reached in this respect. Will the beginning of the final decade of this century be marked by a genuine universal council of all the Christian churches in the form of a festival of the renewing of the divine covenant? God expects nothing less from us "that the world may believe" (John 17:21).

8

Justification, liberation and sanctification in an increasingly rich country

Is it mandatory for the church today to become a "confessing" church in face of the present global economic system? Our enquiry so far suggests that this system notoriously falls short of its mandate to meet the basic needs of human beings (Bonhoeffer's "too little" as criterion for the *status confessionis*). This failure is aggravated and consolidated ideologically by acceptance of the "autonomy" of the economic processes, in plain contradiction to the doctrinal position of Barmen II. At the same time, Latin American biblical and theological insights make it clear that we are confronted here not simply with an ethical question but with a choice between God and an idol, between biblical revelation and an ideology (Barmen.I). Finally, our own examination of the same problem from the angle of the church, its doctrine and form (Barmen III, see Chapter 6 above), shows not only that pseudo-Christian arguments are advanced to buttress the present global economic system but also that economic interests have begun to extend their kingdom even within the church itself and that we have here the makings of a false and persecuting church (Bonhoeffer's "too much" as criterion for the *status confessionis*).

This is clearly not (or not yet) how most Christians and church leaders view the situation. We have hardly reached the stage yet when we feel these questions directly and personally. It is churches in the increasingly poor "two-thirds world", the ecumenical fellowship of churches, and a few individuals, who confront us with these questions. Clearly we are not to expect any sudden awakening in this situation. What is needed in our churches is a movement, a process, in which these questions are recognized, decided upon and answered. But a process of this kind is not at our command and cannot be expected to happen automatically.

We who in structural terms cannot count ourselves among the "poor" cannot simply adopt the approach of the Latin American churches. In our case, the confessional process has a "pastoral" dimension alongside the prophetic dimension which recognizes the "signs of the times" and discerns the spirits. We have to try to grasp, theologically and spiritually, how conversion can take place in our specific situation, how we are to become a "confessing church" and find practical answers in this specific situation.

The best way for us to start, it seems to me, is by reflecting on our own theological traditions. This will help us to recognize that what is at issue here is not something new and unfamiliar but our own essential evangelical church life and being. A Reformation church is rooted and grounded in the message of justification and sanctification, liberation and obedience. These, however, are also the basic theological footholds of Barmen III. What light do they throw on our specific situation?

The fact that the structures of responsibility in the global economic system are invisible and kept that way, and the fact that this system operates anonymously and is even placed "out of bounds" and treated as something "taboo", make our awareness of it a mixture of feelings of guilt and paralysis, as if we were confronted with a fate or a destiny. The "natural" human reaction or, in more precise theological terms, the reaction of the "old Adam", is to deny or repress our guilt. It's not *our* fault, we say. Not everything we've done is bad. We've done *some* good things and now must try harder, and so on and so on. Or else we even deny the ill-effects of the system as a whole, or blame them on circumstances of one sort or another. We invent euphemisms, i.e. cosmetic disguises, such as the "free market economy" to conceal the reality of a system created by violence and ruled by the dictates of the stronger. Or we devise rebarbative pictures of "communism" as the sole alternative, to be fought to the death as the "enemy". All this, moreover, to protect us from real changes.

In this situation, certain routes are blocked:

Firstly, no one can point the finger of scorn at anyone else and say: you're the guilty one! All of us are at the very least customers and users and, potentially at least, savers and borrowers, within this global system. If there are guilty associations in commerce and banking, we are all of us involved.

Secondly, if we still accept the theological notion of something in the nature of "original sin", we cannot in reason and conscience deny such guilty associations in respect of our European colonial history or evade a structural analysis of the present neo-colonial system.

Thirdly, isolated actions of supposedly "moral man" within this clearly "immoral society" cannot quieten the conscience since, patently, no such isolated action or even concerted counter-strategy has up to now proved sufficient to reverse the widening gap between rich and poor, with its increasingly deadly consequences for the latter.

What way remains?

1. Justification and liberation as change of place and allegiance

Thesis 1: If we are to recognize, decide upon and answer the challenge to our own church to become a confessing church, we must first tackle effectively the problems raised by this challenge not only theoretically but also pastorally, spiritually and practically. As a church and church members in a rich country in which we are all of us, willy nilly, accomplices in the exploitation of the poor, we must, prior to all new action, face up to the Pauline and Reformation question of guilt, judgment and justification and do so in no merely abstract way. The Christ who justifies us is the Christ who encounters and welcomes us in his hungry and thirsty brothers and sisters. The question of a confessing church, therefore, is inseparable from the question of our salvation. Not that our salvation is made to depend on a condition, but it takes place in a change of place which is also a change of allegiance. This change is effected by Jesus Christ himself. As the one who voluntarily accepted poverty and suffered death on the cross, Christ places us on the side of the poor and liberates us for the conflict with the godless powers which are destructive of the life of human beings and of the earth. Here, as real sinners under divine judgment (*peccatores in re*), we are saved in hope (*iusti in spe*). Our reading of the Bible, our prayers and our eucharistic celebration are also radically changed, since here too Jesus Christ is no longer buried in abstraction but encounters us in the concrete context of history.

We now find ourselves in the same position as that in which Paul and Luther put their theological questions: that of hopeless bondage to the laws of sin and death — "hopeless" as far as our own human capacities are concerned. There is one difference, of course. Unlike Paul and Luther, none of us has yet striven to do the will of God to the point of supreme sacrifice. It is with some hesitation, therefore, that I focus here on the message of justification as the key to our problem. For how prone we are to accept this message in our national church life as if it were simply a tranquillizer of no real consequence, as if justification had no real sequel in newness of life on pain of spiritual death. But I know of no other way to life than this for us rich: the knowledge of faith that, in his life-giving love in Jesus Christ, God accepts us, entangled and imprisoned as we are in personal and structural sin and idolatry, delivers us from the vain attempt to justify ourselves and liberates us in a radical conversion so that we become free to analyze structures courageously, free to unmask and resist an idolatrous ideology and to work and struggle for justice. Only as our very being as Christians and as church is transformed by the Spirit of God are our individual and corporate acts set free. This, perhaps, is the very core of the biblical message of redemption (liberation) for rich and powerful sinners, for us who trim our sails to the winds of power.

To be sure, God connects this acceptance, this gift of freedom and justice, not to some condition or other but to a definite place, or rather to a change of place. The test of whether we are misusing the message of justification as cheap grace, as a tranquillizer, or really accepting God's justice as a power creating newness of life,[1] is this: *where* do we expect, *where* are we ready for, the encounter with Jesus Christ?

In his address on the nature of the church, Dietrich Bonhoeffer gave a classic formulation of this insight. The tradition of a national or state church in Protestantism tempts the church to settle down in the "privileged places". It fails to ask the question: who and where is Jesus Christ, the crucified, for us today?[2]

The New Testament passage which lights up our situation in this respect is Matthew 25:31–46. Jesus Christ, who gives himself unsparingly for us all and so rescues and saves us, comes to us again and again in the persons of the hungry, the thirsty, the strangers and homeless, the naked, the sick, and the (political) prisoners. What is the theological significance of this?

It is very tempting to read this passage as if it were primarily concerned with "charitable" works in the restrictive sense. Is it mere chance, however, that our Lord should have listed here precisely those items which in economic terms are described as "basic human needs": food, clothing, shelter, health? He adds to these the basic political need: for human dignity and integrity —

indicated negatively by the evangelist in terms of oppression by imprisonment. (These are precisely the basic human needs whose satisfaction the USA Catholic bishops put at the head of their list of criteria.) What Jesus is saying here, therefore, is no more and no less than that *our very salvation itself, and not just our ethical status, is decided by our behaviour in respect of the basic needs of our fellow human beings.*

Our apparent helplessness in face of the problem here consists in our entanglement in a system which, *in principle*, assigns priority to the sophisticated "preferences" of the rich over the basic needs of the poor. In its positive lesson, the story of Zacchaeus in Luke 19:1–10 is saying precisely the same thing: when the rich tax-official welcomes into his home the Jesus who voluntarily became poor and goes on to draw the inescapable economic conclusions from this encounter, he and his household experience salvation. Jesus, presumably, would have much the same to say about *our* behaviour in respect of the living conditions of the poor of our earth today.

How is this related to the question as to whether the present global economic system and its pseudo-Christian justification confronts us as Christians and churches with a specific case of confession and therefore calls for an unambiguously confessing church? Just as Bonhoeffer half a century or so ago boldly declared, to the scandal of many in his day, that "anyone who wittingly separates himself from the Confessing Church cuts himself off from salvation",[3] so today the question must be: Does anyone who wittingly separates himself from the church in solidarity with the poor thereby cut himself off from salvation? In view of the Pauline, Lutheran and Reformation doctrine of justification, the question could be formulated still more sharply: Do we not have to affirm that the crucified Jesus Christ by whom alone we are justified is the Jesus Christ in the poor, i.e. in those whose basic needs are automatically less and less satisfied by the present global economic system? The only legitimate form of the *theologia crucis* today, therefore, would be a *theologia paupertatis*, a theology of the poverty of Christ.[4]

Then, however, the Jesus Christ who meets and accepts us in the poor is also really and truly the saving Jesus Christ, the Jesus Christ who makes us joyful because he delivers us from all fear of renunciation and gives us fellowship and all the signs of the kingdom of God. When he comes to us in the persons of the poor, he brings us the good news that we have been accepted as the sinners we are and can let ourselves be transformed accordingly.

While in our sinfulness we remain under God's judgment and are saved only in hope (*simul iustus et peccator*, and *peccator in re — iustus in spe*, as Luther put it). In virtue of Christ and for his sake, however, we really *are* accepted and the Holy Spirit can begin the struggle for sanctification in us and continues this struggle until the hoped-for consummation.

A fundamental discovery in the ecumenical training process of recent years has been that it is the poor who evangelize us and not we who evangelize the poor. This turns our traditional European view of mission upside down. Having to a dangerous degree distanced ourselves from Jesus Christ by combining our missionary work for the most part with colonial domination and political and economic power-politics, he comes to us once again in the persons of those we helped to oppress and exploit! We are not the benefactors with knowledge to impart but the learners and the beneficiaries. Anyone who has made even just a halting effort to establish close contact with the poor and to share in their struggle can confirm how liberating an experience this can be, delivering us from despair and pride, from sadness and hopelessness. There is no way for us who are rich and powerful, as most of us in the "North" are in one way or another, to be accepted and changed by Jesus Christ which does not include our being accepted and changed by the poor in our midst and the poor in the two-thirds world. This transforms our reading of the Bible, our prayers and, above all, our eucharistic celebrations. Everywhere we rediscover Jesus Christ, for he ceases to be an abstraction and comes to meet us in the actual struggles of history.

This makes it all the more dangerous for us to persist in our European infatuation with power and wealth and to shut our eyes to this reversal of the missionary movement. Particularly disturbing is that leaders of the pietist movement in Federal Germany and elsewhere, claiming to speak for the evangelical majority, should of all people be the ones to reject self-criticism (repentance) and, on the contrary, to persist in the old European direction of mission, failing to notice, above all, how eagerly interested economic and political groups welcome this "unpolitical" Christianity (as they call it) and support it financially as a counterblast to the theology of the Christ who chose poverty and the cross. These pietists should surely be, on the contrary, the ones to understand something of what total conversion means! Happily, there are also pietists who do understand this again, both on the international scene (the Lausanne movement) and also, in a rudimentary way, even in the Federal Republic of Germany.[5]

There is another aspect, however, to this change of place, or rather, this change of place includes a change of allegiance. Finding acceptance with the God who sides with the poor means encountering the God who comes to the rescue of the poor in their (and his) struggle against the oppressive powers. The God who justifies us is the God of justice and mercy, the God of life and not of death, the God of deliverance from and not of helpless bondage to the forces bringing injustice and death. We inevitably come into conflict, therefore, with every openly or secretly idolatrous and therefore unjust power. As individual Christians, congregations and churches, therefore, we must pose and answer, as a matter of urgency, the question whether our global economic system is not just such a power, one which enslaves us all as individuals and as a national church because we are loth to surrender the privileged places.

For the church of the poor in Latin America, the decisions are obvious, since at its place in the periphery it has first-hand experience of the impact of the existing distribution of power whereas we live in one of the centres of power. How can we cut loose from it and really change our place? The first priority, before action of any kind, is for us to recognize this as the central question both theologically and spiritually. From the Bible and the traditional creeds and confessions we must gain confidence for our confession of the faith today. In this way we are equipped for conflict and prepared to face even persecution for the sake of God's love for his human family and the whole of creation.

What will be the concrete form of this confession of the faith today?

2. Sanctification in the global economic context

Thesis 2: This gift of new life necessarily issues in progress in the obedience of faith (*sanctification*) in the form of participation in the church's struggle to practise true discipleship and of cooperation with all who strive to ensure that the basic needs of all human beings are met. (This last partner in cooperation may be seen as a fifth social form of the one people of God.)

In the light of detailed studies of the problems of the global economy, the following steps emerge as possibilities for the church:

— exerting influence in responsible quarters;
— refusing to condone blatant injustices;

— public criticism;
— withdrawal of moral support from irresponsible institutions and value systems;
— cooperation in the development of countervailing power.

The question of becoming a confessing church in face of the global economy has in fact been raised. Our own church must now enter a process in which decisions are required of it. Only as justification, liberation and sanctification are taken seriously and become effective within our church will it be ready and equipped to enter this process.

In the light of Barmen III, i.e. the question of the form of the church's message, order and action as church, the recognition that we encounter the justifying and liberating God in the persons of the poor already carries with it many concrete implications. Like Zacchaeus, we can welcome the poor, the refugees for example, into our homes. We can stand alongside the victims of structural unemployment and listen attentively to what Jesus is saying to us in and through them. We can invite the poor of the two-thirds world to visit us. We can visit them.

The signs of joy and welcome and new fellowship with Jesus which this initiative brings with it enable us to confess our sins and to pray God to change and renew us. We can intercede for the poor in our prayers.

Like Zacchaeus, we can begin to shed some part and an increasing part of what we have acquired unjustly: as individuals, families and communities, by practising a simple life-style; as Christian groups and communities, by testing out new forms of community life which outlaw exploitation; as institutional churches, by eliminating differential salaries and fringe benefits and experimenting with alternative economies. Jesus also liberates us increasingly perhaps from the fear which makes us pay more attention to the departure of wealthy contributors to church funds than to what he himself is requiring of us as his disciples.[6]

All this and much more besides will enable Christians, congregations and churches in the power of the Holy Spirit to make something of the love of Christ visible in themselves. Instead of denying God by their way of life, they will help to glorify God (cf. Matt. 5:16). In the case of the institutional and liberation church model, however, we have to go a step further. The question here is how, as Christians, congregations, groups and churches, we can directly influence the economic institutions and processes in the direction of love to God and the neighbour. The same question arises for the "peace church" model, only here the influence will be exercised "indirectly" rather than "directly".

If the attribution of "autonomy" to the economy must be rejected in terms of Barmen II as a heresy, it becomes all the more urgent to insist, as the basis of all future action, that the church at every level should thoroughly investigate the economic questions, especially in respect of the global economic system, its mechanisms and possible alternatives. It is downright amazing that people should go on repeating that the church has insufficient expertise in this area to voice any opinion while at the same time making no effort to repair this omission and to provide the church with the necessary expertise. To reject or to fail to support an effort on the part of the church to understand economic matters is to infringe Barmen II by default since it amounts to a *de facto* abandonment of the economy to an autonomy exempted from any scrutiny, in the light of Jesus Christ and the God revealed in him, in respect of love to God and the neighbour.

This interest in economic affairs and the efforts to understand it being presupposed, there would seem to be *five ways* whereby the church can and should learn to shoulder its responsibility for the divine mandate to the economy, as part of a conciliar process embracing all levels of the church's life:

a) exerting the maximum influence in responsible quarters;
b) refusing its cooperation in flagrant cases of injustice;
c) public criticism;
d) withdrawing its legitimation from irresponsible institutions and value systems, as part of its renunciation of false gods;
e) helping to establish a countervailing power by cooperation with the fifth social form of the church as the people of God.

We look more closely at these five ways:

a) The examples already given of specific cases of flagrant injustice as well as the arguments advanced by the USA Catholic bishops show that the church in every case shares the responsibility of *speaking to those responsible and of helping the victims*, with the object of assisting to rectify specific injustices. The church cannot wait until radical changes have been effected and simply leave the suffering of flesh and blood human beings as none of its concern. In other words, when the church speaks to those responsible for individual cases of flagrant injustice, this does not exempt it from examining the more fundamental questions of the economic system as such and the changes required in it.

b) When the directors of a firm or bank cling stubbornly to a specific course of injustice and oppression, the churches must also withdraw their cooperation from these institutions and refuse to support them. A classic example of this in recent years has been that of firms and banks buttressing the apartheid system by fresh loans and investments, a situation which was actually declared by the churches of the world to be a case of confession. This refusal to cooperate with such institutions is the oldest form of Christian conduct towards structures which are incompatible with the "laws of faith and love".[7] All churches which include the Augsburg Confession among their doctrinal standards are in fact obliged to this course of action by Article 16 of that Confession. To that extent, it is no longer necessary to argue this point. But churches in Federal Germany and the Swiss Confederation owe us some explanation of why, on this point, they have isolated themselves from the confessional and ecumenical community.

Far more difficult is the question of such a refusal in respect of the global economic system as such. Living as he did in an age which still kept within the medieval tradition with its prohibition of usury, Martin Luther could still roundly reject any participation in the charging of interest and, along with this, any cooperation with the multi-national trading associations. Yet it was possible for him to do so only because, at the time, the basic needs of human beings, and so also those of Christians employed in the church, could be met by a self-supporting economy within the dual-structured total economy. Today, however, the money economy enjoys almost complete power and it is only very slowly that approaches to restore a dual structure, giving the church, too, more freedom once again vis-à-vis the economic power, are being developed.

c) Alongside the refusal of cooperation, there is urgent need to intensify *public criticism* in those cases where flagrant injustice is persisted in. Luther called this: "standing up for what is right" in face of the abuse of power, even if the church itself must suffer injustice and be charged with "rebellion" in consequence.[8] Take, for example, the UNO resolution banning the export to South Africa of articles which could have military uses, and the irresponsibly feeble fashion in which this resolution was handled by the economic ministry of the Federal German government. Here, the churches were required to back their words against apartheid by deeds, since, because of massive economic interests in West Germany, hardly anyone else uttered the slightest protest. Public criticism is by no means without its effects on industrial firms and banks. Industry depends on credit, which in the last analysis means confidence.[9] To give an example: only the announcement that the churches would call for a public boycott of Coca Cola succeeded in putting an end, a few years ago, to the murder of trade unionists in a daughter company in Guatemala. Public criticism as a way open to the churches to act leads on to:

d) The *withdrawal of legitimation* from irresponsible institutions and value systems, as part of the church's renunciation of false gods. Not only Jesus of Nazareth and the "peace churches" with their direct approach to the discipleship of Christ, but even the tradition of the Constantinian churches as well as that of the liberation churches, of course, have always been interested not only in actions in and by institutions but also in the legitimacy of institutions as such.[10] The Augsburg Confession provides the following criterion for institutions: "that everyone manifest Christian love and genuine good works" in them (Art. 16). When this is not the case — when the result of applying this criterion is negative — we must "obey God rather than men" (Acts 5:29).

Here, as I see it, is the most urgent and mandatory task of the churches in the years ahead as far as the global economy is concerned. They must test the institutions against scripture and the confession of faith. The churches can no longer with a good conscience close their eyes to the fact that, *by the very nature of the global system itself*, the gap between poor and rich is widening with each year that passes and with increasingly fatal consequences. To take comfort from the argument that economic power is only abused in isolated if deplorable cases is simply burying one's head in the sand — not to speak of shutting one's ears to the God who speaks to us in the distress and need of our neighbour. What is needed here is a scientific theological analysis of the system (in the light of scripture and reason, as Luther insisted). If the result of this analysis is negative, the church must withdraw its legitimation of the system and with the global Christian family look and work for alternatives. The rigorous analysis of secular institutions in the light of the revealed will of God as attested in scripture and reflected in the creeds and confessions is in principle the plain task of the church. Here, too, it has the maximum potential for influencing the world in the direction of the will of God, and helping to compass the downfall of idolatrous totalitarianisms. While the effects of this withdrawal of legitimation are long-term rather than short-term, they are inexorable. Even the increasingly frequent use of violence cannot neutralize them, as is demonstrated by the accelerating disintegration of the *apartheid* system despite all government brutality.

e) In Jesus' vision of the judgment of the world in Matthew 25:37ff. the "righteous" say: "Lord, when was it we saw you hungry and fed you, or thirsty and gave you drink, a stranger and took you home with us, or naked and clothed you? When did we see you ill or in prison and come to visit you?" The king will answer, says Jesus: "I tell you this: anything you did for one of my brothers here, however humble, you did for me." People who are concerned for the basic needs of human beings are often ignorant of the fact that they have encountered the Jesus Christ who is coming again. We must resist the temptation, therefore, to "incorporate" them into the church, as if they belonged to it or were a "latent" church. God's people is obviously broader than the church. Conversely, many of us who now say "Lord, Lord" will not see the kingdom of God (Matt. 7:21). It is not our business to judge which people will in the end be found in the one group or the other. What is clear, however, is that alongside the four forms of the church in which there is an explicit confession of Jesus Christ as Lord, God has among people of all religions and ideologies a *fifth form of God's people*, with whom God works for the doing of the divine will of love.

The practical consequence of this for the church is this: just as Bonhoeffer worked with secular resistance groups, so too, vis-à-vis the global economic system and all economic questions, the church in all its manifest forms must cooperate with individuals and groups of every faith or none who are concerned for the basic needs of their fellow human beings and for the liberation of the earth from the power of its present economic system.

Here, too, is where the question properly arises of the church's cooperation in the creation of a *countervailing power* which resists the abuse of power. At this point, the practice of the "peace churches" *can* diverge from post-Constantinian approaches. What is involved here is more than even the refusal of cooperation and the creation of an alternative community. In the nineteenth century, the churches in Europe failed to stand by the exploited workers. The question today is whether they are not making the same mistake in relation to the exploited poor of the two-thirds world. The ecumenical fellowship of churches has unambiguously taken sides here and declared its solidarity with the poor and their organizations. It is through them that God will one day accomplish the transformation, for never in history have the powerful voluntarily relinquished their power.

Only in the measure that the churches participate in this struggle have they any possibility of influencing the course of things so that, as the distribution of power is changed, new and genuinely human structures emerge in a new system, instead of merely a continuation of the old system under new management. With this in view, it is vital that the churches should play their part in the theoretical and practical development of *alternative economic models* for the future. There are more such alternative models than we Christians in the rich churches have realized so far — for the simple reason that in countries which are growing richer under the existing global system there is a mental block against infringing the taboo of the present market system. The fact that "really existing socialism" is entangled in similar problems to those of the west is no reason whatever for allowing ourselves to become the hostages of the usual anti-communist fix. All the nations of the world must unite in the quest for alternatives for life, the life of the human family and of the whole earth. To this end, we must "bring them all to the test and then keep what is good in them" (1 Thess. 5:21).

What has been offered here are, of course, no more than initial soundings which require further study and development. The church in all its forms is called to engage in this effort. The pioneers here have been a few discipleship groups and individual Christians who have tried to identify the questions put to the church of Jesus Christ by the global economic system today. They have created research and advice agencies, such as the New York "Center for Corporate Responsibility" (in economic matters) or the Baden "Christians for Work and Justice Worldwide" in West Germany,[11] to enable them to proceed in a responsible way in this field. Even the church diaconal agencies and services were initially voluntary creations before the churches discovered their own mandate and competence in this field.

As far as the global economy is concerned, time is running out, of course. Human beings are dying in their millions and, as long as the "mass murder" of our time is accepted in silence or paid mere lip service, the reality of the church as church is increasingly obscured. In Latin America, many church hierarchies have recognized the challenge and responded to the call. The hungry, the oppressed and the dying are right on their own doorstep. Will a miracle happen, to open our eyes too, even if we can still choose to avert our gaze? If this is to happen at all, it can only be by personal encounter and concrete steps. These alone carry conviction.

In all the social forms of the church, the conciliar process has already begun and advances made towards recognizing, accepting and solving the question whether and in what way the global economic system constitutes a confessional challenge. In its theological substance, as well as in its pastoral relevance, this question is identical with that of our own justification, liberation and sanctification. At the point we have reached in time, no one is excluded from the fellowship of the church which wrestles with this question — except those who by refusing to ask the question at all, exclude themselves.

NOTES

1. On the view of God's justice as the power which sets believers free from the tyranny of the powers of sin and death and thereby transposes them into a new realm of justice and life, see the contributions of E. Käsemann and P. Stuhlmacher on this theme.
2. See above, Chapter 2.
3. *GS* II, p. 238.
4. Even without the assistance of the theological statements of Matthew and Paul, it could be demonstrated from the Pauline theology alone how the doctrine of justification, i.e. the proclamation of the crucified Christ, is always used to support the weak against the strong (on behalf of the weaker Jewish Christians, in Romans 9–11; on behalf of the weak in the community, Romans 14f.; on behalf of the deprived classes in Corinth, etc.).
5. Cf. especially R. Padilla, *Zukunftsperspektiven. Evangelikale nehmen Stellung*, Brockhaus TB 253, Wuppertal, 1977; R. Sider, *Rich Christians in an Age of Hunger*, Intervarsity Christian Fellowship of the USA, 1977; J. Wallis, *Waging Peace. Handbook for the Struggle to Abolish Nuclear Weapons*, Harper & Row, 1983; idem., *New Radical: Autobiography*, Lion Publishing, 1983.
6. A statistic given by the Papal Catholic University of Rio de Janeiro, quoted by L. Boff in his latest controversial book (*op. cit.* is helpful here: "In 1963, 60% of the students described themselves as atheists. Among the main reasons given: the church sides with the establishment which is unjust and which acts against the poor people. According to data collected in 1978, in contrast, 75% of the students described themselves as Christians. This time, the main reason given was that between Medellin (1968) and Puebla (then in preparation for 1979) the church had become the voice of the voiceless and identified itself with the poor and marginalized . . . Thus, by its disinterested championship of the poorest people the church regained its credibility."
7. Cf. U. Duchrow and M. Stöhr (eds), "Boykott als legitime christliche Aktion?", in *EMW Information*, No. 34, 1982.
8. See above, Chapter 1.
9. Cf. Charles Elliott, *The Patterns of Poverty in the Third World: a Study of Social and Economic Stratification*, New York, 1975, Chapter 1.

10. Cf. Duchrow, *Christenheit und Weltverantwortung*, pp. 523ff.
11. Cf. Chaper 9 below.

9

Experience of the Spirit in the Ecumenical Network in Baden

In Galilee, on the margins of Palestine, itself a marginal area in the Roman Empire, God encountered men and women in Jesus of Nazareth. Fishermen abandoned their nets to become themselves a net, to continue growing from person to person, from community to community, until it covered the whole earth. Paul then adds the image of the body, body of Christ, the new Adam, the new humanity, the new creation. The letters to the Colossians and the Ephesians show how, in this way, God delivers the entire cosmos, the whole world from the clutches of the powers of sin and death.

A net — a body — these are so slight, so vulnerable, so slender when set against the divisive and brutalizing power of sin within us and around us! Yet surely indestructible because held and fashioned by the Spirit of God who calls into being what is not and creates life from death.

Not surprisingly, therefore, it has been in the marginal areas, bearing the clear mark of death and the consequences of sin, that the experience of the renewal of the church and humanity has begun within the ecumenical movement throughout the whole inhabited earth. Arising from the division, oppression and suffering in the "missionary lands", as they were called, meaning in fact the conquered and exploited colonial countries such as Palestine itself once was, the dynamic towards the ecumenical movement emerged at the beginning of our twentieth century. In the communities of the poor, not only the voice of the dumb but

---

● Originally published in Danish in H. R. Iversen and others, *Spiritualitet. Festskrift til Anna Marie Aagaard*, 14 January 1985, pp. 233–240.

also the voice of God and the power of His Spirit became audible and evident. The base communities of Latin America and the networks they have created are typical also of many similar experiences in Asia and Africa. The characteristics of this renewal are intensive Bible study, prayer and eucharistic celebration, combined with active involvement in and commitment to the struggle for justice and human dignity.

The longing for renewal gripped even the established churches in the imperial centres of power. There was an attempt to update theology and to achieve reforms in the church. For the most part, however, this effort remained academic and evasive. The sinful exploitation of the workers in the industrial revolution in the last century and the still more sinful uninhibited exploitation of raw materials and human beings in Asia, Africa and Latin America down to this very day, were and are suppressed and forgotten. People wanted no truck with the dry and thirsty land in which the Spirit of God awakens us to love and life. So we became a dry and thirsty land without the Spirit of God. The rare exceptions emerged in situations in which the methods employed as a matter of course in the case of conquered peoples were also applied to sections of the population of the "centre" countries. The efforts towards a confessing church in Nazi Germany or the communities of Christian solidarity in the civil rights struggle in the USA may be cited as examples. But even among those who display solidarity, is there a single one who is not himself or herself inextricably entangled in the structures of exploitation and oppression?

The main question in this situation is how can Christians and churches, prisoners as they are in face of the forces opposed to the Spirit of God, come within range of the power of the Spirit of God, i.e. be the church of Jesus Christ. Here it is not enough just to analyze and deplore the situation; indeed, by itself, this is counter-productive. The law kills; it drives us deeper into the sin of self-imprisonment, self-justification, or fatalism. What is really needed, on the contrary, are visible and tangible experiences of the Spirit of Christ in various forms of new community and solidarity which reflect the decision: "As for me and my family, we will serve the Lord!"

The chief signs of hope are the newly emerging communities in the monastic tradition, since these are the most radical in their repudiation of the acquisitive spirit. Such monastic communities, never extinguished in the Catholic and Orthodox traditions, also became a source of renewal in the Protestant tradition after the

Second World War. The community of the Taizé brothers and that of the Grandchamp sisters became frequently visited beacons of hope for those seeking training in meditation, Bible study, eucharistic celebration and concrete discipleship in a European context. The family communities which have come into existence in the USA and in Europe represent a sort of "secular order" alongside Taizé and Grandchamp.[1]

Within this form of the church ("discipleship groups") I would also include those associations which, while not cohabiting as monastic communities, nevertheless embody certain of the characteristics of the latter. While not completely renouncing possessions, they share what they have; while not abandoning home and family, they open these to others; while not surrendering their own specific location, they subject their career to the call of the Spirit. These distinguishing marks, whose underlying unity derives from the determination to be no longer dependent on the powers of this world, are rooted in contemplation, in the life which is received over and over again from the Spirit of God, and are directed towards voluntary participation in God's struggle for the spread of his kingdom of love in this world. In relation to the local Christian congregation and the organized institutional church, these front-runners of the radical discipleship groups at their outposts within the secular world perform a sort of bridge function. Supported by monastic forms of Christian community whose aim is to overcome the world, they try to find in their secular existence those forms of discipleship which can also be an invitation to every Christian and every congregation.[2]

With its various initiatives, the Ecumenical Centre in Aarhus is one of the pioneering efforts in this direction within the European region. Anna Marie Aagaard has not only made it well-known in the ecumenical movement but also shown that the theological locus in which these efforts are rooted is the experience of the Holy Spirit.[3] Stimulated by this experiment and by theological reflections both in Europe and the USA, an attempt was also made in Baden in the south-west of the Federal German Republic to discover and encourage discipleship groups and to link them up with one another as well as with local congregations and their members.

Planted by the water-brooks

It is important for us to be able to point to specific locations: *Taizé, Grandchamp, Aarhus, Washington, Baden . . . !* Dietrich Bonhoeffer identified the church's rootlessness as the cause of its

Christlessness. In Christ, God revealed himself at a specific place and it is Christ's will today to reveal himself at a specific place.[4] The Ecumenical Network in Baden began with the acceptance of this axiom.

Too many attempts to achieve more clearly Christian ways of living and to make progress in the obedience of faith had already petered out or failed completely. Either they were too vague and "up in the air" or else were beamed too exclusively at the helpless individual Christian. For example, there had been the "Plea for an Ecumenical Future", whereby a few ecumenical enthusiasts sought to persuade the Evangelical Church in Germany to abandon its timorous rejection of genuine ecumenical fellowship. This level and even that of the Catholic episcopal conferences would probably be the last to discover the way to committed discipleship for ordinary Christians. A specific locality, on the contrary, with its local congregations, or a regional church or diocese, are partners who must respond to the call to committed ecclesial existence and who, at the same time, include the personal element in a manageable form which facilitates spiritual communion and renewal.

Another vital factor for the genesis of the Ecumenical Network was the growing realization in the ecumenical movement that we are living in a time, comparable to that of Nazism in Germany and Europe, in which we are being challenged to become a confessing church in all the social forms of the church's life.[5] Apartheid, the existing global economic system and its devastating consequences, weapons of mass destruction, the pollution and destruction of the environment — which are all being justified in the supposed "defence" of the "Christian West" even if condemned by the churches, at any rate verbally — these constitute the crushing global context of the challenge to us to become a confessing church. Memories were recalled of the time when the "fraternals" had been stepping stones on the way to the Confessing Church in Germany. Our first idea was to call the network the "Confessing Discipleship in Baden".

There were, in fact, several stages in the emergence of the network. From autumn 1981 to summer 1982, a dozen or so fellow-Christians from various groups concerned to practise a confessing discipleship in the contexts of justice, peace and the integrity of creation, met together regularly. The Protestants among them already had a head start in virtue of the decision of their provincial synod in the spring of 1981 to promote action towards "church unity in the East-West and North-South divides".

The synod had rejected apartheid on credal grounds and confessed the sin of our own complicity in racism and oppression.

The small group met for discussion and worship. Its most important decision was not to issue and publicize an open invitation to join "an ecumenical network in Baden for justice, peace and the integrity of creation" but rather to achieve this goal by establishing and extending direct personal and group contacts. For use in personal invitations it produced a short explanatory "Basis" and drew up a list of groups and individuals to be approached.

At the end of August 1982, a meeting was held of all those who had been approached in this way. Another important decision was taken at this meeting. The "network" had been conceived of by some as an umbrella organization to coordinate the actions of all groups working for peace, for the third world, and for the defence of the environment. This was not how most of those present envisaged the network's rôle. Not that the idea of such an umbrella organization was in itself mistaken but it was recognized clearly that, in the coming struggles for peace, justice and the integrity of creation, Christians had to be quite clear that, for them, the basis of this struggle was the Christian faith and the Christian community. It was essential that the church itself should emerge more publicly as a partner in the discussion. A prerequisite for critical yet constructive cooperation by the church in evidently desired coalitions with other partners in the achievement of political objectives was a clearly understood identity.

Special attention was paid to the question of the ways in which fellow-Christians could relate to the Ecumenical Network when their commitment to peace, justice and the integrity of creation finds its channels not in overtly Christian groups but in secular associations. Such associations often include Christians who have left a church congregation, having become so marginalized in the congregation or even excluded from it altogether that they have migrated to the no-man's-land of politics. The decision taken here was to welcome individuals and groups which can be strengthened and guided in the network and thus be helped to contribute something new to their secular groups.

This decision did, however, lead to a certain division. Some found this approach too "pious". The rest who decided to continue in this direction found the spontaneous worship celebrations with their rich ecumenical input an unexpected source of joy and refreshment to reinforce their commitment.

It was no accident, therefore, that attention was then focused in the "1983 Pentecost Rally" as the growing Network's next goal. Our hope was that the Network might even become part of a renewal movement and we realized that only the Spirit of God could accomplish this miracle. Inseparable from this hope was also the hope that the Network might become really ecumenical in the sense of interconfessional. In our preparatory meetings for the Rally, we travelled from place to place in Baden seeking to establish as many personal contacts as possible so as to increase and nurture mutual confidence.

At Pentecost 1983, about two hundred people assembled in Kehl, near Strasburg. The programme itself was excellent: a Network "workshop" for mutual introductions, training in non-violence for peace work, discussions on the problems of faith and discipleship in personal, congregational and church life, and, last but not least, splendid acts of worship and eucharistic celebrations. The most important thing, however, was the fact that the Network became a reality, existed, beyond all our hopes. The net held firm and was alive with fish! It was a pentecostal miracle! When we say that something "worked" we mean that its success could not be guaranteed in advance but that, for all the hard work put into it, its success in the end was a gracious undeserved gift. The word mostly on people's lips at the end of these three days together was the word "encouraging" ("I've never before experienced anything so encouraging!" was one testimony.) Others besides Paul Tillich have discovered that "courage" is a gift of faith, indeed, is the very Spirit of God. The Spirit's gifts of joy, peace, justice, were present symbolically in this courage. It was in the strength of this experience that the Network groups in the Heidelberg area held a crowded church service in the Holy Spirit Church, a service of encouragement, on the evening after the German parliament's decision to station new USA medium range rockets in the Federal Republic. After that government decision, many people in the Federal Republic lapsed back into a certain fatalism. Undeterred, the Network groups went on praying and working.

The most important fresh impetus between the Network's annual meetings in 1983 and 1984 was the Sixth Assembly of the World Council of Churches in Vancouver. The Assembly's invitation to all churches, congregations, and networks of Christian groups to join in a "covenant for justice, peace and the integrity of creation"[6] became a focal point for all meetings in this period and stimulated the work of the individual groups in the network.

Specifically, we made an effort to grasp the biblical background to the Vancouver invitation. What is the significance of God's covenant with humankind and with creation? What is the meaning of the *new* covenant? What situations and conditions constitute specific cases of confession for the church of Jesus Christ today? What is the "conciliar process"? These and similar questions were examined not only in the light of the different Christian traditions but also in discussions with the regional rabbi in Baden.

When it came to considering practical steps, we looked for the nodal points where the questions of justice and peace interlock. A wider initiative developed in the "network" known as "Christians for Work and Justice Worldwide". Following preliminary soundings in September 1984, it launched a self-supporting research and advice unit with the purpose of investigating independently the economic links between multinational firms in our own area and countries in which our churches have partner churches. The idea was to make our common calling as God's covenant people so much a living reality in relationships with congregations and groups in those other countries that anonymous economic relationships could be replaced by a network consisting of live and sentient human beings. Another initiative organized a "peace house" devoted to training in forms of non-violent action. Catholics, Protestants from the regional state church, Baptists, Mennonites and Quakers are now living, celebrating and working in harmony in the Baden Ecumenical Network.

The annual meeting of the Network in 1984 was held — this time between Easter and Pentecost — in the *Arche* ecumenical community centre in Neckargemünd. Its theme was "Under the Rainbow — God's Covenant People Celebrates". Many ecumenical guests were present, including to our great joy a group from the ecumenical centre in Aarhus. Sisters from Grandchamp led the daily devotions. Three main acts of worship were planned as parts of a covenant renewal festival: recall of baptism — eucharistic liturgy of Lima — mission (based on liturgical material from Vancouver). The Network "workshop", working groups, and planning discussions were thus anchored firmly within the celebration of the whole range of God's gifts. One participant wrote on a slip of paper in the closing act of worship: "The eucharist yesterday was a foretaste of the great supper of the Lord."

His life for his friends

We were at first surprised when, in the subsequent preparations for the annual Network meeting, someone voiced the following view: "In the services of worship especially, I was unable to come to terms with my guilt. In recent years, we have experienced, to some extent at least, a process of renewal, our lives have been changed, we have practised intercession, we have worked for solidarity with the poor, we have tried to resist the insanity of the arms race. Many people have learned to think differently — to some extent with our help. Yet despite all this, are we not still tragically carried along in the same mistaken direction? Am I not forced to recognize more and more clearly, despite my own commitment, how deeply and inescapably I myself am implicated in injustice, preparations for war, and violence?"

As a result of this questioning, we were led by the Spirit into a new phase of the Ecumenical Network. Week by week, month by month, year by year, we have indeed recognized sufficient resistance in ourselves and around us not to succumb to the dangers of fanaticism. To some extent we have even taken conscious pleasure in the fact that, at long last, the pseudo-Protestant habit of finding fault with the sinful world was no longer on the agenda and indeed that we were beginning to experience some of the promised New Testament signs of the Spirit. We also regarded this as in some sense the hallmark of our network approach, that in it we were more concerned with working hard at our own conversion than with analyzing the guilt of others. Yet the question of an ever deepening awareness of our own guilt even in our commitment, even in our discipleship, led us in a new direction taking us we know not yet whither.[7]

An important task ahead of us, therefore, will be to reformulate clearly the significance of the fact that the Spirit is the gift of justification by faith and, as such, the power of sanctification. The Ecumenical Network and its component groups will also have to learn to live in fellowship as accomplices of structural guilt, and in the power of forgiveness. In other words, how are discipleship groups to demonstrate by their life that it is the gospel with its invitation to joy which empowers us to face up to our guilt instead of fleeing from it, because in Christ we ourselves are accepted as the sinners we undoubtedly are? Only because he, the Messiah, God's anointed Saviour, laid down his life for his friends, are we enabled to envisage clearly our own calling to share *our* life with God's friends, his creatures — even if the cost of our doing so is life itself.

Postscript: the Ecumenical Network from a Brazilian perspective[8]

In September and October of 1985, I was privileged to attend a course in São Paulo organized by the Ecumenical Centre for Ministries of Popular Evangelization and Education (CESEP), along with fifty representatives of base communities from all over Latin and Central America. Many of the positions presented in this book received confirmation, in particular, the analysis of the structures of injustice, of which Brazil is, alas, a classic illustration at the international level. But Brazil also provides an encouraging example of how a church can become, at all its levels and in all its forms, a church obedient to Christ and confessing him both by word and deed, i.e. the salt of the earth. Not without conflicts and trials, indeed, yet nevertheless reflecting fragmentarily the gifts of the kingdom of God. What lessons can we learn from the experience of Brazil for our own situation? Three in particular, I believe:

1. The base communities are not simply discipleship groups but a new form of the local congregation in the closest possible cooperation with the discipleship groups (especially with micro-communities of the monastic orders). Together with the priest, the parishes (at their best) foster this intensive local fellowship between Christians, which has an air of primitive Christianity about it, and the same is true also of the dioceses. From the district level to the national level, it is customary for assemblies of the base communities to be visited by priests and bishops. My first conclusion follows from this. Once the discipleship groups have become recognized by us in Europe as a distinctive form of the one church, the aim should be an even more intensive cooperation between these groups and ecumenically open congregations and congregational groups with a view to winning over as many as possible of our congregations, so often inward-looking in ethos, to labour and prayer for the unity of the body of Christ. Assemblies of the "ecumenical networks" would then become, more than has been the case so far, opportunities for mutual encounter between the discipleship groups and fellow Christians from the local congregations.

2. From the Bible and from their experience of poverty, the base communities in Brazil have learned that the God of Israel, the Father of Jesus Christ, the Saviour and Lord of all peoples, is on the side of the poor and the oppressed. This is axiomatic in Brazil, where nearly two-thirds of the people are numbered with the poor, both in the relative and in the absolute sense. My second conclusion

follows from this, namely that a real convergence between discipleship groups and local congregations in the service of justice, peace
and the integrity of creation will only become possible in our
European situation if the internationally oriented groups unite with
groups and congregations which shoulder the burden of the
increasing poverty among our own people. I am thinking here
especially of those who are condemned to the "new poverty" by
the present developments of the global system, for example, the
unemployed, especially unemployed women and young people.
The New Testament message is that God creates his new people
which lives in justice and peace primarily from the "humble" and
the poor, i.e. from the "two-thirds world" beyond and within our
own countries. Not that people from the bourgeois and upper
classes cannot even qualify for this new fellowship, but that they
are called at the same time to costly solidarity with the poor and
the exploited, and with the world, whose very existence is in
jeopardy (cf. Luke 18:18ff. and 19:1ff.).

3. The base communities, building their fellowship on Bible
and sacrament, proclamation and celebration, set out to overcome
the poverty on their own doorsteps, both nationally and internationally. In consequence, they develop a far sharper analysis of
the social, economic and political situation than we do and are also
able, therefore, to choose far more precisely their covenant partners
in the society around them. Specifically, they are "salt" and
"leaven" within human rights movements and organizations. They
differentiate here between "popular movements" (we would say
"civic initiatives") to secure the basic human necessities (food,
work, land, etc.) and "special issue" groups (e.g. campaigning for
the rights of women and young people). In addition to this, they
identify themselves with trade unions and newly emergent parties
working for the basic rights of the poor (in particular the newly
established workers' party, PT). In every case they run the risk of
conflict with the forces within the social, economic and political
institutions which use their power to continue increasing the profit
of the few at the expense of the many and of planet earth, especially
when the base communities openly challenge the influence of these
forces within the churches by a critique of their underlying
ideology and idolatry. My third conclusion follows from this. Our
churches, too, within their various social forms, must develop a
much more precise social and economic analysis and understanding
of their partners in coalition, if they are really to be of service to
distressed human beings and the endangered earth in obedience to

Jesus Christ instead of accomplices in the abuse of power, i.e. if they are really to become a church obedient to Jesus Christ and confessing him in the world.

The resultant pattern is shown in the following (very simplified) diagram, which may help us in our efforts to participate in the struggle for a more just economic system, as covenant partners of the Christ in solidarity with the poor of the earth.

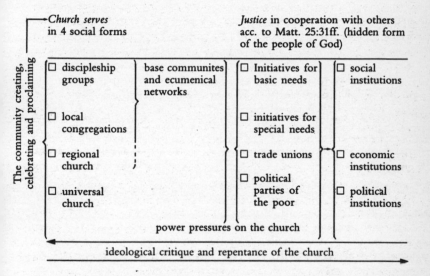

If we in our different conditions are to achieve the kind of renewal and credibility which has been given to the Brazilian church, we still have a long way to go both in theory and in practice. But God will produce in us and among us both the will and the power to accomplish his good pleasure — if we let ourselves be made rich by his Son Jesus Christ who voluntarily accepted poverty for our sake, refusing to clutch his divine riches jealously to himself (cf. Phil. 2:5ff.).

214   *Global economy: a confessional issue for the churches?*

NOTES

1. Cf. among others, D. Jackson, *Coming Together*, Bethany Fellowship, Minneapolis, 1978; H. A. Gornik, *Anders leben. Christliche Gruppen in Selbstdarstellungen* (GTB 344), Gütersloh, 1979.
2. Marita Estor, "Nachfolge: Zeugnis und Bekenntnis in dieser Zeit", in M. Berief, P. Schladoth, R. Waltermann, *"Aus Leidenschaft zur Gemeinde"*, Kevelaer, 1984.
3. Cf. A. M. Aagaard, "The Holy Spirit in the World", in *Studia Theologiia*, 28, 1974; *eadem, Gottes verwundbare Liebe — Heiliger Geist, Meditationen*, Kaiser Traktate No. 66, Munich, 1982.
4. D. Bonhoeffer, "Das Wesen der Kirche", Kaiser Traktate No. 3 Munich, 1971, pp. 21ff.
5. See Chapter 5–7 above.
6. See Chapter 10 below.
7. Cf. W. Krusche, "Schuld und Vergebung — Der Grund christlichen Friedenshandelns", *epd Dokumentation* No. 30a/84, Frankfurt, 1984.
8. Under the title "Was können wir von den Basisgemeinden in Brasilien lernen?" (in *Pastoraltheologie*, June 1985) I have given a fuller account of the ideas briefly summarized here.

10

The ecumenical conciliar process
of mutual commitment (covenant) to justice
peace and the integrity of creation

The Sixth Assembly of the World Council of Churches in Vancouver in 1983 summoned the member churches to engage in "a conciliar process of mutual commitment (covenant) to justice, peace and the integrity of all creation". The Central Committee of the WCC has given a concrete focus to this call by suggesting that this conciliar process might culminate in a world meeting of representatives of all the Christian churches in the year 1990.

As WCC consultant for this process, in conjunction with a staff committeee (including representatives of the Roman Catholic Church), I prepared a background paper for the WCC Executive Committee meeting in Kinshasa, Zaire, in March 1986 (Document No.3 of that meeting). Though without any official status, this working paper provides a number of perspectives for discussions and future plans. What follows in this chapter is a revised and shortened version. At the same time, it is a summary of the main arguments of this book and also opens up the contextual research to the global horizons.

I. The threats to life and the struggle for justice, peace and the integrity of creation

1. The call to an ecumenical conciliar process to promote justice, peace and the integrity of creation has as its background destructive developments at qualitatively new levels.

In respect of justice: racism, sexism, poverty and political oppression have become systematized and reached unprecedented levels of brutality with fatal consequences for the lives of millions of people. Dominated increasingly as it is by multinational monopolies in production, finance, communication and trade, the global economic order produces widespread unemployment, new forms of enslavement, and a neo-colonialism born of mounting debts and international pressures.

In respect of peace: we are confronted with the failure of disarmament efforts as well as with new developments in nuclear technologies and strategies. We have the arms race between the super-powers, the militarization of other countries, the policy of military intervention by the super-powers, the expansion of the military-industrial-technological complex, the devastation of the environment, and the growth of a culture of violence. The penetration of an international military order into every aspect of the world's life has massively affected the world economy and the international system of economic relationships by intensifying the structural dependence of the "developing countries".

In respect of the integrity of creation: no fundamental change has yet taken place in the trend towards the destruction of the created world which is the basis for the life of the present and future generations. Virgin forests are cut down and burnt while others die of acid rain. Nuclear tests continue to contaminate the biosphere and destroy life.

All these forces are interlocked. The constellation of economic interests, technological expertise, military force and regional coalitions between them, constitutes a gigantic conspiracy threatening the continuance of life and human dignity and is rebellion against God, the Creator, Redeemer and Fulfiller of all life.

2. *If witness is to be borne to the God of love and life, the struggle for a just, participatory and sustainable society must be combined with the struggle for peace, and the interlocking forces of injustice, war and the destruction of creation must therefore be confronted and resisted together.*

At its meeting in 1985, the Central Committee of the WCC reaffirmed the continuity between the process towards justice, peace and the integrity of creation (JPIC) and the previous ecumenical programmes: Towards a Just, Participatory and Sustainable Society (JPSS), for justice in a technological world (Church and Society) and against militarism (CCIA). Central in all these is the question of economic power which has been tackled in the study on the church and the transnational corporations (TNCs). In these programmes, the emphasis is on the (messianic) kingdom of God and the historical struggle of the people for the meeting of their basic needs and participation in power. Since the divine Trinitarian love is at work within history, Christians and churches cooperate with people's movements seeking to defend the poor, the oppressed and the victims of militarism, and the life of all creation. This cooperation may bring new experience of Christ's way of suffering love but it may also lead to a new and creative participation in secular institutions.

3. The threat of life at qualitatively new levels and the heretical use of Christ's name to legitimize exploitation, war and destruction, gives the struggle an incontrovertible ecclesiological dimension.

Because Jesus Christ, the Giver of salvation and justice, is the life of the world, he empowers and summons the church as his body to receive and reflect this gift of life in an unambiguous commitment to justice, peace and the integrity of creation. The church does not exist for itself, therefore, but for the world. The threats to life are threats against God. It is sinful for atheistic powers to oppress human beings and to destroy life. It is still worse, however, when the name of Christ is used to legitimize destruction and oppression. As the Vancouver Assembly noted:

> Some fundamentalist sects and church people . . . are against the identification of the churches with the poor in their witness to God's kingdom. The church is thus challenged not only in what it does but also in its very faith and being.

All of this is a radical challenge to our being as the church of Christ. We must rigorously scrutinize our commitment and discover new ways of living out faithfully our oneness in Christ for the life of the world.

II. Becoming the church of Jesus Christ committed to justice, peace and the integrity of creation

1. The process which leads to a church unity based on sacramental unity and the common confession of Jesus Christ is inseparable from the ecumenical process of covenanting for justice, peace and the integrity of creation.

The corollary of this is that, besides the WCC studies on the unity of the church and the unity and renewal of humankind, we must move towards ecclesial unity and commitment. Two specific processes initiated by the WCC have already brought us closer to unity and consensus and, to some extent at all events, have reached all levels of the church. I am referring, of course, to

(a) the Lima convergence documents on "Baptism, Eucharist and Ministry" (BEM), and (b) the programme on the common expression of the apostolic faith. The former (a) is related more particularly to the liturgical dimension of the church (*leiturgia*) and the latter (b) more particularly to the kerygmatic dimension (*martyria*). The key to the conciliar process of commitment to justice, peace and the integrity of creation is to link these two continuing processes to the third dimension of the church, namely, (c) to its *diakonia*, its service in the world and for the world, here specifically to the promotion of justice, peace and the integrity of creation.

But all these three dimensions are also related to a fourth, namely, (d) the *koinonia* of the church. In respect of the liturgy, for example, there is the very important question of the ordained ministry and the ministries within the communion of the church. There is also a *koinonia* dimension to the kerygmatic function of the church, which is sent into the world as a missionary community. In respect of *diakonia*, what is required here, particularly in the critical situation of our world today, cannot be considered as purely social and political but calls rather for the full commitment of the whole ecclesial community in the direction of solidarity. How do the different traditions bear their witness to justice, peace and the integrity of creation as the expression of their very being as the church of Jesus Christ and in mutual commitment to one another?

It was for this reason that the Vancouver delegation of the churches of the German Democratic Republic and the West German *Kirchentag* renewed Dietrich Bonhoeffer's call for an "ecumenical peace council". The challenges confronting the churches and humanity as a whole demand the strongest possible ecclesial response.

Since we do not yet have full conciliar fellowship among the divided churches but still need a committed ecclesial response, finding its expression in the vision of a truly ecumenical council, the present stage in the convergence and covenanting process could be labelled "pre-conciliar". We must therefore avoid using a terminology which would suggest we have already entered into a formal conciliar relationship. So far the term "world conference" has been used of the event it is hoped will take place in 1990. This is certainly much too weak a word for what we hope this event will be. Other possible terms have similar drawbacks. The term "convocation" has recently been proposed.

The New Delhi Assembly voiced the hope that the Holy Spirit

might lead us into a "fully committed fellowship". The Nairobi Assembly defined the unity we seek as that of "a conciliar fellowship of local churches truly united". The time has come to make this definition more explicit, explaining in particular what constitutes a "local church truly united". It is within this framework that the work of Faith and Order finds its place. The same applies also to the covenant for justice, peace and the integrity of creation. Diakonia (service to humankind) is an indispensable dimension of the church and its mission. It cannot, however, be approached in a purely speculative way. Only by working together in this diakonia will we discover all its components and how important it is that we should make progress towards the unity we seek, as defined in Nairobi.

The movement towards fuller unity in order to achieve full unity requires to be made, Faith and Order has discovered, in all these four dimensions of the church. Our hope, therefore, is that, through conversion to Jesus Christ, the Revealer and Mediator of the Trinitarian love in all the convergence and covenanting processes, the truly ecumenical conciliar fellowship of the church committed to justice, peace and the integrity of creation will emerge. In future, therefore, not only the work of Faith and Order but also work in the field of diakonia must be related directly to the unity and koinonia dimensions of the church.

   2. *Whatever we do and say within the WCC context, therefore, must be so structured that non-member churches can participate.*

Jesus Christ has called his whole church to be one. We must confess our sin in contributing to the persistence of divisions in the church. The credibility of our work for justice, peace and the integrity of creation will be limited by our inability to present our concerns as a united conciliar fellowship. Every organizational step planned and implemented in the conciliar process, therefore, must be shaped so as to contribute to better mutual understanding and to the achievement of full unity, possibly in the form of conciliar fellowship and a truly universal council. This applies to all levels and forms of the church. There is a close relationship here between the process and the goal.

It should be noted that the Roman Catholic Church is a voting member of the Faith and Order Commission and thus shares responsibility for the convergence process on baptism, eucharist and ministry as well as that on the apostolic faith. Ought it not to be possible for it to join in the convergence and covenanting processes towards justice, peace and the integrity of creation and on a fully committed fellowship? The same question, the same hope, may also be voiced in respect of other non-member churches, especially those historic "peace churches" which are not yet members of the World Council.

   3. It would seem that, perhaps for the very first time, all forms of the church are ready to join in with mutual respect and support at the beginning of the processes towards greater unity and mutual commitment for justice, peace and the integrity of creation.

These forms of the church include congregations, Christian base communities and orders, church decision-making bodies, and the present expressions of the universal church.

Every form has its own unique contribution to make. The decision-making levels cannot reach decisions without the initiative and consent of the local congregations and churches. But congregations and Christian network groups, too, orders and base communities, should also work patiently for a faithful and responsible decision-making. Without a process in all forms and levels of the church, a world meeting would be meaningless and contrary to the empowering spirit of Christ. A process without a definite thrust towards decision-making in the institutional church courts would be merely sectarian. The World Council of Churches will need to find a pathway between the *two essential poles* of

— ecclesial commitment, which can only be guaranteed by the elected decision-making courts: and
— full participation of all the people of God.

The proposed global ecumenical "convocation" for justice, peace and the integrity of creation in 1990 must be viewed as one vital stage in the pre-conciliar and, hopefully, in the conciliar process of the whole church in all its forms, and as an aid to the movement towards a truly universal council at all levels. The goal, once again, is to become the church of, i.e. committed to, peace and justice. The increase of our own capacity for peace and justice will be decisive here, as will also be the way we deal with power.

   4. Every tradition may contribute to the form taken by this process of mutual commitment within and between the churches and the understanding of it. It cannot be a matter of imposing one systematized pattern from above. "Covenanting" is also only one expression of this process.

To respond to God's gift in faithful obedience, each culture and

Christian tradition may choose different symbols from biblical history as an expression of God's committed love to all creatures and of the binding relationships within the church and between Christians and non-Christians. Such different ecclesiological forms would include: the church of the *eucharistic vision* (BEM, E, §20) or the *confessing* church (responding to a *casus confessionis* by a process of confessing), concepts which played an important rôle in the Vancouver Assembly and also apply to all forms of the church; the concept of *discipleship*, focusing on the doing of God's will as revealed in Christ; the *prophetic* church and the church of *the poor*, where the emphasis is on God's unequivocal commitment to justice in human relationships, and, above all, *conciliar fellowship* combining the dimensions of church unity and the process of settling controversial issues within the practice of Trinitarian love.

The concept of *covenant* highlights at one and the same time God's grace and fidelity to his people and to the whole of creation *and* his call to his people to respond with obedience. "Covenanting" within and among the churches means, therefore, in the final analysis, the process in which the churches express their oneness in the body of Christ and their commitment to do God's will of love.

To invite the various churches and Christian traditions to explain how they express most forcefully, in mutual fellowship as a church, their commitment to justice, peace and the integrity of creation would initiate a third and fourth *convergence and consensus process* (i.e. on *diakonia* and part of the *koinonia* or community dimension of the church) completing the two already in progress, i.e. on the *sacraments* and the *apostolic faith*. Convergence and consensus here would be achieved not only by work on theological concepts but also by a shared evaluation of the actual processes of commitment operative in the various churches and Christian communities.

5. *In the convergence process in the field of diakonia, the primary issues are justice, peace and the integrity of creation. The approach to them will be biblical, theological and sociological. To guide our analysis of our own situation and promote fuller consensus between our different churches, it will be helpful to look more closely at church history. Different churches seem to have developed different approaches to their diaconal responsibility in the world.*

It is possible to differentiate five legitimate ecclesiological approaches to Christian responsibility in respect of crucial world issues:

1. The approach of the *primitive church* and the *peace churches*: renunciation of and resistance to injustices and violence; the creation of *alternative communities* (cf. Matt. 20:25ff. as "salt" and "light" the church influences economics and politics indirectly).
2. The approach of the *Constantinian church*: the *domestication of secular power* by participation in society up to a more or less defined limit (e.g. "just war" and legitimate violent resistance).
3. The *liturgical approach*, especially the *eucharistic representation of Trinitarian love in the world* ("liturgy after the liturgy" with varying degrees of adaptation to and resistance to the "powers" of this world).
4. The approach of the post-Constantinian *liberating church*, combining resistance and the creation of *alternative communities* with the eucharistic fervour of approach 3 and direct *social, economic and political action* of the kind legitimized in approach 2 though not on the side of the powerful but, on the contrary, *critical* of all complicity between the church and the existing "powers that be" and in *solidarity with the struggle of the poor and oppressed*.
5. Another, "post-Constantinian" or "non-Constantinian", approach can perhaps be differentiated, i.e. that of churches which have no possibility of sharing directly in the shaping of secular power. This is like the approach developed in Latin America where in certain situations, Christians are in a minority, either vis-à-vis the state or in respect of the dominant culture or prevailing faith or religion. In such situation, the approach could be labelled, as in Eastern Europe, the approach of *"critical solidarity"* or the *"diaconal church"*.

In actual practice, of course, there will be an overlapping of these different approaches in each case; this differential scheme is no more than an aid to analyzing our own situation. In the convergence process, discussion should not focus on the traditional emphases so much as on their common ground. In other words, we should look for convergence via conversion to Jesus Christ. We should ask such questions as these: Why is it that sections of our church or even we ourselves have become identified with and assimilated to the powers destructive of life instead of faithfully following and confessing Jesus Christ? Where have biblical and ecclesial traditions been misused to legitimize injustice and destruction? The confrontation of nearly all Christian traditions with the ideology and praxis of apartheid is one example, and the rejection of a fundamentalism which legitimizes oppressive régimes and policies in Latin America is another. On the other hand, the theory of the "just war" and the traditions of the "peace churches" are both pushing us in the direction of the rejection of weapons of mass destruction, in opposition to those who defend their uses in the defence of "Christian civilization" against "atheism". The same conflict will confront us in respect of the practical and ideological problems of the present economic disorder and technological developments on a world scale. The question, then, is this: Will it prove possible for the churches of the different traditions to undergo a process of convergence via conversion at all levels and in all forms of the church in order to bear clear witness to the sovereignty of God in face of the threats to justice, peace and the integrity of creation today? This presupposes a deeper understanding and a more committed obedience to our Lord and Saviour Jesus Christ.

6. *The call to patient cooperation between all forms and traditions of the church does not mean minimizing conflicts and controversies concerning the local, regional and global structures of injustice, militarism and the destruction of the earth. On the contrary, the Spirit of Christ and the kingdom of God demonstrate their power by enabling the church to struggle through these conflicts and controversies by self-criticism, repentance, resistance and the development of alternatives.*

There are at least three dimensions of this way of dealing with conflicts;
— an honest search for the points at which we ourselves, as Christians and churches and as members of our societies, are involved in oppressive and unjust structures or mechanisms of war or in the destruction of the earth;
— prayer for forgiveness;
— penitence for the ways in which injustice, war and destruction are reflected within the church itself and in its own power structures (the rôle of women and young people here is crucial);
— participation in the struggle of all movements working for justice, peace and the integrity of creation.

7. *Decision-making within this process has at least three components: becoming aware (seeing) — making decisions — responding to these decisions by obedience to God's will.*

Derived from the experiences of the Confessing Church under

the Nazi régime in Germany and occupied Europe and of the Brazilian church today, this pattern underlines the fact that the process has to start methodically from concrete contextual analysis and will always include, besides efforts to achieve consensus via convergence, action of one kind or other related to the three dimensions indicated:

1) confessing sin and abandoning sinful and heretical alliances;
2) practical covenanting with others who are wrestling with the same decisions for a more faithful discipleship, and necessarily implying practical steps towards becoming the church *of* the poor, *of* peace, *of* the earth and *not* just the church *in favour of* all these causes; and
3) accepting the social and economic consequences in the form resistance must take and in the struggle for alternatives.

8. Since, however, the church is called to be salt, light and leaven in the world and since justice, peace and the integrity of all creation are the concern and responsibility of all humankind, it is essential that, at the appropriate time in the process at all levels, contacts should be made with people of other living faiths and in particular with movements working for these objectives (justice, peace, ecology) in order to assess present cooperation and to test new possibilities of common action and understanding with a view to the achievement of justice, peace and the integrity of creation.

Matthew 25:31–46 shows us people responding to Jesus Christ without consciously knowing and confessing him. They do this as they take care of people's basic needs, whereas the same passage shows us persons and groups who call Jesus Lord rejecting him who comes to them in the persons of the needy. So too, in certain circumstances, confessing Christians who follow Christ faithfully today must identify with movements working for justice, peace and the integrity of creation rather than with certain sections of the church. These sections of the church, however, are not simply to be ignored; on the contrary, the worldwide Christian community should uphold the prophetic and suffering sections of such churches and support them in urging those other sections which are not yet engaged in the struggle for justice, peace and the integrity of creation to cease excluding themselves from the mandatory witness of the church of Jesus Christ and to join in this struggle.

In extreme cases, it may have to be recognized that a certain section of the church has *de facto* excluded itself from the body of

Christ, as happened, for example, in the case of the "German Christians" in the Third Reich and is happening today in the case of churches which support apartheid in South Africa. This could also happen in the case of certain sections of the church because of their position towards other dimensions of justice, peace and the integrity of creation. At the same time, it must be recognized that coalitions with movements working for these objectives are not merely possible but even mandatory. Whenever separations become unavoidable in fidelity to Jesus Christ, everything possible should be done in painful prayer and work to restore communion.

Conclusion

This process of mutual commitment to justice, peace and the integrity of creation on the part of the churches, with its prospect of an increasingly unified witness as the one church of Jesus Christ, is one of the strongest signs of hope in a world in which suffering and danger multiply. Every single congregation, every Christian group and church, can see its efforts as contributing concretely to the common witness of the universal church to this endangered world. As the South African document *A Challenge to the Churches* says, this is an unprecedented "*kairos*". The churches today are presented with a great opportunity and challenge. To summarize the steps that can be taken:

1. All levels and forms of the church can start at once to intensify, or even begin for the first time, the work of identifying their strongest ecclesial approach to shouldering responsibility for justice, peace and the integrity of creation and to engaging in the covenanting process. The World Council of Churches will provide sharing facilities, such as, for example, a newsletter and the exchange of visits. The first international consultation in the autumn of 1986 has made proposals for the convergence process which the Central Committee of the WCC decided on in January 1987.

2. Between 1987 and 1989, regional assemblies will bring forward regional priorities and key issues. Efforts are being made to ensure that these regional assemblies will have the maximum commitment possible.

3. It is also hoped that the world convocation for justice, peace and the integrity of creation in 1990 will be as ecumenical as possible and embody the maximum ecclesial commitment possible, even if full conciliar fellowship is for later.

4. We hope for full conciliar fellowship and a truly universal

ecumenical council at the earliest possible time, *ubi et quando visum est Deo* (as and when it pleases God). For this — that the church should be such a truly conciliar fellowship, universal and ecumenical — is what God and the world expect of the church, that the world may believe.

We must all pray as if everything depends on our prayer, work as if everything depends on our work. The reality of the fully committed fellowship for justice, peace and the integrity of creation can come to us only as the gift of the one God, Father, Son and Holy Spirit.[1]

NOTE

1. In order to ground this whole process biblically Gerhard Liedke and myself have prepared the following study guide: *Shalom: der Schöpfung Befreiung, den Menschen Gerechtigkeit, den Völkern Frieden. Eine biblische Arbeitshilfe*, Kreuz Verlag, Stuttgart, 1987.

APPENDIX I

Baden Evangelical Church: synod message to congregations, 1981

We, the Synod of the Baden Evangelical Church, take this opportunity of addressing you, our sisters and brothers in the congregations. At our spring assembly this year, our main theme was "The unity of the church in a world divided into East and West, North and South". Among the different angles from which we approached this theme was that of "The unity of the church in a world divided by racism". Here we looked especially at the theory and practice of apartheid in South Africa.

On the sinfulness of racism, the position of the Bible is clear. All human beings have been created in the image and likeness of God (Gen. 1:27). The purpose of Christ's death on the cross was justification and life for all (Rom. 5:18). The church of Jesus Christ is not to be divided according to race (Gal. 3:28). As the body of Christ, our calling is not to serve injustice but rather to make our life and our bodies instruments for God and his justice (Rom. 6:13).

The Synod adopted the following declaration:

The Synod recognizes that, as a provincial church and members of a provincial church, we are part and parcel of our industrial society and its quest for prosperity. We are implicated in hostility to foreigners, worldwide oppression and racism. We are slow to inform ourselves with sufficient thoroughness of the basic causes of racial oppression and the extent to which we are accomplices in such oppression. We are slow to engage in the struggle of the poor and distressed for greater justice and the recognition of their human rights.

Recognizing this complicity, listening attentively to holy scripture, as part of the ecumenical fellowship and in partnership with the Moravian Brethren Church in South Africa, we recognize the challenge to our church to unite in the confession of faith of the one church of Jesus Christ in opposition to the theory and practice of apartheid in South Africa. This doctrine and its practice distorts the biblical message, divides the church and violates human rights. On the basis of our faith, therefore, and to manifest the unity of the church publicly and unambiguously, we reject the present system of apartheid in South Africa. Even though they have broken fellowship, we nevertheless appeal to the white churches in South Africa not to remain outside this unity. We summon our congregations and church members fully to recognize as disciples of Jesus Christ their own complicity in this system and to work together as much as possible to change it.

As to the form this cooperation might take in the local communities, we would suggest the following possibilities: intercession services, Bible study, the evaluation of the experiences of the Confessing Church in the National Socialist period, detailed information about the confessional struggle in South Africa, the correction of miss-statements and half-truths about South Africa in the media, and the examination of our own direct or indirect participation in economic, cultural and touristic relationships with South Africa.

We consider ourselves united in confessing the faith as formulated in Article 2 of the Barmen Theological Declaration of 1934:

As Jesus Christ is God's declaration of the forgiveness of all our sins, so, in the same way and with the same seriousness, he is God's mighty claim upon our whole life. Through him we obtain joyful deliverance from the godless bondage of this world for the free, grateful service of his creatures.

Bad Herrenhalb   *Dr Angelberger*
8 May 1981   *President*

APPENDIX II

Example of persecution of the church through cooperation between the USA and Latin American governments: the so-called "Banzer Plan"

The Bolivian government's plan of action against the church

1. Only the church's progressive sector is to be attacked, not the church as an institution or the bishops as a group. In the government view, the principal representative of the progressive sector is Archbishop Manrique (La Paz). The attacks against him should be personal. The effort should be made to separate him from the rest of the hierarchy and to produce friction between him and the Bolivian clergy.

2. The foreign clergy especially is to be attacked — by publicly identifying individuals among them with the Justice and Peace Commission, with the campaign for signatures (to a protest letter), and with leftist political parties, particularly the FLN (National Liberation Army). It is necessary to link them to the Teoponte guerrilla and with Father Prat's activities. We should insistently repeat that they are Prat's followers, that they preach armed struggle, that they are linked with international communism, and that they were sent to Bolivia with the single purpose of moving the church towards communism.

3. Certain religious orders should be closely watched, e.g., Dominicans, Oblates, Jesuits, and their connections with Radio Fides, Radio Pius XII, Indicep, and with religious activities in the altiplano among cotton workers and especially among miners.

4. The CIA, through Freddy Vargas and Alfredo Arce, has

Ed. note: This text is a Latinamerica Press translation of a document circulating among Bolivian church authorities which allegedly was secretly received from an official of General Hugo Banzer's government. It outlines the strategy followed against the Catholic Church and its progressive sectors. (15 May 1975) decided to get directly into this project. The CIA promised to provide full information on certain priests, especially those from the USA. In 48 hours they compiled for the Minister of the Interior complete files on certain priests, personal data, studies, friends, addresses, writings, contacts abroad, etc. Senor Lamasa (John LaMazza) was very helpful in this work. The CIA also has information on other priests and religious who are not North Americans.

5. The replacement of the chief of the Intelligence Service, Colonel Arabe, is part of this plan. He was unwilling to undertake a head-on attack against the church. The new chief, Major Vacaflor, is a hard man, with sadistic tendencies, who has taken part in a number of torturings. He is quite ready to carry out the plan.

6. A special file has been set up for priests and religious, as well as for certain bishops and religious orders.

7. Certain religious houses are being checked into, in order to know where particular priests live and to be able to keep them under surveillance. In like manner, the bishop's office is to be put under observation (i.e., the office of Archbishop Manrique).

8. Religious houses should never be searched or raided since that only leads to a lot of publicity. Priests on the list are to be picked up on the street, ideally in places where no one is around, or in the countryside. The police should be dressed in civilian clothes and move in taxis hired for that purpose. There are also a number of Volkswagens available, without official license plates, but with two-way radio communication.

9. The hierarchy is to be faced with accomplished facts. When the police pick up priests they should do so without any fanfare. They should not bring them to the Ministry or to the DCP, but should contact the intelligence service by radio. The best procedure is to take them to remote places outside the city until the ministry decides what steps are to be taken. The bishops are to be informed only after the priests have been expelled from the country.

10. Arrests should be made preferably in the countryside, on deserted streets or late at night. Once a priest has been arrested the ministry should try to plant — in his briefcase and, if possible, also in his room — subversive literature and a weapon (ideally a large-bore pistol), and his dossier should be ready in order to discredit him before the bishop and public opinion.

11. Complaints should be published in the communication media (particular *Diario*) to discredit Bishop Manrique and those

priests and religious who represent the church's advanced thinking. *Presencia* should be firmly intimidated so it will publish only sketchy accounts of what happens. Any reports published should be required to carry a signature so we can know from where they come and who wrote them.

12. Friendly relations should be built up with churchmen like Bishop Prata, Fr Mestre and certain Bolivian priests so that the public won't think the church is being systematically persecuted, but only a few of its members. The importance of having a national church should be stressed.

13. The police have been told that those who perform well in this plan will be given any belongings that are confiscated in the houses of certain priests.

14. The list of the ten priests to be seized has already been drawn up.

15. The Ministry of the Interior has an accusation against the Justice and Peace Commission signed by ten Bolivian priests and religious.